CASS LIBRARY OF AFRICAN STUDIES

MISSIONARY RESEARCHES AND TRAVELS

No. 21

General Editor : ROBERT I. ROTBERG

Massachusetts Institute of Technology

MISSIONARY TO TANGANYIKA
1877–1888

Edward Coode Hore, Fellow of the Royal Geographical Society, Master Mariner, Missionary at Lake Tanganyika from 1878 to 1888. This photograph is reproduced from an original in the archives of the Congregational Council for World Mission, Westminster, England.

MISSIONARY TO TANGANYIKA

1877-1888

The Writings of
Edward Coode Hore,
Master Mariner

Selected, edited and with an introduction

by

James B. Wolf

Department of History, University of Colorado

FRANK CASS & CO. LTD.

First published in 1971 by
FRANK CASS AND COMPANY LIMITED
67, Great Russell Street, London WC1B 3BT

Distributed in the United States by
International Scholarly Book Services, Inc.
Beaverton, Oregon 97005

Library of Congress Catalog Card Number 72-171259

IBSN 0 7146 2924 3

Printed in the Republic of Ireland by Cahill & Co. Limited,
Parkgate Printing Works, Dublin

CONTENTS

ILLUSTRATIONS

GENERAL EDITOR'S PREFACE

Anyone who has done research on the problems of nineteenth-century eastern Africa knows how uncommonly often the name of Edward Coode Hore, master mariner and missionary, appears. He was a forceful representative of evangelical initiative at Lake Tanganyika—a friend and counsellor of explorers, adventurers, imperialists, and African and Arab merchants, and the fulcrum of the pioneering London Missionary Society from 1878 to 1888. For a time he was the West's chief representative in a critical region of the interior, and one well-placed to affect the course of Euro-African relations on the eve and during the so-called scramble.

Hore was a more complicated and influential man than he often appears. Among missionaries, too, his sensibility stands out. A biography is long overdue and, in time, Professor James Wolf of the University of Colorado hopefully will produce it. Hore himself published *Tanganyika* (London, 1892) and his wife published the strikingly titled *To Lake Tanganyika in a Bath Chair* (London, 1886). But neither account bears reissuance in full. The second is a slight, if humorous period piece. The first, ostensibly a likely candidate for inclusion in this series, lacks lasting interest and is unrepresentative of the quality of the man and his work. When Professor Wolf, whose dissertation was a study of Hore's mission, and I discussed this problem some years ago we soon realised that Hore's best material was buried elsewhere—in an unpublished journal to which Professor Wolf had accesss and in his published articles. For this volume Professor Wolf has therefore edited a collection of the less well known but more substantial parts of the Hore *oeuvre*. The authentic nineteenth-century practical man of God emerges in context.

R.I.R.

1 April 1970

Cambridge, Massachusetts

ACKNOWLEDGEMENTS

The editor wishes to thank the directors of the Congregational Council for World Mission, formerly the London Missionary Society, for permission to publish the journals of Edward Coode Hore, and to extend particular personal appreciation to Miss Irene Fletcher for her help and co-operation in 1967. The Department of History, University of California at Davis, and a grant from the Council for Research and Creative Work at the University of Colorado, helped to finance the costs for this collection. The editor is responsible for all material contained in the footnotes.

J.B.W.

1971

I

INTRODUCTION

Edward Coode Hore, a sailor with ten years' experience in the merchant navy, was one of two artisans appointed in 1877 to the pioneering expedition of the London Missionary Society (LMS) to Central Africa. His duties, once the caravan had reached its destination, were to complete the geographic survey of Lake Tanganyika begun by Richard Burton and augmented by Verney Lovett Cameron and Henry M. Stanley, ferry missionaries and supplies to the various parts of the lake where stations would in time be established, and receive, assemble, and command a steamship to be transported piecemeal overland to the lake. If it were not for the need to service an indeterminate number of lakeside mission stations by steamer, the foreign secretary of the society would not have been so anxious to employ a sailor skilled in handling steamships as well as sail, nor would have Hore been so pleased to accept, for it was exclusively as the master of a ship that he desired to give expression to his religious dedication.

Perhaps the major factor behind the flurry of missionary fervour in Great Britain, which so affected Central Africa in the 1870s, was David Livingstone's death at Lake Bangweulu and public burial in Westminister Abbey and the publication in 1874 of his last, dramatic journals. When Livingstone had requested help in 1857, few had followed him back into the interior of east Africa, but his death sparked Scottish and English missionary societies to abandon their previous hesitation, alter their priorities, and plunge enthusiastically into Central Africa. No doubt their decisions were favourably affected by the logistical changes brought about by the opening of the Suez Canal; no doubt their directors were heartened by the increasing British influence with the Sultan of Zanzibar who implied suzerainty over the Muslim traders and settlers in the interior. But it was primarily as a memorial to Livingstone that two Scottish societies undertook activities in the Lake Nyasa region; it was the search for Livingstone which first had brought Stanley to Africa, and it was on his recommendation and virtual guarantee of success that the Church Missionary Society obligated itself to the establishment of a mission in Buganda at the north end of Victoria Nyanza.

1

The " Sea of Ujiji " (Lake Tanganyika), probably in Europe the best known of the great inland lakes, remained beyond the missionary assault until the end of 1875. Then Robert Arthington, a rather eccentric Quaker from Leeds who was dedicated to no less an effort than the early evangelisation of the world, noticed the gap and, using his capital as an enticement, requested the London Missionary Society to fill it. If, he suggested, Livingstone's former society agreed to establish a station at Ujiji, a town so popularly linked with Livingstone's name, and if that mission included a steamship, a means for inland transport in which Livingstone had great faith, then he would contribute an initial £5,000 to the endeavour. The financial lure worked, and, while it took another twelve years to get *The Good News* steaming under her own power on Lake Tanganyika, her promised arrival was the reason that Hore was among the first three missionaries to arrive at Ujiji in August, 1878.

For the next decade the Central Africa Mission was dominated by the endurance, determination, and self-assurance of this sailor missionary. Reinforcements and replacements, often disagreeing and sometimes overruling Hore as to the direction and focus of the mission, did not survive the rigors of the tropics; if they lived, they were invalided home in failing health and flagging spirit. But Hore stayed on, dispatching home optimistic reports, which suggested that all that was needed for success was better quality missionaries: ". . . I would say you ought to send a lot of old sailors out here. . . ." [1]

While the London Missionary Society stations were the only British outposts at Lake Tanganyika, two other European agencies were present during the 1880s: the Association Internationale Africaine, sponsored by King Léopold II of Belgium and the Roman Catholic Société de Notre-Dame d'Afrique (the White Fathers) based in Algiers. With Hore at its helm, the LMS mission seemed to have more in common with the secular representatives of the former than with the White Fathers.

Hore and his society were in agreement that the missionary vessels served only an auxiliary role to the religious and educational purpose of the mission, but, as neither missionary nor mission station could be long sustained, the auxiliary became the primary characteristic by default. Evaluating the political significance of the small Protestant flotilla, Coupland believed that British influence was greatly extended by flying the British ensign from one end of the lake to the other.[2] It is true that, while the Arab leadership at Ujiji forbade flying the British flag on land they permitted it on the lake, but Coupland was misled as to its significance, for neither

Her Majesty's Government nor the directors of the LMS had the slightest desire for friction with the Muslims in the interior, nor any political ambitions which could lead to an official British presence so distant from established bases of power. Although Gladstone's government was willing in 1880, on the advice of Consul John Kirk at Zanzibar, to name Hore " consular agent " at Ujiji on Lake Tanganyika, the foreign secretary of the LMS rejected the appointment to even so vague a post. It was too political. When Lake Tanganyika was affected by the European partition of Africa in the mid-1880s, Hore was among the last to know which empire encompassed his Karema island station. On receiving word of the creation of the Congo Independent State and British recognition of German claims to influence beyond the east African coast, he lamented that, given permission, he could have brought a strip of east Africa as wide as the length of Lake Tanganyika and stretching from the upper Congo to the coast under British jurisdiction.[3]

While Hore might have felt politically impotent, the Central African Mission's only impact was in the secular realm. Against Hore's recommendation, the directors of the LMS committed the transport of the steamer to the African Lakes Company, a secular adjunct to the Free Church of Scotland's Lake Nyasa mission. The company's intention was to open a route (the " Stevenson Road ") over the plateau connecting the two lakes. Part of the agreement obliged the LMS to establish stations at the south end and on the Stevenson Road above the lake. In 1888 the African Lakes Company, in order to protect its commercial future along the plateau, used armed force to prevent Muslim traders from blocking the route north; in 1890 the German government recognised the Stevenson Road to be within the British sphere and the southern end of Lake Tanganyika as part of a British protectorate. The LMS mission, essentially a partner in the road and the physical presence of the British at Lake Tanganyika, significantly influenced the division of territory at the time of the partition.

Two observations by members of the mission in late 1890 and early 1891 indicate the dimensions of the failure of the mission as a proselytising influence in its first dozen years. Alfred Swann, Hore's replacement as head of the marine department, commented to a visitor that she should not be surprised in the future to find all the shores of Tanganyika Roman Catholic;[4] and, shortly thereafter, Kalulu, the first convert made by the mission, while still dressed in baptismal white, requested a Martini rifle similar to those of his European brethren.

The observer of the first years of the Central African Mission must agree with the official historian of the first century of the LMS that it was an example of " how great missionary enterprises ought not to be attempted ",[5] and with Cairns, who, sixty-five years later, wrote, that it was " a continuous attempt to repair folly evoked by zeal without discretion ".[6] However, to give the directors credit, when Hore left the lake for the last time in June, 1888, a directive already had been dispatched from London with instructions to his successor to transfer emphasis from the lake to the Nyasa plateau. Although *The Good News* remained LMS property until 1895, its limited use after Hore's departure confirmed its reputation with missionaries in the interior as " a white elephant ". The directors unquestionably agreed, selling it to the African Lakes Company for a fraction of its actual cost.

Although there appears to be agreement on the minimal contribution of the mission at Lake Tanganyika, no such consensus exists concerning the contribution of Edward Hore. Depending on whether they were fellow missionaries or not, his contemporaries either disliked or admired him. His brethren found him officious, demanding, domineering, and generally hard to get along with; complained one, " All credit is due to Captain Hore for his theoretical knowledge, but one cannot give it that only a sailor man knows anything. . . ."[7] A foreign secretary of the society, analysing Hore's difficulties with personnel, blamed his perfectionism: " He does not seem to make sufficient allowance for personal idiosyncrasies and does not see that if all men have not quite his lofty ideals, the wise leader will try to make the best and happiest use of such material as he can get."[8] The crux of the matter was that men coming to Lake Tanganyika expected to work with Captain Hore, while he expected them to work for him.

In contrast, his relations with individuals travelling through the region or with representatives of other European enterprises based in the interior were excellent. Joseph Thomson, exploring central Africa for the Royal Geographical Association in 1879, wrote glowingly about his encounter with Hore:

> . . . I felt that I had found a missionary of the type which Livingstone longed for, and could so seldom find—a man who did not waste his time wandering about with his Bible in his hands, trying to teach the natives to talk mechanically about things they could not comprehend, but who loved the essentials of his religion; whose word was as good as his bond; whose advice was worth having, and could be trusted; who could teach them how to build better boats, to dig their fields to more advantage, and to be ashamed of committing a bad action . . . The necessity of having men like Mr. Hore cannot be too apparent. Missionaries must

be thoroughly practical men, learned with a wide experience of
the world, and not merely that of theological colleges . . ."[9]

A member of the Karema station of the Association Internationale
Africaine volunteered to the LMS that with Hore at Ujiji they had
" the right man in the right place ",[10] and the French explorer,
Abbé Michel-Alexandre Debaize preferred Hore's hospitality at
Ujiji to that of the French White Fathers, who, in turn, found Hore,
if not sympathetic, co-operative and helpful. E. J. Baxter of the
Church Missionary Society's Mpwapwa station, was hopeful that,
if the LMS withdrew support from their failing Lake Tanganyika
mission, Hore could be persuaded to stay on as an Anglican
representative.[11]

Both the criticism and the praise reflect the man. While the
LMS supported the idea of the individual missionary's indepen-
dence, with direction coming from London, Hore saw himself as
the secular authority (in both senses of the word) at the lake, as
well as competent to make whatever policy decisions situations
demanded. It is no wonder that his brethren resented him, or that
he considered them insubordinate? Nor is it surprising that his
endurance, confidence, and seamanship won respect from men who
encountered him at Lake Tanganyika.

Hore treated his responsibilities with the Central African Mission
as he would a ship under his command, including keeping a
thorough log book. Often added to daily, this journal was the
source from which he drew material for his letters and reports to
the foreign secretary and later for his lectures, papers, and book.
As would be expected the focus of the correspondence and public
writing is secular rather than religious. Their purpose was to record,
with as much precision as possible, the physical and social
characteristics of the interior.

It has significance today for three reasons. Hore, during ten years
at Lake Tanganyika and while in charge of six caravans to
or from the coast, had an opportunity to observe a variety of
peoples of the interior. Although his impressions and comments
were affected by his preconceived ideas of an idealised African
society being corrupted by coastal influences and by his dependence
upon Swahili-speaking interpreters, he provides the student of
African history with a new source of heretofore unavailable data.

Secondly, his circumnavigation of Lake Tanganyika provided the
first accurate information on its nearly thousand mile shoreline,
including confirmation of Cameron's suspicion that the Lukuga
River on the west bank was the sole outlet of the lake. The maps
he presented to the Royal Geographical Society in 1881 reflected

B

his attempt to transliterate place names; with the exception of several capes in the south identified by Cameron in *Across Africa,* names were " obtained by careful inquiry of natives on the spot— I had no Ujiji pilot ".[12] He found there was no specific indigenous term for inlets, bays, and the like, so, in addition to " Burton Gulf " in the northwest and " Cameron Bay " in the southwest, his charts and all subsequent maps of Lake Tanganyika, show at the southern most part of the lake, the eventual British sphere, " Hore Bay ".

Lastly, Hore's writing indicates still another example of the prolems Europeans encountered in the attempt to establish themselves in the interior of the continent. For a time, the Central African Mission enjoyed the unique position among missionary enterprises of being located squarely in a centre of Muslim power, Ujiji, and of functioning at the sufferance of the Arab settlers and traders who lived there. It is for these reasons that Hore's writings, in spite of their stilted style, merit publication.

Two selections, not written by Hore, are included in this collection. The first, a complementary biographical sketch published in an evangelical journal in 1892, contains information unavailable elsewhere which reflected Hore's own impression of his background and accomplishments. The second, a chapter from his wife's book, *To Lake Tanganyika in a Bath Chair* (1886), contributes a naive account of mission life by the first European woman to see and to reside at Lake Tanganyika.

Having just turned forty and in failing health, Edward Hore left central Africa for the last time in 1888. During the next six years he attempted to make personal capital of his experiences in Africa, first as a public speaker, then as owner of an African exhibition in London, and finally as an advisor to a utopian socialist scheme of European settlement in East Africa, based upon Hertzka's *Freeland.*[13] When all had failed, the London Missionary Society offered him a berth as first officer on the new missionary steamer, *John Williams IV,* sailing from England to Sydney, New South Wales, and then on semi-annual tours of the island mission stations in the south seas. At Sydney, because of the illness of the captain, Hore was put in command until his continued poor health and usual inability to get along with his officers and crew forced him to resign. He retired to a life of unsuccessful farming in Tasmania. In the last months before his death in 1912, Captain Hore, impoverished, insane, and institutionalised, imagined himself living in a luxurious palace. " The Directors have placed me here," he raved, " on account of my work in Africa." [14] It was madness, for he had outlived his fame by more than a quarter century.

1. Hore to the Foreign Secretary of the LMS, June 1, 1883.

2. Reginald Coupland, *The Exploitation of East Afria, 1865-1890,* (London, 1939), 264.

3. Hore to the Foreign Secretary of the LMS, August 15, 1885.

4. Jane Moir, " Correspondence ", *Journal of the Manchester Geographical Society* VII (1891), 73.

5. Richard Lovett, *The History of the London Missionary Society, 1795-1895* (London, 1899), I, 670.

6. H. Alan C. Cairns, *Prelude to Imperialism* (London, 1965), 14-15.

7. Brooks to the Foreign Secretary of the LMS, October 12, 1885.

8. R. W. Thompson to the acting Foreign Secretary of the LMS, March 25, 1897.

9. *To the Central African Lakes and Back* (Boston, 1881), II, 86-87, 88.

10. Carter to the LMS, February 8, 1880.

11. Baxter to the Church Missionary Society, September 11, 1885.

12. Hore, in an appendix to " Journal of the Voyage to the South End ", 1880.

13. Theodor Hertzka (trans. Arthur Ransom), *Freeland : A Social Anticipation* (London, 1891).

14. Cited by his widow in a letter to the Foreign Secretary of the LMS, June 3, 1912.

II

THE MAN

Edward Hore was a particularly cold and guarded individual who revealed little of his personal background in either his missionary correspondence or in his published works. Generally disliked by his colleagues, it is not surprising that he is seldom mentioned by them other than in criticisms of his policies and attitudes. Only his wife in *To Lake Tanganyika in a Bath Chair* (1886) and Joseph Thomson in *To the Central African Lakes and Back* (1881) hint that there was a relaxed, unofficial, human Edward Hore. But again, they say nothing of his past. Even the archives of the Congregational Council for World Mission are void of information, for, as Hore was hired originally as a paid artisan member of the expedition to Lake Tanganyika, he did not have to submit the standard application which requested professional and personal data.

The following biographical sketch was written shortly after his return to England from a decade in central Africa; it is the only known source of knowledge of his roots, youth, and professional experience. Here is, without doubt, an accurate reflection of how Hore viewed his early life. Although somewhat idealised, it reveals a drab, economically insecure, urban boyhood relieved only by exaggeration of his family's historical importance and by escape into the adventure stories of the period.

Physically, Hore freed himself from that close environment by going to sea, but psychologically he was bound to the Methodist, lower middle class values instilled in him by his mother, Charlotte Hore. While his professional advancement was rapid, his social adjustment to his shipmates was not. Their freedom annoyed him, and he protected himself from their crude behaviour and irresponsibility by turning to religion. His attempts at proselytisation amongst them, not surprisingly, proved unsuccessful. Frustrated, Hore saw his only alternative as association with committed Christians in a missionary enterprise, preferably in some naval capacity.

But even after he became a member of the London Missionary Society's Central African expedition in 1877, his inability to relate harmoniously with his fellows plagued him. He become increasingly isolated, directing his energies to fulfilling his concept of the mission at Lake Tanganyika while belittling anyone else's contribution.

Our Portrait Gallery*

Edward Coode Hore, F.R.G.S., Master Mariner

Our portrait this month represents a gentleman whose name is already well known in connection with the London Missionary Society's Central African Mission.

Edward Coode Hore was born in Islington, July 23, 1848; his parents were of two old Cornish families, representatives of whom had settled in London shortly before. One of those families has been well represented in the army and navy; of the other, several were amongst the West-country seamen-adventurers of the reigns of Henry VIII and Queen Elizabeth, who helped to reveal and settle the shores of the New World.[1] And if something of heredity may have aided in the eventual choice of a wandering, seafaring life, the environment of a Christian family, and especially the devotion of a pious mother, has in God's good providence, resulted in a missionary sailor. The circumstances of life permitted but a few years of education, chiefly in a school at Cambridge, before the responsible duties of life were entered upon. Destined at first for a London business life, Edward found nothing congenial in it— there seemed to be nothing important ahead. His mind was already full of longings for other scenes, and especially some books of travel in inner South Africa, and of voyages to other parts of the world, had interested him, and although still somewhat vaguely, settled his determination. Eventually he was bent upon going to sea, as perhaps the only possible means of travelling abroad; and after some time his parents yielded to his continual solicitations, and apprenticed him, at the age of sixteen, to the owner of a London ship, " to learn the business of a seaman." His very first voyage was to a port in South Africa. Two lads in the same vessel yielded to the temptation to wild adventure and fortune, and deserted; but Edward declined to accompany them. His early teaching was still strong upon him, and he had been impressed by the parental admonition that, having been sent out into a profession of his own choosing, he must continue and persevere. And this deter-

*From The Evangelical Magazine (London), new series, XX (April 1890), 184-187.

1. He believed himself to be a descendent of Richard Hore who, in 1536, commanded two ships on a voyage to Newfoundland.

mination has been constant, for, although becoming eventually a missionary to the heathen, it was strictly in a department of the work where the aid of his profession was specially required.

Steadily working on then, visiting nearly every part of the world, serving on more than twenty different vessels, from the small coasting schooner to the first-class mail steamer, he passed through all the grades of apprentice, able seaman, boatswain, third, second and chief officer, and master-passing all his examinations in his own port of London.

During this period he first made public confession of faith at Sydney, N.S.W., joining the Seaman's Church there, the pastor of which had come from that Bethel at Sheerness founded by Mr. Shrubsole, whose son was one of the first secretaries of the London Missionary Society. In such a connection it is not surprising we should find the subject of our sketch busy for the spiritual welfare of those around him. On shore we hear of his visiting the ships, and getting the men to come to church; at sea, as a foremast man, writing out and binding an edition of hymn-books, giving " temperance readings " and lectures on geography, aided by a globe he made himself, to his fellow-sailors; and, again, as chief officer of a large vessel, holding services around the capstan on the quarter-deck, each man (of a dozen nationalities) provided with a Bible or Testament in his own language; or on board a large steamer, conducting a Sunday-school for the young men and boys.

But his most earnest desire was to join a missionary ship. For this purpose he once when in Sydney went on board the *John Williams* and offered himself as able seaman.[2] Twice in London he was just a day late in applying on board the *Harmony,* and once he went all the way to Australia for the purpose of joining the *Dayspring.* That vessel, however, had already sailed on her annual round, and taking a voyage to Japan as chief officer, Mr. Hore left his ship there on account of refusing to take part in what he considered dishonest practices, and worked his passage home once more before the mast. In London he had charge for some time of the missionary cutter *Evangelist,* belonging to the East London Institute, with which he was connected for a few months.

Preparations for the Central African Mission were just then proceeding. Dr. Mullens[3] replied by return of post, and at the ensuing interview it became practically settled that the hour and the man in this case coincided. The ensuing interval of a year (before the

2. In 1894 Hore became the Master of the *John Williams IV*.
3. Rev. Joseph Mullens, Foreign Secretary of the London Missionary Society, who himself died as he attempted to lead a relief expedition to Ujiji in 1879.

final start), during which no other more suitable person had been found, convinced Mr. Hore that this was his call, for which his previous life had been a training. His subsequent history is practically that of the Central African Mission. Except the station of Urambo, founded more particularly by Dr. Southon,[4] whose portrait has already appeared in these pages, Mr. Hore has shared all of its dangers, difficulties and successes, up to the time of his return to England.

As in Polynesia, South America, on Nyassa, Nyanza, the Niger and the Congo, seafaring men have led the messengers of Christ to the furthest homes of the darkest heathen; so on Tanganyika, by the same means, first in a native canoe, and now in the beautiful steam yacht the *Good News*, the Christian sailor has made the friendly acquaintance of the distant tribes of inner Africa—surveyed and mapped that inland sea, and proclaimed to its dark peoples the love of God in Christ Jesus, preparing the way for others who may go forth to the same work.

---

4. E. J. Southon who, between 1879 and his death in 1882, was the LMS missionary with Mirambo of the Nyamwezi.

III

TRAVERSING EAST AFRICA

In September 1877 the foreign secretary of the London Missionary Society entertained high hopes for the pioneer expedition making its way from the Indian Ocean to Lake Tanganyika. This, "a great experiment", by introducing the South African bullock wagon into East Africa, would appreciably reduce the cost of transport and open a new highway for European civilisation into the interior. But the tsetse fly was on the road, and, as the oxen died, enthusiasm in London and on the expedition itself waned. Two of the party dropped out, one, Rev. Roger Price, the expedition leader; the reduced transport capacity meant more and more supplies had to be left along the route. Clarification of goals and reorganisation of the expedition were needed, so, as the monsoon rains began, a temporary camp was established at Kirasa.

While the expedition had suffered a serious setback, Edward Hore found his responsibilities and his importance increasing. A conscientious worker from the start ("He's worth his weight in gold to us," wrote Price), Hore managed all aspects of the caravan except the oxen and wagons, and, as the great experiment failed, Hore returned to Zanzibar to hire more carriers. The following is his account of the expedition from the time he left the coast with the additional carriers to his arrival at Ujiji in August, 1878.

The journal is divided into three segments. The first is a letter to the foreign secretary of the society which was composed after Hore had returned to Kirasa. The remainder is a daily, unedited log of the expedition: one section to Urambo, the Nyamwezi capital, and the other to Ujiji. Probably because he received a cold reception from Chief Mirambo, Hore kept no record of the time spent at Urambo.

Technical and repetitive passages have been omitted and are indicated by ellipsis. In some instances Hore's handwriting, variations in the spelling of place and personal names, and the condition of the manuscript have made editorial correction and standardisation necessary.

15

The Journey to Kirasa*

. . . We had unusual difficulty this time in procuring the required number of men as carriers at Zanzibar having to wait three weeks after everything else was quite ready for the road. We eventually started on Christmas day [1877]. Perhaps, you will say this was too bad, but after waiting so long it would not have been wise to keep 140 men in unnecessary idleness for one day. We longed for nothing so much as a start and, having no materials at hand to make a plum pudding, there were no allurements of other kinds to detain us, so off we started after the usual bustle and ado of apportioning out the loads and packing up those things which are always left after " everything " has been packed. Shortly before this the N. East wind had set in with cold sharp squalls which swept round our verandah, sometimes most chillingly; I suppose one of these must have laid hold of me whilst clad in airy garments so that I caught a cold which proved rather troublesome. Mr. Dodgshun was still in possession of the good health which up till then we had both enjoyed.[1] We started with 147 men and lads, being with ourselves 149 persons all told.

No great natural difficulties had to be encountered in the early part of the road tho' a muddy path and bogs in the hollow places served to remind us that it was different travelling than earlier in the season.

An Arab who visited us at Ndumi, having coming from Zanzibar to look after a runaway slave, told me that, had he known the state of the country, he would not have left Zanzibar for " one towsan slave ".

On arriving at Pamagombe it was evident we had made too long a day's journey for a great number of the pagasi [carriers] were knocked up [ill]. I had arranged for a shorter stage myself, but the head man saying they were quite able to go to Pamagombe, of course, I did not stop them; however, it was now evident we must

*From a letter to the Foreign Secretary of the LMS, February 15, 1878, in the archives of the Congregational Council for World Mission (formerly The London Missionary Society).
1. The son of a major contributor to the London Missionary Society and considered to be a missionary of great promise, the Rev. Arthur Dodgshun did not survive the rigours of the journey to Lake Tanganyika. In charge of the slow supply caravan, he did not reach Ujiji until the end of March 1879 and died barely a week later on April 3.

17

have a day's half. Next day, however, a new trouble arose. The pagasi all demanding that a shukka[2] of cloth should be a day's allowance for six men only instead of as heretofore for eight men, pleading that, the matama harvest being over, food was dear. After obtaining information from the chief of the village and inspecting a few sample shukka's worth of food, we found that food was really a little dearer and decided to allow a shukka for *seven* men. This offer the men refused, the next day refused to start until they got food at the rate they demanded; this we determined *not* to give them and in the afternoon (too late to start) they gave in to our terms. The next day was Sunday, so three days were spent here. On Monday we had still worse trouble for on my wanting them to go further than they had made up their minds to do, about thirty or forty took up their beds and walked off. I at once sent my active second man Farajella after them and he succeeded in bringing back all but five. After this we had a grand palaver [conference]. The men demanded that they should not be made to walk after 11:00 a.m., I told them this was all I wished, knowing that if this was done every day we should do excellent work as it gave four to five hours for the day's journey. (We generally roused out about 5:30 getting started by six or half-past.) Then there were sundry grievances to be righted and a great, and sometimes angry, talk about nothing.

The day after this the pagasi surpassed themselves for they marched right on to Kandigwami, a distance from our last camp of nearly twelve miles, but so hot and trying a journey was it that during the night three more men ran away frightened at the rate at which they had to go. When not in very good health the travelling as the sun gets high is very trying especially in the forest where there is but little movement of the air. On finding there were absentees in the morning it took them some little arranging and scheming to divide the staff fairly between those remaining. One empty packing case was presented to the chief at Kandigwami, and after arranging all the other things I gave the order to march, but, as the men were starting, we found that another man had run away while they were waiting. He had been carrying a truck which had originally been a load for two men but which for the last two days he had voluntarily carried by himself. This was rather awkward. The men were moving on with their loads and here was this box without a carrier. I tried to strike a bargain with two natives but after a long palaver, and just when I thought the bargain completed one of them said he must go home and drink pombe [beer] before he commenced the work. I now opened the box and packed

2. Two yards of cloth.

some of its contents into a piece of canvass one man was carrying. Farajella took up the box and remaining goods, and so we went on our way.

We had to march through a good deal of swamp each day but not deep water. All now went well till we got to the Rukigura river at Mbuzini. The bridge of which Mr. Price speaks in his printed report is broken down and the river is unfordable.[3]

We found Mr. Mackay of the Church Missionary Society and his party encamped on the further bank, having floated their goods across in carts raft-wise the previous day.[4] Mr. Mackay himself, however, had gone back in search of runaways.

By a little further necessary contraction of our loads we rejected here three packing cases but found the CMS party would be very glad of them which was good. It became evident now that we must use our ropes to get across; accordingly, I sent the end of a rope across by a swimmer, and had it made fast to a palm tree in a suitable position. Then my end was also taken round a tree and by thirty or forty men hauled as tight as possible, (I had previously rove the rope thro' a single block). A pair of small shears, about twelve feet, were now rigged and forced up under the rope between the tree and the river, making the rope very tight and giving it a little slope towards the other bank. I now built a platform of Morton's provision boxes under the rope on which I could stand and reach the block, had two small ropes fast to the block one to each side of the river and the apparatus was complete. The loads were now one by one lashed to the hook of the block and hauled across by the small lines, going most of the way by their own gravity. Mr. Dodgshun who had previously swum across the river superintended the work of receiving and unlashing the loads as they came across while I secured each load to the hook and sent it over. After the men had got into the way of doing the work it went very rapidly to the great admiration of the natives. This, I think, was the hottest day we have experienced; a great number of our men sick, or unable to swim had to be hauled across on the line.

The following Sunday we had the pleasure of spending with

3. The Rev. Roger Price, in command of the expedition at its start, made a preliminary journey in 1876 from Saadani to Mpwapwa to test the possibility of using bullock wagons rather than carriers for transport of goods inland. Because he concluded that the tsetse fly was not on the road, the LMS committed itself to pioneering a wagon road. His report was published by the LMS in 1876, and it is to this that Hore refers.

4. Alexander Mackay was forced, because of poor health, to delay his journey to Lake Victoria Nyanza. On recovering he was instructed by the Church Missionary Society to apply his engineering skill to cut the wagon road from Mpwapwa to the coast.

Messrs. Copplestone and Titherley of the CMS having our camps close together in a pleasant piece of forest half a mile west of Matungu. On Monday morning both caravans started, the tiny CMS carts with nearly 1000 lbs. being drawn along apparently without effort over this level piece of country, but by fourteen oxen. We had not gone far before the scene changed altogether: softer and softer became the soil, first black mud thinner and thinner, then bog, and, last of all, the real water itself. We travelled on in this way sometimes awhile deep in water, sometimes in mud, and then thro' a dip over knee deep until half way across the pori. Here there is a considerable hill which of course is dry. We gave the pagasi leave to camp here if they liked, but they agreed to go on a little further on to another rising ground.

Accordingly we descended to the nullah thro' which Mr. Mackay had made a cutting. This was now a river full to the brim thro' which the pagasi waded breast deep, then on thro' mud and mire and then water again, a large expanse gradually deepening until our tallest man could only just keep his chin out of water. The pagasi train was now a row of black heads on the surface of the water each surrounded by a load. As soon as we emerged from this dismal place I scribbled a hasty note warning our friends of the CMS not to bring their goods beyond the hill until they had surveyed the country in front, and sent back a messenger with it. We now soon got up onto the rising camp where I found Mr. Dodgshun already arranging camp in a convenient dry place, and very glad we were to change garments and drink a cup of tea. The remaining half of the pori we found on the morrow to be covered with water generally about knee deep but many little rivers three or four feet deep, by the time we got to Kidudwi we were pretty experienced waders.

At Kidudwi we were very soon told that we "could go no further for there was very much water". We have, however, got so far experienced travellers that instead of rushing to look with great anxiety on hearing this news we said, "all right", and sat down to our breakfast (if a meal at noon may be called such). After the great heat was over we walked down to view the *magi teli* (much water). Waidinguzu, our head man, went with us, and behold, where formerly we knew nothing but dry lands was now a large and swift river; where we were led to see the river it was spread out nearly 100 yards wide. Waidinguzu was in a great fright about the crocodiles which some of the natives had spoken of, and we soon found that this stupid man had so encouraged the rumour that all our men were equally frightened or pretended to be so with himself. They had made up their minds for a day's halt, and from this Waidinguzu made no effort to dissuade them. We soon found, also, that he had led us to the very widest and worst part of the river in the neighbourhood, for on walking down river a little I soon found a place less than half the width and with a noble tree in the middle upon one of whose lofty branches I was sure a rope and block could be fixed so as to swing our loads across. I now got some men and an axe and cleared away the brushwood and creepers to give us room to work on the morrow. Darkness then came on and we returned to camp. In the morning I found that not a single man would swim over with a rope for fear of crocodiles. I then went to Makumulo, the chief, and asked him for a couple of men who would swim across and fix the ropes, whereupon the old gentleman quietly said if you will pay me I " will medicine the river so that it will go down and you can cross tomorrow ". This made me place faith in the native report that two days fine weather would cause the river to subside; it being, I suppose, a mere rain drain of the adjoining hills. I told the chief that I must cross today; he then said he could get seventeen men who would *walk across the river* with all the loads! but I must pay down twenty cloths at once and the work could not be done till tomorrow. I told him that was very much money, and so the matter ended. This business took about two hours, the chief and myself each sitting on a low three-legged stool whilst we slowly deliberated over the business, for in this sort of dealing nothing can be done in a hurry.

I now went down to the river knowing there must be a better crossing place than I had yet seen and soon found the place where the men who were to walk across must have intended starting. It was the narrowest part of the river in the neighbourhood and is spanned by a large tree which had evidently been cut down for the purpose. The near half of the tree was still submerged some three feet, although the river had already subsided three feet since the day before. While surveying this spot a native appeared on the other side whom hailing I offered a shukka if he would haul over our rope and make it fast to a tree stump. The man accepted the offer at once, and I sent men off to the camp for the rope. Several other men and boys now appeared and commenced bathing and playing in the river, swimming about with evidently no fear whatever of the crocodiles; The men I had sent up to the camp for the ropes had evidently spread the news that I had discovered the crossing place for with them came down a number of the villagers among them the big man who was to have been the leader of the seventeen and, whom it now appeared, was the owner of this " bridge ", he having cut the tree down. This man now spoke to the one to whom I had offered the shukka, and when I called him

C

to take the rope he declined to do so, saying that he did not want the shukka.

I again remonstrated with those of our men who were present, among them the head man Waidinguzu, but not one of them would venture in; Waidinguzu earnestly protesting that the men who were bathing had first medicined the river and so were unharmed. The big man, aforesaid, was evidently wishful to thwart my plans and my own men were useless, so after watching where the natives who crossed got their footing I took off coat and boots, and taking the end of the rope started over myself, succeeding in holding up against the current and making the rope fast on the other side. As I stood in mid-river I did not forget from that standpoint again to give the men a bit of my mind, but they continued constant in expressions of fear of the crocodiles. When halfway over coming back and steadying myself by the rope which several of our men were holding tight for that purpose I heard a volley of angry words on the side I was going to; a native was shouting and throwing his arms and pointing to me and to the rope. He then laid hold of the men who were holding it as if he wanted to shake me overboard. I got over as quickly as possible and found that this man had a garden on the other side in which the young corn was just coming above ground and he was afraid if we crossed here that the pagasi would trample it down. I quickly assured him that I would tell the men to be careful and if after getting across any damage was done I would inspect and pay for it.

There was evidently an ill feeling at my success so far, and I myself felt very indignant both about the crocodiles, which appeared to be an invention on the part of the people and had thoroughly scared our pagasi, and, also, that they had kept this crossing place secret. The rope was now ready for the next morning either as a handrail if the bridge were exposed or if the water rose it would be ready for the block and hauling lines. The owner of the bridge now demanded two doties[5] for the use of it and came into the tent to palaver. I expressed my feelings and asked him to be seated. I told this man that I could not even see part of the bridge yet it being under water and that the loads and men must be all across before I could tell whether it was a real good bridge, also, that if it rained hard in the night I should not be able to use the bridge but should cross on my own rope. I, also, told him that I must see my rope all right in the morning and requested him to see that nobody touched it. This seemed to quiet him, and he retired smiling. In the morning we were rejoiced to find that the waters

5. A doti is four yards of cloth.

had retired leaving the bridge dry, but we found assembled there, in addition to the owner of the bridge, the man of the shamba (garden) and his friends. The owner of the bridge now demanded his two dotis, and the man of the shamba backed by his friends, and all appearing very angry, demanded another doti before we could cross into his garden. In vain I remonstrated that I would keep my promise of yesterday—to pay fairly for any damage that might be done. The man persisted in shouting and talking very angrily and with his friends blocked up the way on and around the bridge.

I now agreed to pay the big man his toll but told him he must send these men out of my way, but he now demanded *three dotis* at which I was very indignant and told them all to wait a little.

I now went quickly up to the village to see old Makumulo, the chief, who was supposed to be our friend. I found him squatting on the ground, and the following conversation ensued:

" Jambo."

" Jambo."

" Are you a friend to the white men?"

" Yes, why do you ask that?"

" Because some of your people are at the bridge. They are very angry and say I cannot pass without paying four dotis. If you want still to be our friend you will settle this business for us."

" It is fair to pay the big man for his bridge which he had great work to cut down."

" I am willing to pay a fair price."

Upon this the old gentleman deliberated a little, and then procuring a staff beckoned me to follow him. When we got in sight of the noisy crowd at the bridge Makumulo turned aside in quite a different direction, my faith in him began to waver, but I followed him and found he was taking me to another crossing where he thought the water was now low enough for us to cross but we found it was not. And well I knew that our pagasi would not wade thro' even a foot of water in this river for fear of crocodiles. We now went to the bridge, but the old chief evidently did not know how to decide the matter being apparently equally frightened to offend either us or his own people and on some trivial plea shortly took his leave.

I now knew that if I would not waste the day I must speedily settle the matter somehow so I offered the big man two dotis to let me cross, telling him very positively that he would not get another inch. This he at once accepted. The man of the shamba now demanded two dotis but I told him firmly he should have none until I saw if any damage was done and, advancing towards him and his friends with as fierce an aspect as I could command, asked them to show me the man who dared stop me. This move had an unexpectedly good result, for they all seemed to collapse and disappear, whereupon the pagasi pushing forward at once commenced the passage. When about half were over I paid down the cloth telling the man I now saw that his bridge was good.

After everybody was clear over I crossed myself delighted indeed to be done with it. I found the shamba to be a very small one. The man's demands were perfectly ridiculous, for we passed thro' gardens much bigger nearly every day getting nothing from their owners but "jambos". The man pointed out to me *four* young shoots of corn which were trodden a little on one side, a most trivial complaint; however, in case anyone either of the natives or our own people should consider a non-payment as premeditated by me after the promise I had made, I cut off a kitamba (one yard) of cloth and offered it to him, but he refused it, and at once set up his noisy antics again making a rush at Waidinguzu and seizing his turban. I recovered the turban at once and warned him not to touch any of my men again.

Waidinguzu was very frightened and wanted to give the man a shukka himself, but I would not allow it and sent him away. The native stood making angry talk and gesticulations but being the only one of us two desirous of a quarrel, no harm was done, and I walked off followed by his angry voice.

For about a third of this march we had some swamp up to knee deep with horrible black mud but after that a fine dry path all the way to the tembe (square village) by the Mona river which we reached about noon.

From reports I had expected to find this river had gone down very much, but we were disappointed for on reaching it we found it full of water at the bridge, which rickety concern was submerged at either end. Single passengers, however, managed to get across with some difficulty.

The tembe was so entirely surrounded with shambas upon which we could not camp for the young shoots of corn and the ground beyond so stifled with tall thick grass that we were compelled to camp inside the tembe.

As soon as the sun had declined a little I went down to the river to survey and soon came to the conclusion that with a little work we should be able to cross by the bridge. Accordingly, sent for the ropes at once. Stretched the big hemp rope tight across and then went over myself and lashed the rope at intervals to trees and other portions of the bridge in such a way as to render it available as a handrail the whole way. To do this I had to stand in the water up to my waist for about half an hour. The east side of bridge had now to be repaired by lashing a lot of logs together. It is a wonderful thing how this old bridge stands at all in such a large and swift body of water, but there are several trees against which it bears which are growing in the river. Before dusk all was ready for next morning.

It was just about all the pagasi could do to struggle across this bridge. It certainly afforded but poor footing: part of the bridge being three feet under water with a good swift stream flowing across and even where the footing is in sight it is terribly unsteady. We took a very long time crossing; six or seven men said they were sick (frightened to go across), and several more could not carry their loads over which others took at the last. After all had got over Farajella and myself stopped behind to undo the lashings and recover all the ropes again which involved a lot of work in the water again; however, I took care to have dry clothes waiting for me on the other side.

After going a very short distance we found the ground covered with from one to three feet of water and this nearly the whole of the way to the tembe by the little river Kigulumbezi. The tall coarse grass here is very thick and luxuriant, and the thick reeds which gave us so much trouble with the carts were now in two and three feet of water thro' a great part. Many of the cornfields are under water. Over the little Kigulumbezi [river] dry ground again and so on to camp on a little round knoll close to a small village. Thunder and lightning with threatening appearance of weather in the evening.

Next day we marched on to the Mukindo but found it too deep to ford and had to go back to a bridge all the way to the village we had camped at. Waded thro' a reed swamp and then across the tree bridge, rather a climb. When I got to the other side I found my daily box had been dropped into the water and opening it found everything soaked and some inches of water still in it, several good books much spoilt, wrung the things out as well as I could and packed up again. Got to Mkiropa in good time and camped. Weather fine in the forenoon; in the evening violent squalls of wind and rain with incessant thunder and lightning.

Next day was Sunday and very glad indeed were we of the day's rest; same weather as yesterday.

On Monday, we found the valley thicker than ever with tall grass, sugar, maize, etc. Halted a short time at Mvomero and then went on and camped about three and a half miles towards Mongubu—(Ngubu). Here for the first time we had bad water, finding fishes and tadpoles in our drinking mugs. Siwaki the cook had disappeared this morning, a good riddance, and next day two more men ran away.

We arrived at Msoero without further adventure on the 17th. It seemed quite an event to get back here, all the country beyond being quite new to me, and it was from here that I had twice started for the coast. On the morning of the 18th I felt so ill that it was decided to remain tho' I don't think the pagasi would have travelled had I been well. Mr. Dodgshun, too, had an attack of fever.

The old one eyed chief of the town and the superior chief whom we call " the king of the country " paid us a visit today and after a long roundabout told us that they should allow no more waggons to pass this way because they spoilt the gardens. This chief certainly seems an active man and has some well worked gardens so that this can hardly be thought unreasonable; I have no doubt a road round can be found. They both expressed themselves friendly to white men and quite agreeable to the passage of foot travellers and pagasi but could not be argued into seeing the benefit of leaving a waggon road instead of a footpath thro' their gardens.

Next morning the pagasi refused to travel, there being several men very sick and objecting to leave here. Had a long palaver and at last they took a notion and all hands declared for an immediate march back to Zanzibar, refusing to take the allowance for the day. After a very long talk and a little persuasion of a few who I knew were still faithful I succeeded in quieting them, and they agreed to go on with the journey on Monday. I now mustered the sick men and administered Epsom salts to such cases as it was suitable for. The rest had to trust to Nature.

Monday Jan. 21st. There are quite a number of respectable villages about Msoero, and the path from that place to the river winds through a number of well kept gardens and a larger village, all belonging to the Makua people and so down to the river, a broad and shallow tho' swift stream. Another village at the landing place and more good gardens—from here the road leads W.S.W. thro' alternate long coarse grass and thin forest. Passing Mbumi village we come to the Sangata, a small river which we crossed on Mr. Thomson's bridge, still in good repair. Here were goodly numbers of people working in their gardens and we were very pleased to see that they had had the good sense to leave an ample road for the passage of waggons instead of as usual only the bare vestige of a footpath.

At our camp just beyond we were pleased to receive messengers from Mr. Thomson bearing a lot of mutton and two loaves of bread on which fare we regaled with some satisfaction. The next day we had a really splendid walk thro' beautiful undulating forest land passing many large shambas and so on to the very large village of Rudewa—quite a town. Thro' here we descended into a nasty waste place with swamp and then a walk thro' gardens brought us to the Wami river thickly fringed in with tall coarse reeds and grass. We found that a strong man without a load could just manage to get across the river which was neck deep and flowing with a good current but no loaded man could walk across.

I was very anxious to get across the river that day so the rope was brought along and stretched tight across the river and with the help of this good handrail the pagasi were induced to wade across and eventually everything was got over in safety tho' the stronger men had to come back and take the loads of many who were too weak or timid to venture in.

We now considered the real difficulties of the journey over. On Wednesday we reached Farahani and next day Patupa thro' country thickly covered with long coarse grass which makes weary travelling, and on Friday we entered the Mukondokwa valley. Coming all at once upon the river fringed in with reeds we turn sharp round to the N.W. and walk up the valley—verdure covered mountains on either side and so we continue sometimes N.W., sometimes W.N.W. right on to Kirasa. Arrived at Muinyi Usargara on Saturday about eight miles from Kirasa having just previously met Mr. Hutley and M. Broyon who had come out to meet us. Here I used every bit of threat and persuasion I could muster to induce the men to make an afternoon march to Kirasa and should have succeeded but that more than half of them were away in other villages buying food and I was compelled to remain. Messrs. Dodgshun and Hutley, however, walked on. Considering all the attendant circumstances I deemed it admirable for the first time to move on Sunday morning. I arrived at Kirasa about 9:30 a.m., and I think it was about the nearest approach I have had to getting home in reality. It was indeed delightful to get to this pleasant little settlement. Everything appeared to me most civilised and homelike after the rough work of travelling.

On Monday morning I prepared to settle business matters with the pagasi, make up their accounts, etc. For this purpose I called them all up, intending to overhaul each load in the presence of its carrier and see that all was right. Before however any work was commenced they had a great talk among themselves being evidently in a state of discontent and some of them thinking that they still had to go on to Mpwapwa, the result being that they got up in a body and expressed their determination to make tracks for Zanzibar there and then! barely giving me time to warn them that by this foolish action they were forfeiting all their pay.

Shortly afterwards we sent down to their camp for Waidinguzu and the seventeen head men (these are the leading men of each

kambi or mess and are looked upon as a sort of leader or spokesman) to reason with them. When these men arrived they at first
seemed willing to be reconciled (indeed it would have been for
their own benefit and not ours that they should be so), but, when
I began to question them before everybody upon sundry occurrences on the journey, matters resumed a different aspect.

I first asked them what they had to say about the detention they
had wilfully caused to the caravan at Pamagombe. To this they
could make no definite reply. Then I asked them what they could
say of the desertion of about thirty of their number from the camp
at Magubika and picking out one of them I said, " This was one
of the deserters and he took his gun with him but was caught and
brought back, what can you say to that?" They were all greatly
astonished and frightened at this especially the poor man himself.
They little thought my eyes had been used so sharply.

Just at this juncture Waidinguzu (who well knew that the next
question would be a demand to know where the gunpowder was
that I put in his flask at Ndumi and which he had since made away
with) whispered in his mysterious way to several of the men and
they all got up together and cleared out. Shortly afterwards we
heard their horn sounding down the hill and knew that they were
really underweigh for Zanzibar.

I did not deem it necessary or advisable (indeed such would have
been quite fruitless) to make further effort to stop these deserters,
our goods having been delivered complete at our door, they therefore bear upon themselves the loss of pay and character which
their childish action has brought about. Farajella, our second man
who had been my factotum and boatswain's mate and everything
that meant activity and work thro' out the journey, had proved
himself a very faithful and hard working man, and I did not like
to see him losing his pay. I therefore called him aside and gave him
an order on Mr. Buchanan for his pay, etc., and an allowance to
buy food on his way to the coast.

The journey of 180 miles was accomplished in thirty-three-and-
a-half days being only one day and-a-half longer than the former
caravan which considering the extra difficulties in the last journey
may be considered as very good work. . . .

We are all in very good health at present. As for myself I have
only had one slight attack of fever since October 24th, but I have
suffered somewhat on this journey from a succession of colds kept
up by the continual wading and then working in the water at the
rivers, as I expected, I have quite recovered again now. . . .[6]

6. This concludes the first segment of the journal.

Log of the Expedition to Urambo*

Thursday May 29th 1878—Roused out at five a.m., served out the loads, packed up all final odds and ends and found that several men had run away, and, thus, we were compelled to leave behind twenty-three loads which it had been arranged to take with us. To do this I had to descend the hill to where the men and loads were assembled, and, catalogue in hand, select what should be left to the best of my judgment. Had I not been thoroughly well acquainted with each load and its contents this selection and re-arrangement would have delayed us another day; as it was we were able to proceed and all got away about eight o'clock, Juma MacKay leading with the flag.

Whilst crossing the Mukendokwe river one of our three oxen was drowned, although some of the men exerted themselves well to save it, two of the oxen were swept down river against a half sunken tree and, becoming entangled while after much struggling, the other was swept away down the river and was finally recovered on the other side.

Several of our men are sick and we are fairly loaded, I have some anxiety as to being able to carry on eventually what we have with us.

Little Majelewa, with the smallest body amongst our men, seems to possess, perhaps, the greatest energy and spirit amongst them, with another man he is trudging along with a big double load beside which he appears quite a small object. His outfit, beyond the muslin-like loin rag he wears, consists of a white shirt given him by Mr. Dodgshun and which is duly lashed on top of the load. On coming up to the little man today and speaking encouraging to him, he said, " O great Master I shall die today and then you must get another man to carry this load ", and with that he started on quickly and whipping his load with a stick imitating a bullock driver's chant to the oxen and went off smiling; I will make bigger men carry this tomorrow. Arrived at camp one mile short of Kadete river and tried to get things in order a little. I found that a load of lead had not arrived which I knew a man had carried away from Kirasa, and concluded he had bolted with his load; so, sent off Widmajera and Abdulla Songoro after this man and the

*In the archives of the Congregational Council for World Mission.

Kirasa runaways. They shortly returned with both man and load, the man having had an attack of dysentary. Ordered the same two men to start early in the morning after the Kirasa runaways. . . . Mr. Baxter of the CMS is with us having come from Mpwapwa; he arrived at Kirasa yesterday.

Thursday 30th—Great trouble in starting this morning; four or five men had run away during the night; our double loads also are very unpopular, being the cause. I am afraid of some of these men running away. After most of the men had got loads, I found there were still four or five of these double loads without men and only a few sick men remaining. I crowded other loads together as well as I could, and sent Juma MacKay on with main body of caravan. . . .

I tried hard to make a bargain with two Wasagna who were travelling our way, but they wanted too much cloth. Meantime a large caravan of Wanyamwezi came along bound coast-wise with ivory (some 1200 carriers had passed by yesterday), and we were obliged to wait to let them cross the river and pass by. They are bearing an immense quantity of ivory and have very many large tusks. I tried to get a few of these Wanyamwezi as carriers but could not. After this caravan had crossed we got all the things across, and then by pressing the servants and Farajella into the service contrived at last to get away with all the things, but I had almost to force men who I knew to be sick to carry loads, and then it could only just be managed. It is evident we must either get more men or send some loads back; two men dropped on the road, and all the head men came into camp loaded. Arrived with last lot of men at camp on Ugombo Lake, about 1:30 p.m., all very tired. The first sight of this little lake was, as Mr. Henry M. Stanley had said, very refreshing, especially as it was immediately followed by the arrival of a man carrying a calabash full of its water.

Came to the conclusion that we must make some rearrangement of matters and talked to the men. They refused the offer of one doti extra per month for any who would carry double loads right thro' to Ujiji; we decided to leave light loads here under charge of Mr. Hutley.[7] Mr. Dodgshun to proceed post haste to Mpwapwa (Dr. B. accompanying him), and endeavour to engage some Wanyamwezi pagasi, and also send back some natives to bring on the eight loads. Mr. T. and myself to proceed with our journey to Mpwapwa. . . .

7. Walter Hutley, a joiner, was the youngest man on the expedition. As did Hore and Dodgshun, Hutley kept a detailed record of his experiences in Africa; his journals, in private hands until 1969, are being edited by James B. Wolf.

Saturday June 1st—Underweigh as early as possible but again had much trouble in getting loads taken away the double loads being very unpopular, and several sick men. My man Joseph and one Saidi Stanley carried Mr. T., myself keeping close to him. It proved very hard work for these two men, and they had to take frequent rests. At Simbo we halted for two or three hours, and I prepared some soup for Mr. T., who is getting very ill with continued vomiting, rejecting medicine. Got on again in the afternoon after another hard job to get all the loads taken up, several men staulking to the front without loads. Got all fixed at last. Joseph still carrying Mr. T. with Rehani. After frequent halts arrived at sunset within eight or nine miles of Mpwapwa. Mr. T. is very low and requiring constant attention as also do these 250 wild children, and all our valuable property, which otherwise in their hands would fair sadly. One of our bright head men Juma MacKay (I found when I got to camp, myself tired and Mr. Thomson helpless) had pitched the tent right in the middle of a thick scrub with the door looking right away from the stack of loads and the road. I laid Mr. T. on the ground and, comforting him as best I could with promise of a speedy adjustment of things, by dint of a little shouting and gesticulating got a man to every tent rope and by one movement slewed it round into position without taking it down. Then, all at once, I had to see the loads stacked, the things in the tent, undress the patient, make hasty pudding and acid drinks which he managed to take; later on I gave him a big dose of Chlorodyne which gave him some rest. Called our head man Juma and told him to pick out two of the best men to carry Mr. T. to Mpwapwa early tomorrow morning. Our water now ran short and I had to serve it out to Mr. T. in little sips so as to leave some for his journey tomorrow. A fine starlight night and gratefully cool (to our men baridi sana—" very cold ").

After Mr. T. was asleep and the camp quiet I had a stroll outside. The scene was quietly impressive; some thirty or forty camp fires lighted up the forest, the now bare and weird looking trees looking still bare and more weird in the fire light, scrubby undergrowth filling the space below with patches of blackness beyond, and above, the dark blue star lit sky. All was quiet, save the pleasant crackling here and there of the fires and the voice of man, not yet asleep, in a low chant to the accompaniment of one string, telling a mournful tale about the " Bwana Mdogo—who was left in the wilderness."

Sunday—Up with the first streak of dawn and at once got hammock men prepared and sent Mr. T. off in the care of Juma, our head man (sending also Feraji with the small drop of water remaining and one or two others with Mr. T.'s clothes, etc.), in the hope that he would reach Mpwapwa and obtain the attention of Dr. Baxter two or three hours before I could arrive with the caravan. And this proverbial circumstance should be remembered that at this critical point in the most serious illness that had yet occurred amongst us the patient was enabled to arrive at the CMS station at Mpwapwa and obtain the assistance of a medical man, Mr. T.'s case the more complicated as from weakness and fever; he was unable to retain such medicine as I administered long enough for its diffusion, and his lips and fingers revealed alarmingly his great loss of blood.

I had a harder job than ever to get the loads all carried this morning, but finally arrived at Mpwapwa after a hot tiring march. Found Mr. T. snugly housed in Mr. Copplestone's house and Mr. Dodgshun diligently stacking the loads as they struggled in. The men were all very tired and thirsty and many lay by the roadside taking long rests. Mr. D. kindly sent his servant out to me with a kettle of water for which I was extremely grateful; I divided the remainder of the water in small sips amongst such of the pagasi as I overtook. When I came to the dry sandy watercourse of the Mpwapwa river, it looked like a bare broad road, some natives were driving along a very decent herd of small cattle while numbers of our pagasi lay prone under the shade of the trees declaring that they could go no further till they had water. I encouraged them on as best I could and myself hurried on to Mpwapwa and sent back men with water. The temporary collection of buildings of the CMS at Mpwapwa looked to me very much like a roadside inn, farmstead, and outhouses in the Australian bush, and it proved as welcome to the weary traveller. Our tents were pitched opposite Mr. C.'s house. Moderate breeze increasing to fresh and gusty, towards noon and midnight.

Monday—Busily engaged unpacking double loads making some lighter, and others into single loads. Sent off nine men to Mr. Hutley to bring on loads left with him. Heard news of Ludi (our messenger to Mirambo) being within two days with 500 pagasi for us.

Tuesday June 4th—Still busy packing, etc. Mr. Thomson getting slightly better. . . . Went up on the ridge behind the CMS houses with Dr. B and Messrs. C and D. This ridge is a large spur of the hills over which the Lubugwe roads enters the Mpwapwa district. The CMS has three temporary houses here in a beautiful district. Our men refused their rations today, wanting a higher rate, which, on consideration, we refused; they having now a shukka for every seven men according to their own agreement with us at

Kirasa. Afterwards, believing that many were not disaffected but perhaps under a misunderstanding, sent a message to them for all who wished their food to come for it; nearly all came and took it, but next day nearly twenty discontents were missing.

Wednesday—A few of the best men spoke to me thro' Juma quietly in the way they had been told to do in any such case, and I promised them that this time if I found this was not enough I would give them their poshos after six days had expired instead of seven (having found that food was dear here).

Thursday June 6th—Ludi and Mahabutu, our messengers to Mirambo, arrived with 120 Wanyamwezi pagasi who are bound coastwise with orders to engage themselves to any white men who may be coming Mirambo-wards.

Friday—We tried to make a bargain with forty of these pagasi to come with us now, but on consideration of their demands and the diminution that would be caused to our stock of cloth by paying them we have determined to let them all go to the coast for the benefit of Broyon,[8] and go on with such Zanzibar men as we could retain in our service.

Saturday—Had long consultation as to ways and means. I am of opinion that, taking probable risks into consideration and the fact that now the great bulk of our goods being with Broyon, twenty-three of the loads we had calculated to take with us having been left at Kirasa, and forty-two more must be left here (all in consequence of men running away), that it would not be well for all four of us to go forward with *any less goods* than we have here. . . . The result of consultation was that Mr. Dodgshun, on his own suggestion, should remain behind and come up with Broyon; Messrs. T. and H. and myself going on with what we could. By this arrangement one of our number will be with the goods we have left behind, which will certainly be a great advantage. We also decided what loads to leave behind, marked off twenty-five for that purpose, finished about one p.m.

Sunday—Mr. Thomson getting much better; in the evening he conducted service and we celebrated the Lord's supper altogether.

Monday June 10th—Plenty of work, repacking and rearranging everything to suit new order of things. Hutley building storehouse for safety of goods left behind.

Tuesday—Preparing for start tomorrow; put goods to be left into LMS storehouse, hoisting small mission flag thereon. Packed

8. A Swiss trader, Phillippe Broyon, had been serving as Mirambo's agent, and at this time was in charge of a caravan containing goods for the Unyamwezi chief.

pots and kettles and private baggage, all ready for a start. Mr. T. better.

Wednesday June 12th—Underweigh shortly after daylight, taking all the loads estimated and still having, apart from the head men and servants and two men carrying Mr. Thomson. Ten men not carrying our goods. They were of course however loaded with mats and bundles, etc. belonging to their comrades. Descended Mr. Last's road to the river, now a shallow stream flowing here over the sand but under which it soon after disappears. Passed along the terrace formed by the first rise of the plain towards its mountain border making thus a semicircular course towards the Chunyo pass, which we could see plainly from the CMS station. Passed several tembes and over many small water courses with red soil and some forming deep but narrow chasms six to eighteen feet deep. To our left the enclosed Mpwapwa plain, close on our right its mountain border, to the South the lofty Rubeho stretches as far as the eye can reach. The camping place at Chunyo lies just in the western discharge of the pass on a little level patch about 300 feet above the plain of the Marenga Mkali, upon which the pass opens. To the N & S rise the mountains steep and pointed and on the northern side there is close at hand a high bluff, semi-detached hill which is conspicuous. Away to the West there is yet but a limited view of the Marenga Mkali, much of the view (until we entirely emerge from the pass) being shut out by scattered hills which in the distance appears as a smaller range running N & S. These hills generally of long gradual slopes, but withal generally detached, form a general feature (with the flat plain with which they are surrounded) from here right thro' Ugogo. In the Marenga Mkali these plains are covered with a thick scrub of stunted trees and dreadful thorns, now looking fierce and dread in their wintry garb. The Chunyo river, descending as a torrent thro' the mountain gorges on the Southern side of the pass, crosses the pass and emerges upon the plain along the Northern portal. The much dreaded waters of this river, now formed in isolated pools in its otherwise dry sandy bed, are indeed nauseous and only endurable as tea or coffee taken medicine-wise; our pagasi, however, seemed to put but little restraint upon their use of it.

Shortly after getting to camp a messenger arrived (one Abdulla, Moslem, dressed partly in the uniform of the Royal Marine Light Infantry) with the news of having brought to Mpwapwa ten more men for us; Juma was at once sent back for these men with orders to bring on with them six more loads left at Mpwapwa. An Arab caravan of 300 men shortly after arrived, and the Arab wished to

join caravans with us for strength thro' Ugogo. Tried without success after some Koodo (deer) on the southern hill.

Thursday June 13th—Preparing for a start in case of being able
to go, but when Juma arrived he brought with him Maktub with
our mail who had brought to Mpwapwa another nineteen men (!),
and Mr. Copplestone, seeing this change of course before us,
kindly sent on by Juma eighteen loads instead of six. These men
being too tired to proceed today on the long forced marches necessary on leaving here determined to wait till tomorrow, enduring
thus an extra day of his horrible water. Slight shower during the
night. Served out light rounds of ammunition to the men with
guns.

Friday June 14th—Got underweigh this morning and commenced the passage of the dreaded Marenga Mkali. The road
descended from the pass close round the southern portal of the
pass and on thro' rough scrub and thorn bush with few bare open
patches for eight miles when a halt was called. This morning I
have suffered the effects of the Chunyo water. The journey tired
Mr. T. very much, and he was carried for the remainder of the
day, very glad of the short rest at the halting place. Had the
poorest ox killed for the benefit of the pagasi. After about two
hours started again and made another eight miles to camp, same
country.

Saturday 15th—Made about the same distance as yesterday,
arriving at camping place at Ndebwe about noon. The same scrub
and thorn continues to within a couple of miles of Ndebwe, when
it suddenly ends, and the open country is seen for a wide space—a
few scattered hills bound the view, and Ndebwe is entered thro
long and wide spreading gardens of Matama and Meweri. *Ndebwe*
is a scattered collection of forty-one tembes on a flat, and now
almost barren, plain of rough burnt grass stubble, dotted with
baobab trees, under one of which our camping place is situated.
Very tired, men all knocked up from their long forced marches so
it was some time before the tents were pitched and all made snug.
Found that a load of mixed cloth had been opened and a piece of
Amerikani gone, Juma found out the carrier who, after a few
smart blows from that party's stick, expressed himself willing to
show where he had put the cloth. Farajella returned with him and
the cloth in about two hours; the lad alleged that he had only
taken it out of the load to relieve himself of the weight. Here was
brought to us for sale fat, ground nuts, beans, and pumpkins.

Sunday—Enjoyed a quiet rest. The Wagogo not troubling us
with their impatience half as much as we had been led to expect.

Monday 17th—Eight miles to *Mvumi* over several nullahs and two dry rivers of good size, same country. We are now fairly in Ugogo, and alas, within the clutches of the hongo-squeezing Wagogo.[9] The large plain, not unlike a dirty bare common in England, is horrible with the filth and refuse and ashes of many caravans. The little huts of branches, reeds, and grass having done duty for many travellers, each new caravan enlarging or shifting the little huts, either sometimes bodily or sometimes piece work to suit their convenience and the size of the Boma they may require. We made our camp close to that of a Wanyamwezi caravan bound coastwise. The day after we arrived they announced by beat of drum that their hongo (which had consisted of eight days' work of carrying firewood, etc.) was completed.

In reply to our advances we received a message from the chief that as yet we had scarcely arrived in his country, and he could not think of commencing business till tomorrow. Our camp became as at Ndebwe just like a bazaar or fair with a touch of the zoological gardens : the people gathering round the tents just exactly as people in England look at the animals there. Their observations, of course, covering all our belongings as well as ourselves. The remarks passed upon as being very similar. One instance as an illustration : some young men were gazing intently into my tent when one laid hold of his friend very earnestly saying, " O come over to the other tent there's one there with a big beard ". Old men and women, young men and maidens, are all the same : stare stare stare. I have tried several times boldly to show them out, and only succeeded in one instance when, I suppose, I must have managed an expression of a superlatively injured and astonished character and a woman persuaded several people that they were rude, but I was much disappointed when the same woman, who was the last of the group to leave, herself turned back to take a parting stare. Nearly all these visitors however have something for sale, and most patient they are in promenading the camp, sometimes all day with their wares on their heads looking for customers, matama meal, pumpkins, eggs and milk, the two latter in very advanced stages of their existence. The tembe of the chief is some distance off. As sunset approaches the crowds of people disappear, before dark not one is to be seen but our own people.

Tuesday & Wednesday—Bargaining over the hongo the old chief was to be seen by white men and making exorbitant demands for cloth. Finally, settled hongo by paying one coil of brass wire, about

9. Hongo was tribute paid to the various Wagogo chiefs to insure safe conduct for the caravan through their territory.

seven lbs. of white and pink beads and 75 doti (300 yards) of cloth.

Thursday 20th—Underweigh in the morning, very glad to be away from this tiresome place and arrived at Matamburu after a march of eight miles. Still the same flat plain between hills, which, tho' there are often many of them and at a distance look something like a chain, are still isolated hills with a distinct plain between. From Mvumi to Matamburu there are many tembes and gardens, and scattered scrubby bushes are dotted over the plain; in addition to the numerous small nullahs we passed over two good sized river beds. As one camp was being formed the old Chief himself appeared with a troop of noisy warriors, and commenced an altercation with several of our pagasi about their having removed some huts from another camping ground resulting, our men afterwards told us, in their having to pay a penalty of Amerikani. I went up to the old Chief at once and saluted him with " jambo " which he heartily returned and shook hands. I then said to him that he should leave such small matters to some of his men and come and sit awhile in the tent of the Masungu, thinking it a good opportunity of getting an early commencement of the hongo business. We, accordingly, came into the camp, and I introduced him to Mr. Thomson, but no business was done today. The chief is a jolly old fellow, if such a character can be reconciled with demands for hongo.

Saturday 22nd—After great business we settled the hongo today but to do so I had to hand over to the Wagogo my double barrelled gun, and then, instead of the 150 cloths they demanded at first (for ourselves and the caravan of Wanyamwezi who travelled with us and who desired us to make one business of our hongo and theirs), they now were satisfied with ninety for the two caravans. The total hongo for the two caravans thus amounting to forty-two rings brass wire, one dressing gown, about six lbs. beads (white & pink) and sixty cloths paid by ourselves and thirty-five of a very inferior kind by the Wanyamwezi. The hongo being finished, the next business was to settle matters with the Wanyamwezi and this proved as big a job as the hongo itself, for they were very unwilling to part even with a single cloth, while to settle matters we wanted from them thirty-six good cloths and twenty-five circles of brass wire. After haggling for a whole day with these people I succeeded in acquiring out of them twenty rings of brass wire (which wire, being thicker than ours I was satisfied on that score) and twenty cloths but these cloths were very inferior to ours, and they cheated us with short measure and other deceit, and the matter ended by their refusing altogether to

D

pay the remaining twelve cloths. It was only because they were in Ugogo that they dared to do such a thing, knowing that we dreaded a disturbance. At this point they commenced taking away their loads, making a separate camp. Before they were all gone however I mustered our men and surrounded them (the loads) refusing to let any more be removed till our debt had been satisfied. The Wanyamwezi were frightened, and, had it been anywhere but in Ugogo, would, I think, have paid their debt, but they well knew, that we knew that if the Wagogo heard the row they would make a great fuss and perhaps stop both caravans and demand more hongo, and knowing that we therefore dared not prolong the position, still refused, or rather put off, until at the urgent advice of our head men who said the Wagogo would assuredly be down upon us otherwise I ordered the men to be dispersed, and so we suffer greatly from force of circumstances this open robbery of our goods.

Sunday June 23rd—Mr. Thomson still very ill, but nearly every day he gets better and then relapses. We had prayer together in his tent this evening, after I have finished haggling with the Wanyamwezi.

Monday 24th—Underweigh this morning, past several tembes. First two miles threading our way amongst numerous hills, the path closed in often by thorny scrub. The rest of the way rugged and winding thro' thick jungle, the latter part of our road being along the bed of a small stream for some distance, we finally emerged out of the jungle on to a sandy river bed in which sundry holes supplied the water for the folks of Bihawana. There was only the one tembe near our camp but several further on. Here we killed the calf that old Matamburu had given us, the hongo was settled with little trouble and consisted of thirteen cloths in all, eleven of them being of the inferior cloths received from the Wanyamwezi.

Tuesday 25th—A short march of four miles this morning brought us to Kididimo. Mr. T. had an interview with the Chief. Large corn fields abound all over the country while butter, milk, eggs, matama meal, ground nuts, beans and honey are brought to the camps for sale. Many beehives are deposited in the trees; they consist of split trunks of trees hollowed out, the ends being left open and the two parts finally lashed together. We managed to get the hongo settled today for twelve doti of cloths, six being of those received from the Wanyamwezi.

Wednesday 26th—After leaving Kididimo we seem to enter a new country, more resembling the best aspects of the coast region.

Here is a fine grass and for the first five miles in pass thro' the jungle not so scrubby and thorny as districts in Ugogo. We pass many tracks of large game which is said to be very plentiful. We halted at the same spot where Stanley stopped on his first journey. After a good long rise we suddenly descend into a sort of bay where the water is retained in a sort of basin; just below is the river bed of which Stanley speaks, and very fine grass and soft verdure is abundant here. We stopped till noon having rest and refreshment. The head man of a small Wanyamwezi caravan came to me here having two coils of copper wire which he wishes to sell. I drove a hard bargain with him, finally getting the two coils for ten of the cloths we had received from the Wanyamwezi at Matamburu. His bargain took a full hour to complete. Both buyer and seller, tho' it is hard to say which is which, depreciating the others goods' the old Wanyamwezi overhauled each cloth and remarked the slight defect or damage, while in return I pointed out each flaw and crack in the wire.

After leaving this halting place at noon we rise a little with a really beautiful forest thro' which the road leads us the whole day. Good soft grass abounds, and tho' the winter is far advanced there is still enough green to make the scene pleasant. Here are large forest trees again much as we have not seen since leaving Mpwapwa and such a fine collection of straight trees so suitable for building and other purposes we have not seen in the country before. Many acacias also and the ebony and other trees remind one of the pleasantest part of the coast region. Nearly all thro' this forest a sandy soil is revealed by the path tho' animal and vegetable deposit has rendered the place competent to the production of the most luxuriant vegetation. The large baobabs are still here. Altogether a very fine forest on either border of which, indeed in a clearing of the forest itself, would I think be found some most desirable places for a settlement. In the middle of the forest water is obtained very near the surface in little holes, and I should say that a constant supply would easily be obtained for a settlement by the construction of wells. A journey of good twelve miles today and we camp in the forest; there is still thorny wood enough for a boma to be quickly constructed, and we are glad of rest and refreshment after being underweigh all day.

Thursday June 27th—A march of three more hours brings us with a slight descent on to a similar plain to that of Eastern Ugogo: an open and level plain dotted with baobabs and scanty bushes and covered with white saline deposits. Palm trees are now seen in the far distance and numerous tembes with far stretching and straggling cornfields testify to a considerable population. As we approach the large tembe of Pembera Perah, the chief of *Nyambwa*, we pass by a fine large tamarind tree, the first I have seen in this region, and a few castor oil plants are also encouraged in the close neighbourhood of the tembes. The numerous rivers or river beds of Ugogo, winding as they did in every direction defy anything but a most careful local survey to correctly lay down, and a season of unusually copious rain will most probably very greatly change their form and direction. Here again the sand is genuine quartz as near the coast and the general surface feature in eastern Ugogo was more clayey with many gravelly conglomerates, tho' the granite crops out all over the country. The granite and quartz, as near Mpwapwa, is seen in almost every variety of quality and composition, and I think a careful search for the more valuable varieties would be rewarded. I fancy a " prospector " would be more hopeful in Eastern Ugogo than in any part we have yet passed thro'. Making the best selection we could amongst the old camping places, our pagasi were soon once more busily building our little camp town.

The hongo business was commenced as soon as possible but, as the Chief was in a state of drunkenness, it proved a most humiliating business. It was finally settled however today after the payment of one coil of copper wire and thirty-nine cloths, but this proves after all to be not final. Just as I had completed my observations for latitude in the evening, the camp was disturbed by a Ugogo messenger who on approaching the camp cried out to know where the entrance was. Now as the Kigogo for door is " mesigo " and " mesigo " in Kiswahili means a pagasi load, cries of " mesigo " connected with the words of Masunlu and Wagogo quickly brought me out of my tent with revolver and lantern, only to find that a messenger had arrived from the drunken chief demanding further tribute from the white man in the shape of a volley from the white men's guns. Today to the closing festivities of what he termed a " good day "; doubtless the cloths were good for him as for us it was a sore point. A non-compliance with this request would very likely have prevented an intended start next morning, so I started off with Farajella and four other men to the big tembe where the drunken Pembera Perah was holding the final revels of his " good day ", not knowing how long this drunkard might detain us or how much of our precious gunpowder might have to be expended. I sent a message as we drew near the tembe that with the white man seven was a good number and, therefore, we should fire seven shots only and no more (which message seemed to be taken in). We found a few people outside the tembe wall. We were desired on our arrival to fire two shots; the old gentleman evidently wanted to take the pleasure of gun shots in little bits, and he now sent out a message to me that if I wanted to see him, I must give to each of his two wives a good cloth, and that I might also have the pleasure of seeing them (the wives). I replied that we had already given him all the cloths he had demanded, and that it was now his turn to give us something. Of this he took no notice but still demanded the two cloths. After haggling in this way for about an hour, during which time many messages passed between us, amongst which was one from him that the other white man had brought him many cloths out of his tent but that I had brought him none (!), and one from myself to the effect that tho' the other white man had given him the cloths they had all come out of my tent and now everything was packed up and the people had gone to bed and that I had no cloths with me except the shirt I wore. After this we were told we might fire off the other shots and return. My men were all glad as myself to terminate this humiliating affair, and firing off their guns in every direction made me think that some of them were dangerously close to my head. They are like a lot of children with guns. While we were waiting outside the tembe I was supplied with a stool to sit upon and secured the good feeling of the people outside by opening and shutting the shade of a dark lantern, much to their amusement and surprise. Shortly after coming in camp again and, thus when everything was quiet, we were again aroused by a lot of shouting from some Wagogo who were trying to scare a lion which was supposed to be prowling about; (they told us there was a noted man-eater in the neighbourhood who lately had carried off several people). We accordingly retrimmed all the fires and set a watch.

Friday 28th—We got away as quickly and quietly as possible this morning fearing all the time lest we should be again stopped by the drunken chief but we got away all right. The corn fields of the Nyambwa folk lined our road for the first mile after which the broad open plain extended as far as the eye could reach on either side, with scattered tembes and cornfields the whole route and palm trees now took the place to a great extent of the baobabs. A few scattered bushes broke the monotony of the salt encrusted plain, at the westward now appeared a ridge looking like a blank wall right before us, a termination to the northward about 3 points N. of our path merged off into the haze; southward the ridge extended as far as I could see. Not a vestige of this sudden ascent (for it is really one immense steep *step* of 800 feet and the plateau beyond) which has such a striking appearance rising abruptly off this level plain. Half way on our road we pass between two little sharp hogbacks of granite extending in a line about N.W. and S.E.

with a quarter of a mile between them, and now as we draw near *Mizanza*, the palm appear in great numbers.

Stanley has truly described *Mizanza* as being situated in a grove of palm trees. Numerous and large tembes, and cornfields, herds of cattle, and a small troop of donkeys add to the lively scene. This place presents its romantic appearance only spoilt by the refuse and filth of the camps of many caravans. We camp amidst the palms and are politely told that no hongo can be treated for today, for the people must have a chance to barter with our pagasi and get their cloth. On approaching Mizanza the ridge to our Westward reminded me forcibly of the cliffs of England being approached from seaward. As no hongo was to be done today I started off for the hills with Farajella and another man, passing many tembes and large corn fields; these latter extending close up to the foot of the hills which are abruptly off the level plain. We commenced the ascent where a spur enables the traveller to make it gradually and arrived at the top, 800 feet above the plain. Immediately beneath us and further north the hillside is almost wall like, a pathway made by the natives in traversing the hills in search of building wood, leads right along the forest clothed ridge. The baobab, ebony, numerous acacias and other trees thickly clothe the hills, a good soft grass covers the ground, and partridges, guinea fowls and doves abound. To the west the plateau extends at first somewhat brokenly. This ridge, or edge of the plateau, lies nearly true N.S. A view of the level plain of Ugogo was limited by a border of haze which prevented a distant view, and we returned to camp at dusk.

Saturday 29th—In the early part of the day I was busily employed repairing some of our loads and preparing cloth for our men's posho, a job of some extent, some 230 two yard pieces of calico having to be measured and cut off. The serving out however takes up the most time, but it is now greatly facilitated by the use of the tin tallies with which we have supplied the men; every man as his name is called showing his number. This matter settled I had to hand out the hongo in installments corresponding to the caprice of the chief's headman (and of our headman) who had the business in hand. It was finally settled today after the payment of forty circles of brass and copper wire and thirty-nine cloths. Cleared up decks for Sunday.

Sunday—Enjoyed a good day's rest. We met together in my tent in the evening for prayer and worship.

Monday July 1st—Underweigh early, our road leading towards the Northern point of the ridge before us. . . . For about one and a half miles just before arriving at Lugossy we pass over a piece as perfectly smooth and flat as a skating rink or asphalt pavement.

We have the advantage on these plains of being able to see at one glance the whole of our caravan. As we near Lugossy immense herds of long legged water birds are seen in a few pools to the Northward, the remaining moisture of this vast marsh, and more ostriches. Lugossy consists of about sixteen tembes under the Chief Mgono Kamonga, a tall slender person of considerable importance in his own eyes. A few scattered palms in the immediate neighbourhood of the tembes relieve the otherwise monotonous scene, for there is nought else from N.W. to N.E. save the same bare plain. The people's gardens are close up against the foot of the hills. The Wagogo and Wahumba seem to live together here in amity. The Wahumba are certainly a distinct race having their own particular features and manners. Here, as all thro' Ugogo, plenty of food was brought into the camp. The Chief visited us this evening bringing his battered and broken powder flask; he begged a new one, and his prime minister, a cunning old Nyamwezi, carried two pistols for repair, but I could do nothing to them for they both wanted new nipples. He sent us milk this evening.

The Chief however would not commence the hongo business today saying he wanted to see something of the white man before he could let us go. He, moreover, warned us that the people hereabouts were great thieves and advised us to shoot anyone we found stealing. Precautions were accordingly taken for the safety of our goods. A sudden and strong breeze lashing half an hour swept across the plain at 7:30 making the tents shake again.

Tuesday July 2nd—Got some nice milk this morning, and paid the first installment of hongo by giving some cloth to Chief's young wife and his prime minister. It was finally settled today after payment altogether of a powder flask and one lb. powder, small piece of tobacco, about two lbs. of various beads, 135 cloths, and finally my purple and gold Good Templars badge which afforded great satisfaction. The Chief's wife came into camp afterwards wearing it. I shot a bird in the marsh this afternoon. . . .

Wednesday July 3rd—The step onto the plateau along which our road passes becomes now less steep until further west when it makes the ascent beyond Mukondoku. There is a far more gradual (tho' still steep) slope out on to the plain forming a border of forest and tangled vegetation between the plain and the hills. The people here are a thorough mix-up of Wanyamwezi, Wahumba, and an inferior class of Wagogo. The Wagogo tribe here abouts smear their bodies with white clay in various hideous devices, a favourite one being whitened skin and thighs with parallel wavy lines so scratched as to show the dark skin, also white dabs or beauty spots on cheeks and temples. We could do

nothing towards settling the hongo today. Here for the first time
the people, apparently immensely astounded, ran by the side of
the caravan as Cameron describes. Messrs. Thomson and Hutley
being in front some distance had passed by before attention had
been thoroughly aroused, but by the time I passed the first tembes
they came running to see the Masungu (Englishmen), and I was
closely followed by a curious and increasing crowd. One woman
who with her children was standing by the roadside looking at
the passing caravan had not observed me so that her first view
was on her happening to turn round when I was about six feet from
her, when she gave a scream and bolted with her family at her
heels to the great amusement of all hands. Once or twice I just
turned my head to look along the line of the caravans; this illicited
a shout from the crowd of Wagogo following me, who to a man,
warriors and all, turned and ran, but soon recovered themselves
when everybody laughed. After passing the first village we made
a short halt, and I became the centre of a staring crowd who
watched every movement I made, and when I started off they all
cleared out of my path very quickly. Mr. T. and myself walking
out of camp in the evening met one of the Chief's headmen, and
he in a state of drunkenness. He promised to give us an ox and
settle the hongo tomorrow, and pressed us hard to drink pombe.
In this village, as at Nyambwa and Mizunza, neat water troughs
are moulded of clay for the oxen to drink from, plastered thresh-
ing floors, plastered walls, bins and large baskets for corn, etc.
Besides the neat ornamenting of calabashes and cloths with beads
and cowries, show an advance of intelligence and industry beyond
that of many of the coast tribes. I also saw here two seats and
a table of smooth sun baked clay, the table about four feet long
nine inches high and indented with holes adapted for a game of
two players, which I have seen played near the coast.

Thursday July 4th—Hongo business commenced and settled
today by payment of one dressing gown and twenty-six cloths, and,
this being the last hongo place in Ugogo, one cloth each was given
respectively to Juma Nasibu, Ludi bin Ali, and Macaugera
(Mirambo's man), besides three yards of Amerikani to the Kigogo
interpreter Wadi Kilemta, for their services in the hongo business.
Shortly after the hongo business was settled, a bit of a row was
caused, originally, by a young Ugogo insulting some of our men.
This young fellow being very impertinent and refusing to leave the
camp on being ordered by our headman. I laid hold of him and
put him out myself, which proceeding emboldened our men to
press their desire for redress still further, and, coming round in
numbers, the Wagogo warriors also began to gather, and a noisy

altercation ensued during which many hard words were passed and a row became imminent. At this moment we ordered all our men back into the camp, and Juma went off with the delinquent's spear to complain to the Chief. All Wagogo were now kept out of the camp, not without some little trouble however. The Chief afterwards sent a messenger, and peace was restored, we being requested to secure and bring to the Chief any depredators or offenders and to shoot any night thieves. Soon afterwards there were as many vendors and gazers in the camp as ever and no further disturbance occurred. A fine evening.

Friday July 5th—Started at daybreak in the morning, very cold. Marched about one and one half miles and halted on outskirts of Mukondoku, here, tho' no hongo, they made us pay a few beads for the use of the water. Had a crowd of gazers here the whole time till we started off again in the afternoon. Went on about 10 more miles. The last mile being the commencement of the ascent. Entered a forest which here forms a border between the hills and the plain. There is a very thick undergrowth in places. Camped in pleasant forest ground on ridge.

Sunday 7th—Off again at daybreak (men without food), arriving at Koi Kirondah about 11. Camped about a half mile beyond the town. Until two miles from the village the same fine forest land which then opened upon large clearings on a greatly undulating country covered with larger corn fields and giving a well-to-do aspect to a large Tembe of Wakimbu, many of whom we found industriously employed cutting the large posts of which their tembes are made. Others were fashioning boxes, or rather bins of bark, like huge bandboxes forming most excellent receptacles for grain, etc. They are stored on the roof tops. The maize pods in bundles are elevated on poles in the same position. They also have a sort of rack about four feet off the ground but depressed in the middle on which the matama is exposed and dried. These people being almost devoid of ornament, although clothed more *decently* than the Wagogo, appear to the traveller (fresh from Ugogo) as being almost in undress. The forest here supplied splendid wood for building purposes and also all the useful barks, such as those used for lashings and for boxes, etc., etc. After crossing another wide undulation of spreading corn fields, we arrived at the main tembe of Koi Kirondah. This is the largest and best built tembe I have yet seen in the country. Here is a little colony of Swahili or Mrima men, and I must say that unless they are engaged in slaving (and we saw no sign of it) they must be an immense civilising influence upon the more savage races of the locality. Under the influence of these coast men. This tembe presents the appearance of quite a respectable and good-sized town; all the homes, or rather compartments, are half as high again as those solely of native architecture, while there is a great deal of respectable workmanship bestowed upon the building: comfortable doors and verandahs, plastered walls and many other little additions to household comfort and cheerful appearance. There are also several clusters of houses. In the centre space one large house is built with huge wooden posts and an extensive verandah; it is the residence of some of the well-to-do hunters, some resident, some guest, and here we squat on little stools or sit on the clean mats and talk with these people who on the whole seem a very respectable lot of men. They have learned to imitate the Arabs in everything, having much of the same dignified exterior, stately movement and formal, tho' pleasing, courtesy of that race. There is a native chief in the town who lives in an inner and strong enclosure. One of the Swahili men showed us over the town and took us in here but the chief was not at home; two huge drums stood in his courtyard. But in the town generally the native element seems comparatively small and nearly all either working for or in some way connected with the coast men. Our pagasi were quite at home here and in their best garments paraded about the town as if they were in Zanzibar. Many had friends to greet and all had bargains to make, for here is great plenty of beans, and maize and matama, pumpkins and sweet potatoes to say nought of the pombe and tobacco in which they revelled during our stay. One enterprising townsman killed an ox which was cut up on its skin in the public square, and, being disposed in quantities suitable for small purchasers, the meat was transformed very quickly into good Amerikani. I noticed the Sami-Sami seeds collected here in quantities for the manufacture of oil. Plenty of oxen, but few sheep, goats and chickens. Some of the coast men in the town politely sent to our camp each of the two mornings we were here a liberal supply of good sweet milk, which proved very acceptable to us. About fifteen of the late Lieutenant Smith's men were here on their way to the coast and from them we had news of Mr. Mackay's progress.[10] Here we obtained some Indian meal to make porridge enabling us to enjoy that good morning refreshment without using the objectionable matama meal.

Monday July 8th—Remained all day at Koi Kironda to let me rest and buy food for the journey of a whole week before us without inhabitants. They complained again (tho' revelling in plenty) wanting an extra day's portion but I reminded them that

10. Shergold Smith and another CMS missionary had been murdered on an island in Lake Victoria Nyanza as they prepared to return with supplies to Buganda.

a shukka here bought a great abundance, that they were much better off than if they were with Arabs who would buy the food and dole out to them the bare measure of matama corn. Also, that I was well aware of the far superior value of Amerikani here in the interior, that I knew they were trying to impose on men, and reminded them that further trouble might cause them to get beads instead of the far more desirable Amerikani. I heard no more about it, but knew well that they had a great abundance of food. Pombe, tobacco, and extensive feeds kept the men awake and noisy to a later hour and myself fidgeting lest some should remain behind at this, to them, very desirable place.

Tuesday July 9th—Turned out some time before daybreak afraid lest some of the men should be going North. Sore heads and bellies caused a sorry spirit for the caravan, the men hovering over the fires till actually driven away and many pleading sickness. Marched on thro' fine open forest the whole journey, the baobabs now are few and far between, fine straight wood for building. Camped at Muhaley, water for some distance in bed of nullah, crossed a dry nullah half way on march.

Wednesday July 10th—A raw morning, hurried out early but made a very bad start especially as a long day's journey is before us. Many men pleading sickness; great discretion is required to distinguish between loafers and the really sick, trouble also on the road of the same kind. Not all in camp till 1:30 p.m., very tired. Mr. T., knocked up, had arrived long time previously. Anticipated complaints and troubles by making a great fuss about the careless handling of loads, many being torn.

Thursday July 11th—A much better start this morning but as three men had to be told off to carry Mr. Thomson, I was obliged to engage one Wanyamwezi porter, (there is a little party travelling with us), there being still several men sick and weary and they having much food to carry. . . .

Saturday July 13th—Trouble again at starting; the men hanging round the fires till driven away. After considering this matter a good deal I have determined to commence to enforce fines tomorrow for those who do not come out of their huts to take up the loads. . . .

Sunday July 14th—After the bulk of the loads had been taken up (very quickly as they generally are) I sounded my whistle, and Ludi announced that any man who did not come forward before the next whistle sounded would forfeit half his week's posho (allowance of calico), this brought them along rather quickly but nine were fined, to the great amusement of all hands but themselves. About two miles from Camp we passed a small village of square flat roofed houses. Food abundant, gardens carefully laid out with bean plants on ridges. Next the little palisaded town of Lura with its fortified gateway and platform above for defensive warfare, food abundant. Finally, camped beyond the village (also palisaded) of Perce. Serving out the posho as quickly as possible.

Monday 15th—At work repairing loads. One man, Mbaruti, was reported to have run away today taking with him the posho cloth belonging to five or six of his messmates. On the evening the man was captured at the town, an Unyamwezi native having reported that the cloth was deposited with him by the runaway. Mbaruti, having been convicted of the theft and desertion, was sentenced to five lashes for each offence and I had to interfere to prevent his being mobbed, the popular feeling in the Camp being very strong against him. Today the bright weather we have enjoyed too long gave way to a dull cloudy day threatening rain.

July 16th—The fine system promises to answer well. This morning we got away unusually early, and I did not even have to sound the time signal, every one of the loads being picked up at the start. Road generally thro' the same scattered forest but more varied now with open glades and broken ground. Fresh breeze during the day with flying clouds, night fine and clear. Camped in the fine open forest; these forest camps (when good water is at hand) are the best we have. The old camps and bomas near villages are abominations.

During the afternoon, while I was quietly seated in the tent repairing our flags, a cry was raised that one of our men had been carried off by a lion. I rushed out with my gun and with about 150 men armed with guns, spears and clubs, and went off in pursuit, of course such a wild army cleared the lion away very quickly, and he abandoned his prey which turned out to be a zebra. The party I was with traced the lion a good way, but of course he was off far out of reach. Meantime, a party of our Wanyamwezi friends found the zebra, and by the time I arrived he was being jointed; in another few minutes all was shared out. Our Zanzibar men of course could not partake of this meat, but I see they do not refuse some of the spoils, his mane and tail and pieces of his skin being secured as dandy decorations for some of the swells.

Wednesday July 17th—Off early again. Half way on march came upon the Kuale River flowing here E.N.E., slowly and thigh deep. Large body of water in the rains (does this feed the Nile? Malagarasi?), delapidated bridge. On thro' some forest to camp, having been (in rear of caravan) ten hours on the march. Very tired, but on this, our longest march yet accomplished, our men on the whole did remarkably well. Fine clear night with a few light passing clouds. . . .

Friday—Seven miles march arrives at Hitura, eight or nine flourishing villages with extensive corn fields and gardens; the latter laid out in high ridges for tobacco, beans, muhogo etc. Camped in a corn field. Friendly chief, food brought for sale.

Saturday 20th—A march of six miles brought us to *Kurkwa* the capital of Uyui, a very large village, or rather town with many evergreen trees inside. The mild bush bridges round the village giving it a very pleasing appearance. We camped about a quarter of a mile beyond the town although as we passed, Said bin Salim sent out to invite us inside. Shortly after pitching camp Mr. T. and myself went to visit the Shiek, meeting on the way messengers from him bearing a tray of rice and curry and a bowl of milk. Said bin Salim, the late governor of Unyanyembe, we found to be a very respectable looking old gentleman who, although not living in the style to which he had been used in his more comfortable circumstances, still has the air and manner of a well to do Arab. There are several other Arab and half castes and a goodly number of Zanzibar men and other followers who all are respectful to and seem to revolve round the Said as their patron. Said bin Salim received us most amicably, and we conversed about the road, etc., and also about his deposition from the government of Unyanyembe, Said complaining that he had had all his things taken from him while Mr. T. explained to him that he had come to look at the country, etc. Shortly afterwards I was obliged to leave in order to serve out our men's *posho*, and Mr. T. then presented his letters of introduction.

Wednesday 24th—Started after the usual trouble and drive one mile N.W. by W. brings to the N. Gombe nullah, the water standing in pools. . . . Crossing the nullah we now enter the district of Ulikampori. Just before coming to Kwikuru (the capital) the forest opens on to a plain dotted with hills and revealing a populous and flourishing country in the numerous well to do looking villages and surrounding cornfields; much of this plain however is still boggy.

Eight miles from camp brings us to the stockaded village of *Kwikuru* in Ulikampori. Inside the stockade this village is abundantly shaded with crowded plantain trees and milk bush, gardens with tobacco, beans, etc., outside. Speke's Ulikampori must be south of this; the natives say there are other towns of Ulikampori to the south. . . . We halted a short time to bring up the stragglers and started across the plain in a winding path for our camp in Unyambewa. Treading one way thro' cornfields we closely skirt three villages all stockaded and thickly shaded and hidden with plantains and with bush. The houses inside are some oblong with flat roofs (like pieces of tembes), others round with neatly thatched conical roofs. The people came out to stare. Some are delving in their gardens, and others are already bringing food to sell in our camp. Outside two of the villages were little blacksmiths' shops. I went to one to see the operations. They showed me a coil of iron-wire which had just been drawn, and, except that the iron was of inferior quality, the work was very good. The wire is drawn thro' little blocks of iron with holes of the sizes required; the blocks are inserted firmly in a post. At some distance is a crude, but effective, windlass. A stout bark rope is secured to the end of the wire to be drawn and being taken round the windlass is thus drawn. The forge was not here, and I only saw a few rough tools, hammer, tweezers and chisel. The people seemed pleased for me to examine their things. Camped on level ground at foot of one of the small hills and just thro' the strip of thorn scrub joining two hills and which with those hills separate Ulikampori from Unyambewa.

Arrived at camp 1 p.m.; I was very hungry having had nothing since 5:30 a.m. we found to our dismay that the basket with our victuals, plates, etc. had not arrived, and it turned out that the man carrying it had thought to take a short cut but instead of doing so had lost the road. Basket and man were finally recovered during the afternoon, while we made a good shift with what we could get together with pieces of tin and large dishes for plates. In the evening two men arrived from Mirambo's with greetings for Mr. T. Obtained some good plantains here (a great treat).

Thursday 25th—Hazy and cold morning. Just when we were ready to start a wild looking fellow (whom I remembered yesterday with his face hideously smeared with white clay) came into camp, and, flourishing his club, announced with orders from the chief of a neighbouring village that we must stop, for that chief required to see the white man before we could go on. No persuasion, I well knew, could move one pagasi now till this matter was settled. Mr. T. accordingly proceeded to the village with Macaugera (Mirambo's man) and the two head men, and found that the said chief wanted hongo. With the help of Macaugera the demand was pooh-poohed.

Thursday 25th—Hazy and cold. We proceeded a full hour after sunrise, one quarter mile brought us to the large mud plastered tembe of Kirkuru of Unyambewa. Before us was a rolling country with thick and varied vegetation, but fewer trees. Thro' cornfields, large grass and between several hills, about N.W.; 11 more miles brings us to camp in thick grass and scrub. A short distance from *Kanors*, between the hills, we had to wade thro' several bogs of black mud, which is disagreeable after a long journey on dry, hard ground. Passed the ruins of two villages which we were told had been capsized during some of Mirambo's battles. One had been an extensive place; the vegetation around was very thick, and the ruins of the village itself were completely buried in a dense mass of vegetation amongst which were plantains, corn, beans, milk bush, potatoes, and creepers matting the whole together. Many of the various uganga [charms], with which all the Wanyamwezi villages are supplied, still remain on the ends of some of the long stockade poles which rise up above the debris: old pots, calabashs, horns and skulls of game, etc. Many of our men stopped here and ransacked the wild gardens with some success, many obtaining potatoes and tomatoes. About half way on our march I heard angry voices in front and ran on, for I had heard rumours already this morning of ruga-ruga (robbers). Farajella, who was close behind, followed, and we found some of our Zanzibar men, some of our Wanyamwezi, and two other Wanyamwezi engaged in angry talk but still going on in the path, and it is found that some Wanyamwezi who were travelling with us had been robbed of their loads, but none of ours were touched.

Friday 26th—Ludi sent forward to greet Mirambo and announce our coming. A raw morning. Our road first ascended over shoulder, or rather saddle, of hill; same country, in the valleys black mud bogs. Over the shoulder of another hill and then another and two miles now to one of Mirambo's villages. One mile west to camp under olive trees, close to another village. . . .

Saturday 27th—all lively and cheerful for the start to Mirambo's town. Descending gradually thro' grass and scattered bushes and past a fine spring pouring, and upon the road we came to the North Gombe nullah here are evidences of this river being in the rains an immense body of water which just here must cover (at times) a large tract of country. There remains here about half of a long bridge said to have been built by Mirambo. It consisted of two rows of about 150 forked poles which are four to six feet apart; there are beams across covered with other poles longitudinally forming the road. From here we ascend gradually about two miles to a large stockaded village where I passed the people were all out to greet us and I was followed for a quarter of a mile by about 150 women of all sizes and ages making the most terrible din and screeching, yelling and singing at me and dancing and running and flinging themselves about in a strange style. I was completely mobbed and was told it was no impertinence but genuine rejoicing at the arrival of the Wasungu. They followed me till they were tired out.

And now with slow and stately step we march towards the great man's tembe. Our new Union Jack creeps along in the front, for it would not be dignified for the caravan to hurry now, in the opinion of our headmen. As we approach guns are fired, and warriors and people run and prance about like mad folk. Alongside the tembe we find a square house, in the course of erection, is set apart for our accommodation, and the great Mirambo welcomes us to his *Kwikuru*.

So is completed the second stage of the journey of the LMS Tanganyika Expedition.

To *God* we would give the glory and praise for our safety and many mercies.[11]

[The visit with Mirambo was an unpleasant one for Hore, as he believed that Mirambo looked down on him because he was Rev. Joseph Thomson's inferior. Only on Hore's return to the coast in 1880 as the senior man with the mission was he received well by Mirambo.]

11. This ends the second segment of the journal. Hore made no entries during his stay in Urambo.

Log of the Expedition to Ujiji*

August 5th Monday—Got up very early to start caravan. Despatched our mail to the coast. . . . The men came along for the loads in very good time and all seemed wonderfully refreshed by their stay here. Mirambo came on astern shortly after we started with Mr. Thomson. We walked off over a greatly undulating elevated plain, and this is certainly by far the best bit of country in the neighbourhood of Mirambo's town. . . . Camped in the village of Uyva which contains a large mud-brick house belonging to Mirambo who keeps one of his wives here; the house is called Kanongo. There are ruins, also, of another house of the same kind. The village contains some neat little round houses and is surrounded with the (now) inevitable milk bush hedge. Went to see Mirambo at his big house. Before he left to return to his capital, he came into my tent to say goodbye. I held out my hand to him, but he looked very solemn and hesitating a moment lifted his forefinger without moving his hand. In Mirambo's opinion I have passed thro' his country without giving him any presents, and his marked coldness to me after the first day or two of arrival bodes anything but a pleasant return for me (should I be alone) thro' his country.

Tuesday 6th—Got out of the village with the usual excitement. Our road is over the same elevated undulating plain. Passed by eleven villages on the march, many of them consisting almost entirely of mere beehive grass huts, tho' Wanyamwezi make very nice bark boxes of various sizes with attempts at ornament and have a good notion of preserving provisions in them and various other receptacles. I saw a bark box or bin today four feet in diameter. Sweet potatoes are very abundant, long grass in places, scattered bushes, and stunted trees except a few palms and tamarinds. Villages stockaded and having milk bush hedges, five miles on road we leave Urambo, and enter Usange. Water in a few pools and puddles; camp at village Kirkuru of Usange; time on march five hours, fifteen minutes. This evening two messengers arrived from Mirambo to tell us that the little party of Wahita we saw at his town had left suddenly, and that from this and some information let out by one whom he made drunk for the purpose he warned us to hurry on to the Malagarasi River with all speed lest the Wahita should have hostile intentions towards us. Beyond

* In the archives of the Congregational Council for World Mission.

the Malagarasi it is thought we shall be safe, the country being thickly populated. . . .

Friday August 9th—This hard travelling is beginning to tell on our men, making it difficult to get away in the morning. Alternate forest and open glades with scattered bushes, almost level but rough ground over the hard baked deep mud foot marks of man and game; the elephants and rhinoceros have left immense holes in some places where the mud has been soft. At two and three quarter miles passed a village on our left hand then the large stockaded town of Kirkuru of Ugala, where for the first time I saw human skulls stuck on poles. These large villages have mostly a huge hedge of the milk bush and clumps of plantains forming a barrier outside the stockade of the village. The intervening space being used as garden, and often consisting of a tangled and overgrown mass of ground nuts, sweet potatoes, yams, tomatoes, pumpkins, etc. which, together with the stream from numerous small standing waters, render the close neighbourhood of these villages anything but salubrious. The next village we passed was in the district Uvungu and is ruled by the Chief Karangu; he is commonly termed " Mtoto Mirambo " being some relation of the great man's. When we passed this village it was only partly completed, surrounded by a fine strong stockade, and the people busy erecting round homes as at Urambo. We camped between the hedge and stockade of another large village called Ugala, in a luxuriant garden in which our oxen were permitted to roam at pleasure and thus got a fine feed of green young shoots. We are told that the lions are numerous hereabouts, but did not hear them during the night. Troubled very much by swarms of mosquitoes. Six hours and 50 minutes on march. . . .

Saturday August 10th—Great trouble to get the men and loads away, many being sick and tired, so we made a late start. Passed thro' thick forest and many palm trees to the village of Kanijipo, after which we descended slightly and waded for two miles ankle deep and sometimes knee deep in water. The distinct and permanent water marks upon every tree and bush form a perfectly straight line as viewed in the distance; from the ground to the water mark being of a much darker shade than the rest of the wood and the line is also continued most distinctly round many little hillocks which in the rains are islets. As we made along here the water mark is a clear foot above my head, and this level extends away to the north to the Malagarasi, the line of verdure bordering which is now clearly discernible. To north of us, about half way across this depression (which here receives the overflow of the Malagarasi, there are no signs of a flow or rush of water) is a little village of eight or ten houses. The stockade of this village and the thatch on every house roof clearly record the water mark four feet above the ground; the people say they retire to higher ground during the Masika. The chief and a few of his men were busy here making a solid wooden door for the village; it was of one piece nearly semicircular; the ends left on one side to revolve in holes in logs, top and bottom, and was decorated with a rudely, tho' distinctly, carved lizard in bold relief. This was the first village in Uzanza. The next was a larger one, and governed by a chief who had seen the world, he having travelled to Bagamoyo. Soon after leaving this village we enter Uvinza, and camp beside a large village abounding in stockades and hedges and overgrown gardens: Kasabula's in Uvinza. The north Gombe nullah, here the eastern arm of the Malagarasi, flows parallel with our path, one and three quarters miles to the northward, with low banks, indicating the presence, in the Masika (rainy season) of immense marshes. This village of Kasabula's is of good size and very much divided up, the people evidently having an idea of little private gardens fenced round with their houses. They have several arrangements for making salt here. The dirty mess of mud and sand and water in a large bark box on top promises little, but the clear salt water is dripping out beneath. I went out a little way with our Mirambo's guide to look at the river about a mile and three quarters N.; it is called here the *Nyika*, but they are sure about it being " the same water as the Gombe Nullah "; that " it is not the Malagarasi "; but that " it runs with that river a little further down ". This village, they say, used to be called Usenye, and I think it perhaps, is the Nasange of Burton and Speke. . . .

Sunday 11th—A day of rest and wonderful quiet considering we were inside a village. We have always been enabled to meet together in peace and comfort in my tent. The people listening wonderingly to our hymns. Now Mr. Dodgshun is not with us to conduct the music, we use Sankey's hymn book and always manage somehow to raise a tune.

Monday 12th—Very glad to get the caravan out of the village. I have a dead set against camping with the caravan inside a village. It is all very well when one is travelling alone and light, but not with a caravan. Kasabula, I am glad, has now advised against doing so. March thro' thick growth of grass and bush and stunted forest. At three miles passed across another patch of overflow one mile with eight feet water mark; at seven miles came a ruined village said to have been destroyed by Mirambo, district of Usunsu, and shortly afterwards arrive at the first of Katalumbula's villages, beyond which we camp. Heaps and heaps of sweet potatoes, the people busily cutting them up to dry in the sun. Katalumbula is leaving or has gone on ahead to the ferry, but the hongo man or representative of Msogera, the Sultan of Uvinza, is here, also the representatives of said Katalumbula, besides brothers and other important persons who inevitably put in a claim for very large hongo which is finally settled by paying them twenty-three doti (two pieces) Amerikani, twenty-three doti (ten pieces) of Kaniki, three durbwani, three soubayah, three sumpunga, three doti handkerchiefs, and one sahari.

Tuesday 13th—Many sick (?) men this morning but as we had roused out pretty early were not very late in starting. Hazy morning. Had a winding road thro' forest of varying feature and uneven ground passed several ruins of villages and one very small one of a few beehive huts but with a great abundance of food. Saw tracks of lions today and iron ore, a sandy soil of two distinct kinds today, a coarse red and a loose fine white, also in one bog much iron making a rusty shine, a small pool of water in forest and a large round hole with water near one of the ruined villages. The first land in sight for several days now rises ahead, apparently an elevated ridge running N and S and dippling a little ahead of our course. Camped in the bush.

Wednesday 14th—A winding and descending road thro' little bogs over shoulders of small irregular hills, past several ruined villages, and so thro' more hills and broken ground down to the river which from here looks like a vast marsh inhabited by flocks of large white birds. As we round into the river valley we pass another village of Katalambula's in Ugaga, and camp near another small village in the district of Ugaga on the east bank of the Malagarasi. The camp is on the slope of a hill and looks right over the river below us. It looks from here rather like a huge swamp. Settled hongo for the river today by paying 30 cloths *viz*: eleven doti Amerikani, ten doti Kaniki, two sumpunga, two sahari, one dowli, one durbwani, and three soubayah, also two fringed soubayah—one each for Mzogeya and Katalambula.

Thursday 15th—Waited an hour owing to delay of the boatmen, but, after a good looking up and agitation, were enabled to get off and down to the river about 8 o'clock. A descending path of quarter mile brings right into the marsh which here borders the river on either side. From edge to edge including the river is threequarter mile. The deep water where we crossed was divided in two by a central patch of mud bank over which the canoes have to be dragged. Only these two central deeps are at all clear of the long tangled rope-like grass with which the rest of the river is covered and to a great extent masked. We had to wade thigh deep for 500 or 600 yards thro' this marsh in order to reach a little hillock or island which was made the starting point for the boats. To the South the river contracts into more reasonable dimensions being confined on either side between small hills; these small hills are terminated on the eastern bank by a small round isolated hill which forms an elbow round which a sharp bend of the river turns and, on the western bank, at the ferry to which we cross. To the North of these points is a large level expanse over which the river must spread in the rains to a great distance. The passage of the river by our caravan occupied five-and-a-half hours, there being about fourteen bark canoes, eighteen feet long by eighteen inches beam, and three dug-outs rather shorter, broader, and decidedly more substantial. On the arrival of the canoes at the starting place, we found that we should have to pay each canoeman for every passage he made, although the Chief had promised yesterday that the hongo he received should cover every expense of the crossing. In this paying of fares I expended forty-eight yards of calico and about six pounds of beads. The boats generally took two men and their loads at a time for which were paid a half to a yard of calico or a few beads; the beads however were at a discount. For our three oxen, one calf, and two goats I was compelled after about two hours of haggling to pay four yards of cloth, their passage being considered an extra difficult job, and even to get the obstinate boatman into a sufficiently good humour to finally complete this bargain I had to give him a pipeful of tobacco and fire it withal with the object lens of my field glass. In many cases, men, and loads had to get in and out again of the boats during expressions of indignation on either side in the progress of a bargain. Each boatman on each passage had to be separately bargained with, ourselves standing knee deep in water, and the pagasi and their loads crowded together on the little hillock or island. Fortunately, I had handy in a bag a piece of " satean " (very inferior cloth); this and some old and damaged pieces which had been used as wrappers for other cloth I cut up into short lengths for this business, so that only a few yards of good cloth were expended. In two cases only could we make a more extensive bargain: ten men and loads for two yards of cloth, the boats making three or four journeys. It was nearly 3 p.m. when, all the men and loads having been got off, I myself embarked; just when I was ready to go a canoe arrived bearing for me a dish of stewed fowl and potatoes which Mr. Thomson had considerately forwarded from the other side. With Juma and another man (the bargain having been completed) I stepped into the canoe, but the boatmen refused to proceed because one man was sitting with his face towards the stern;

this having been put right we started. The canoe had to thread its way thro' long alleys of the tangled grass, being poled along. The paddle was only used in crossing the two deep central portions. On the bank dividing . . . we had to disembark for the canoe to be dragged across. The western shore was steeper but with a short extent of marsh. Our camp was a quarter mile from the landing, high removed from the low, damp, mosquito infested river bank. Two small villages of Mpete this side. I found our Camp to be in Lat 5° 5' 27" two miles North of the place where Burton and Speke and Cameron crossed, but still the crossing was from "Ngaga" to "Mpete", those being the names of the districts in the east and west lands respectively.

Friday 16th—Got started this morning in reasonable time. The road bad thro' thin forest for the first six miles with broad slabs of sandstone. Sometimes a slight descent led across little bogs fed by streams of fine but iron impregnated water. After this the road began to wind about fearfully and I soon became aware, by coming upon the caravan halted and disputing about the road, that the track was lost. Here I was told that Mr. Thomson and those with him (the vanguard) had gone on a path which led N. by E. but I was sure this could not be right. By compass I soon decided which was the right direction, and we proceeded past two villages and arrived at a large village on the edge of what we were told was a very long and waterless pori, having gone already ten and a half miles.

Here was another debate. Mr. Thomson had gone by a north road and had not been heard of. The natives tried hard to make us stop here, but after making sure that the village (beyond the pori) was the place to which we had arranged to go, I started the caravan off in that direction and arrived in Camp after another five miles, about 3:30 p.m., and at once fired off two guns and dispatched six good men with guns and food in search of Mr. Thomson in a Northerly direction. Messrs. T. and H. however arrived approximately two hours afterwards by the same road we had come, very weary and having come back to the village the other side of the pori and then followed us. It appears the guide provided for this part by Said-bin-Salem had proved altogether incompetent, and had led them far astray. Served out the men's posho, and decided to remain here Sunday.

Saturday August 17th—This is still one of Lusunsu's villages; some call it "the Klambi" and one or two other names making it doubtful. Repaired a lot of the loads today. One of the pagasi remained behind at the other village, sent him back a little cloth and beads for food. Fine breeze.

Sunday—Makanjira, our leading pagasi, has been sick several days with inflamation of the chest, and had neglected to come for medical treatment tho' repeatedly told to do so. He is now so bad that he is unable to proceed so gave a doti to head man of village who promised to shelter and attend to him; I gave the man himself a little cloth and beads.

A great row occurred this evening. One of our men, Salimini, insulted a woman who turned out to be a wife of the Chief. The woman made a great outcry and came to the camp to make complaint. She had a very long tongue, and was evidently determined to make a good thing out of the business, not being willing to regain any other comfort or satisfaction than some of the Kisungo's white man's cloth. A doti and a half had to be handed over to settle the business, and the woman went off satisfied with the cloth over her shoulder. The delinquent Salimini had disappeared entirely. . . . We descended to the river down a rugged little gorge in the sandstone which here presents a great variety. . . . A few salt pits rut up the ground near the stony bank. The river here was 125 feet wide, and confined without swamp, tho' the tricklings from the western rise beyond descended in little strips of bog here and there. The river was just fordable, being at its deepest just to a man's middle and running about two and a half knots. I was snugly carried by two men. Poor Joseph, who is very sick and whom a friend volunteered to carry across, was toppled over friend and all in midstream to his no small discomforture and to the great amusement of the crowd on each bank. From the river we rise up again on to the elevated plain, and two miles brought us to camp. In the rear of the caravan I was ten and a half hours on the march the fording of the river took the caravan two hours. I anxiously followed with my eyes each load in its transit; some of the weakly men enter the river with fear and trembling, but there are many willing stronger hands to help and at last all are safely across. Got to camp at 4:30 p.m.

Tuesday 20th— . . . Yesterday's long and tiresome march has told on our men. This morning there are many sick and weary ones, and after a great deal of trouble in getting the loads away. I left some eight or ten of them with their own things and marched off. This had a better effect apparently than a great deal of coaxing and other persuasion, for they all very soon followed us in haste fearful of being left behind. . . .

Arranged this evening for Mr. Thomson to go on to Ujiji in order to find a suitable camping place. Overclouded all day and at night. . . .

Thursday August 22nd—The men are all anxious to get to Ujiji and were ready for a start this morning before daylight. First three miles thro' undulating forest and then alternate ridges and valleys and broken ground. To our north the mountains of Uhha. Crossed three small rivers, feeders of the Ruiche . . . The last one formed the boundary of Ukaranga. The last three miles of march over a hill broken up into holes and steep slopes covered with bamboos. The hollows and ravines full of a luxuriant growth of palms and jumpers, plantains, etc., forming thick, dark, damp masses of vegetation. A pleasant little brook meanders thro' the hollow, and we camp after a march of eight and three quarters hours. One mile west of the old site of Niamtaga, we are close to the same little brook which winds in and out of the depressions of this wildly broken up bamboo hill. The elephants have been gambolling about among the bamboos which, I suppose afford their food. In the forest on first part of march grass ten and twelve feet high. On the whole we have descended considerably this march. The men have all expressed their willingness to push right on to Ujiji tomorrow. I have hoist our two good flags and given special instructions for the halting of the caravan on nearing Ujiji for all the people to come up.

Friday August 23rd—Everybody, myself included, in a great hurry to get to Ujiji. We got away just before daybreak. Crossing the pretty little brook which winds round the broken bamboo hills, over another bamboo hill, and then, along the side of a long slope thro' scattered forest with great variety of stone fragments, we slightly ascend until at four and a quarter mile we are on the top of a ridge and began to descend towards the winding valley thro' which the Ruiche flows. From here we get the first view of the Tanganyika, and we overlook Ukaranga Bay, and plainly see the point Kasimbo. . . . From where I stood the valley was hidden by the tree tops beneath me so that it looks like a great gradual descent of tree tops right to the lake. Perhaps I should have taken off my hat and shouted, had mouth and hands not been both fully occupied at the time with a bone of mutton which formed my breakfast. As it was I sat down on a camp stool, and finished my breakfast with this glorious view before me. Juma coming up at the time came in for the remainder of the shank bone that I might spend the remaining moments before I hastened on in gazing at the lake.

The pagasi were rapidly descending the rugged and stony path, and I must keep up the impetus. We had never marched like this before. Hurrying up to a party of men I would shout to them to go on, and as I passed them shout to them again to come on, and Juma hurried them from behind, and Farajella, alternately laughing and scolding at them, seemed to be everywhere. We passed over two smaller hills in descending and then, instead of striking across the valley straight to the ridge of hills overlooking Ujiji as Stanley seems to have done, we made a long detour to N.W. to avoid the bog into which the river is spread out here, eventually crossing the river at eight and a quarter miles en route. The Ruiche was here from ten to forty yards wide, a very winding course with many elbows; lower down it spreads out in places into wide marsh. The river has many deeps and shallows. Where we crossed it the first half was thigh deep, the second knee deep and a swift current. I can quite understand now how one of Burton and Speke's routes crosses the Ruiche twice; Mr. T. who went over it this morning early tells me he crossed it four times. Now a wide detour N. to W. to S.W. brings us, after crossing several hills and a considerable feeder of the Ruiche, another small stream, and two small but deep pools, to the Ujiji gardens: a dense plantation of plaintain palms, beans and little open gardens of maize and potatoes. Winding thro' these gardens, a long ascent, at last brings us up to the heights overlooking Ujiji and the glorious Tanganyika beyond. Between the Ruiche and Ujiji this elevated ascent and ridge is dry and wholesome (except to the N.W. where there is a hole and little swamp), and the air seems good and fresh. The valley of the Ruiche on the one side and the hollow of Ujiji, filled up as it is with damp groves of palms and plantains on the other side, are bad.

Here the caravan halts according to my orders that all may come up and proceed in proper order. Threequarters of an hour brings all hands together (except that Mr. Hutley and his party, the vanguard, have missed their way and not yet turned up. I sent Farajella and another man after them). Ammunition has been served out to the men for the march thro' the pori after leaving Mirambo's, and, as I know it would never be returned after the journey, I thought we might as well have a little benefit out of it somehow, so I gave the men permission to make the usual display and noise as they entered Ujiji. Meantime I had retired to the bush, and donned clean attire (after having first carefully ascertained that there was no more bog on the road), and gave the order to proceed.

As we descended towards Ujiji, the open descent, bare of trees, showed off the whole caravan to good advantage at a glance, and never in my life have I seen a procession which has given me such joy and pleasure. Yonder is Ujiji towards which we have so long marched and waded, and here in due order are our goods intact and marchers in excellent health, and 225 men in single file each, save the head man, with his load on head or shoulder. In front walks the portly and consequential Songoro, bearing the Union Jack with white border; then the pagasi's Kilangozi with lofty head dress of nodding ostrich plumes, . . . working his legs, to give due sound to the iron bells hung round his knees; then come box and bale, bag and bundle, tents, pots and kettles, and little bundles of matting and cloth (the bed so easily walked off with). In the centre of the procession Juma MacKay displays on long bamboo the dove of peace with olive branch. After the last load, I march in orthodox position as Master of the Caravan, followed by the head man Juma with his three stripes; and his mate Sudi closes the rear with the English Ensign. As we near the town the people run to look; it is a great day for them (and indeed it is one for us). Some of our leading pagasi shout to the rest who answer in chorus, and Juma fires his gun as a signal for a salute, bang, bang, now in front now behind and anon a " pistola " vies (with its big charge of powder) with the larger weapons. Juma and Sudi close behind me seem to be trying who can make the most noise with their gun. The excitement resulting in Juma firing into the Ensign and giving it a sad tear, and at that, I well know, they are congratulating themselves that I am in an excellent humour. We entered the town and camped in the garden of Bwana Musa. Mr. Hutley turned up shortly afterwards and the men who had lost their way, came in before dark. PRAISE GOD!

IV

UJIJI

As an entrepôt for Arab traders operating in the upper Congo region, Ujiji enjoyed a renown in Great Britain unique to central African communities. The Arab settlers had been helpful as well as hospitable to Burton and Speke and later to Livingstone and Stanley, and their published accounts had captured a measure of public imagination. In part it was due to Livingstone's association with Ujiji that the directors of the London Missionary Society had been receptive to the idea of establishing a station there. Unlike the previous European visitors, however, Hore and his companion Walter Hutley, a twenty-year-old builder and joiner, arrived at Ujiji intending to stay and were received, therefore, with suspicion. The Arabs, enjoying an economic boom in the mid-seventies, saw them as the thin end of a European wedge aimed not only at abolishing the traffic in the slave trade, but at ending Muslim economic hegemony in the interior as well.

Hore's vivid account of Ujiji society and commerce between 1878 and 1880 was published as a chapter of his book *Tanganyika: Eleven Years in Central Africa,* unfortunately an otherwise stilted and unimpressive work. Although the thousand pages of manuscript referred to by Hore in the preface to *Tanganyika* have never been located, the following contains several valuable excerpts from what must originally have been a substantial manuscript.

Ujiji*

Although one of our number still remained behind, the Mission might now be said to have arrived at its destination.

The events of the succeeding two years may be termed the consummation of its purpose, being indeed a sort of shaking down into its place in the country, eventuating in the establishment of three stations in carefully selected localities, and the reinforcement of its *personnel* to working strength.

The progress of the Mission into the country had not been achieved without a reduction of its numbers, and long-continued labour and hardship. And in its establishment the faith and endurance both of its workers and supporters were also to be severely tried.

Ujiji, it should be remembered, is really the name of a large tribal territory, bordered west and south by the Tanganyika Lake, north by Urundi, and east by Uhha and the River Ruiche, and occupying a gap in the mountain barrier of the lake, as well as a part of the elevated country itself.

It is divided into about thirty-five districts, or counties, each with its chief (*mteko*), answerable to a smaller council of some of their leading ones (*mutwali*), and to the Sultan or head chief (*mgassa*), who, however, during our experience, being a minor, was a mere puppet. The town commonly known as Ujiji straggles far into two of these small counties, Ugoy and Kawele, as London spreads into Middlesex and Surrey. But from a distance (although Ugoy is sometimes used, and still more rarely Kawele) the term Ujiji generally means the big town.

The traveller would naturally expect on arriving at Ujiji to look to the westward over the lake; but the lake view is due south, where on a clear day Capes Kabogo and Kungwe may both be seen, and sometimes even the mountains of Marungu. From the southern-looking beach the low part of Ujiji stretches in undulating hill and plain to the foot of the mountains, north about six miles. East, the gap is just visible across the Ruiche River, through which Ujiji is reached from that direction. South-east, the shore of the lake, in a long vista of capes and bays, disappears in the

*From *Tanganyika : Eleven Years in Central Africa* (London, 1892), 67-107.

dim distance. Westward, if clear, the sharp profile of Bangwe Island, the south-west promontory of Ujiji, brings into sight the lofty tableland of Goma, forty miles away on the western shore of the lake.

The big town occupies a central position on this southern-facing shore, and numerous smaller villages are dotted both along the coast and here and there over the low country. On the hills the real native settlements are still more numerous and rich in cattle.

Ujiji for over half a century at least had been the terminal depot for those Oriental colonists, travellers, and merchants (chiefly Arabs), who have so long exploited for us the ivory of these regions, and from whom chiefly we have information and assistance enabling us to enter them. From this point their expeditions and their influence extended farther afield, and now their terminal depot is Nyangwe and Kasongo in Manyuema, and Ujiji has become rather a station on the road to those places than a position of independent importance. For variety of people, languages, and customs, Ujiji is quite a little Egypt. Representatives of all the tribes come to it for trade and diplomatic purposes. The Arabs have settled down upon it, and, although nominally still native territory under the rule of its local chiefs, the Arabs practically rule, and the chiefs are puppets in their hands. By Arabs, of course, I mean all those—pure Orientals, Waswahili, Beloochis, and half-castes of every shade—who have come there as civilised people from a distance. The natives recognise the fact that the Arabs are a solid protection against native foes, and secure them the benefits of trade, improvement and extension of arts and industries; and this renders bearable the frequent injustice and disturbance they suffer at the hands of the lower class and slaves of these foreigners.

Thirty or forty large flat-roofed Arab houses (*tembes*), mostly hollow squares with massive walls and broad verandahs, form the principal feature of the town, and, with erections of every kind between that and the little grass bee-hive hut,—very irregularly placed amidst straggling oil-palms, bananas, and fruit-gardens,— make up the metropolis of Ujiji. A few winding tracks between these, worn down by common consent and use in the direction of greatest general convenience, form the streets or roads, mostly converging eventually upon the market-place. The market is essentially a native institution, and as such may be seen here and there over the whole territory of Ujiji and Urundi. But here in the town it is the meeting-place of all the various classes. The real native Mjiji from the hills brings his goats and produce; the poor Mswahili builds a little booth of palm leaves, and investing all his capital in a goat, displays his joints and penny lots of meat, warranted as being killed in true Mohammedan fashion. His wife may be close at hand with a jar of palm oil, which she retails in tiny gourd measures for cooking or lighting; towards the cool of the evening she lights a little fire under the jar to keep the oil liquid. Equally minute lots of salt, tobacco, fish, and vegetables enable the poor man to give variety to his fare, and afford facility for barter in every direction. Nor are the Arabs themselves above sending a slave woman to the market to retail fruits and vegetables from their gardens.

Here is a gaily-clothed Arab slave with bright-coloured cloths and a few yards of calico; he takes the place of money-changer, selling his cloth for the beads (which form the currency) accumulated by the retailer, or converting the purchaser's cloth into beads. The amount of cloth in the town, and what comes on the market in the morning, decides the exchange for the day, on which all transactions are based. The standard is the *doti of satini* (four yards of common Manchester calico), for which nine to eleven bunches of ten strings of beads, called a *fundo,* was the exchange in 1878. In 1888 this was reduced to three or four bunches. The arrival of a caravan with cloth gives scope for endless financial scares and schemes, while the visitors who come to town influence both the price and supply of everything. A few Waswahili tradesmen have come from Zanzibar; one is quite prosperous as a carpenter, and may be seen superintending his journeymen and apprentices making doors and windows out of the beautiful and durable *mininga* (African teak), or patching up on the beach some of the venerable and grotesque-looking craft of the Arab merchants. One is a maker of sandals and belts and pouches, and is always busy. Another, as a gunsmith, is highly favoured in the personal service of an Arab. There are beggars; there are itinerant musicians and singers. Fishermen bring their loaded baskets from the lake; women bring their fowls and eggs and butter to market from the country.

Here and there amongst the natives is one who has been to the coast; he is like a countryman in one of our more obscure villages who has been to London. Here and there amongst the Arabs there is one who has lived at Zanzibar, or who has been to Muscat, and is a weighty man in council in consequence. But to the chief part of this people the outer world has all the mystery as to its shape and character, all the unlimited possibilities that it had for us in the Middle Ages. With no revelation of God's love, their spiritual natures are yet groping for light amongst fetiches and so-called magic rites—grovelling before every display of Divine power as a spiritual influence capable of evil towards them—lying in darkness.

And over all that other cloud of blackness and terror, slavery and the slave-trade, perpetuates their ignorance and their barbarity, and prevents advance in any direction towards the higher and the better. That gaily-dressed man with riches of cloth for exchange is a slave; and the poor woman who has brought her basket of meal into market to sell looks up to him in awe and envy as she walks past with her companion who carries her wares and is *her* slave. This party of naked savages just landing are half of them slaves, who will shortly be sold by the others; and a chance disturbance in the market, or some crisis in political affairs, and they themselves may become slaves too. At one point you may see a gang of poor creatures (newly captive) chained together in their misery; at another, a party of poorly-clad native porters carrying loads, and led by an amply-dressed and armed superior, who is, however, a slave, while they are free hired labourers. A most complicated system, the details of which require years to understand; but the terrible degradation, misery, and death consequent upon the fearful traffic are plain enough.

In any other part of this earth there is such darkness of life and thought, such oppression of man by his fellow-man, such naturally promising and enterprising people so shut out from the benefits of civilisation, so beclouded in their spiritual view as to specially appeal to the efforts of Christian philanthropy, here it is, and here they are, in Ujiji town—" the true heathen ".

No wonder that our missionary brethren, coming into this motley and wondering community, should be the subjects alternately of irritation, wonder, and suspicion, which language, if they had it, could scarce allay—which could only be lived down by them, the observed of all observers, by Christian life and action. But for many a long day we could scarce expect to do better than on the day of our arrival, when, by the very influence of our presence, the *Ujiji slave-market was closed.* I do not mean that the slave-trade was stopped, but a conscience was created in the matter which rendered the trade illicit while we were there.

The Arabs, as the actual leaders of this strange community, were the first to have dealings with us. To them as such, and as having letters of introduction to them from the Sultan of Zanzibar, and having already some knowledge of a language they understood, we also addressed ourselves. There has always been something of a fellow-feeling between Arab and European meeting in these parts of Africa as " civilised " amongst the " heathen ".

Having a personal introduction to one of these, Moosa, from Said-bin-Salim, the deposed governor of Unyanyembe whom we had met at Uyui, he invited us temporarily to camp in his garden,

a wide domain of banana groves, oil-palms, and fruit-trees surrounding his house. Scarcely were the tents pitched when messengers began to arrive from the principal Arab houses bearing
numerous trays of dishes with all kinds of cooked food, a most
appetising display to travellers from the bush. Friendly greetings
came from all, and numerous offers of unoccupied houses, but
Moosa told us his friend had put us " on his head ", and he expected us to accept his hospitality for a time. Three days after our
arrival there was a great assembly of all the civilised people. We
attended, our letters were read, and we explained as far as we could
our purpose in coming into the country. To this the Arabs unitedly
replied, " that the Sultan in his introductory letter had said nothing
about our *staying* in the country; that we, having been placed
' upon their heads ' by the Sultan, they could not think of our living
for the present anywhere out of the town of Ujiji, where we should
be beyond their protective influence; and, on the other hand, that,
fearing what the Sultan might say to such proceedings, they could
not risk offending him (not yet knowing what we might be going to
do) by allowing us to acquire a possession in the country, either
ashore or afloat, until they heard further from him. We must therefore write to Zanzibar, and they would do the same, to hear what
the Sultan might say about us; and until that time we could
purchase neither house nor boat, but were at perfect liberty to
secure the temporary use of any house or boat in the place; and
further, for the same reason, we must not build either, but could
go to and fro on the lake and on shore whither we would ".

In fact, in their ignorance they suspected that after all we were
something of the nature of Government representatives inserting
the thin edge of the wedge for the abolition of the slave-trade and
European annexation.

But few of them were from the coast, or understood much of
international affairs—" far away ", as they said, from their Sultan,
when he was quoted to them, they were, although professing great
loyalty, not in present fear of him.

Irritating, however, as this position was to us, it did not really
prove much hindrance to the progress of the Mission; for we were
able to move on to other stations when we were prepared to do
so, and the two years spent at Ujiji resulted in a friendly acquaintance with the natives far and wide—as extensive, perhaps, as if
no hindrance had been placed in our way. In the course of years
the restrictions themselves disappeared as suspicion was allayed.

Individually, the Arabs continued as friendly and as hospitable
as ever; indeed, the rival attentions and intrigues of the different
parties and individuals in the endeavour of each one to make us

F

believe that *he* was our special friend were very embarrassing and difficult to deal with.

One of these Arabs, Nassour-bin-Cassim, was just then finishing a large *tembe*, and this we secured on hire as soon as it should be finished. It was situated in the highest part, and on the outer verge of the town, and was certainly the best in the neighbourhood.

While the house was being completed a temporary enclosure was made of a quantity of poles (some of the builder's materials), and this, partly roofed over with grass, forming a shade for the tents, made a temporary and indeed very pleasant habitation as long as the rain held off. In like manner, in accordance with our circumstances, a solid log canoe, built upon in Arab fashion, was hired for a year from Said-bin-Habib. In a little over a week from our arrival we were already engaged in the work of settling down : one making furniture and fittings for the house, one repairing and fitting up the boat, and one studying the language and making the acquaintance of our numerous visitors.

Mr. Thomson had never fully recovered his wonted strength and energy since his serious illness at Kirasa and Mpwapwa, but he was thought to be recovering, and indeed during the latter part of the journey, and on arrival at Ujiji, had taken a leading part in all affairs of the Mission. Three weeks after the arrival at Ujiji however, he became again very ill: a very few premonitory symptoms, and then a fit of an apoplectic nature laid him quite insensible. Consciousness returned after an interval, but after another fit he passed away on Sunday, 22nd September. He had lived to prove the ability, devotedness, and self-denial which enabled him to carry out his important duties, which had carried him forward, fearless of all perils, and made him faithful unto death.

The loss of its senior member, of one out of three of its present representatives at Ujiji, was a severe one to the Mission. What the effect of that loss would be on the distant representatives was perhaps anxiously wondered, alike by the two at Ujiji, the one yet in peril and anxiety on the road, and, on *their* part, in regard to *us*, by the directors and supporters at home. In due time we each became aware of the independent testimony and determination of the others, which, differing in words, were one in sentiment, as expressed in a resolution of the board of directors, that in it they found a renewed call to the work, and an appeal for filling up the vacancy.

Increasing anxiety had long been felt for the safety and progress of Mr. Dodgshun. One of the first things attended to at Ujiji was the establishment of a means of communication. From time to time, while working with the waggons, and on the subsequent quicker march, certain of the smartest of our men had had some training in carrying letters. The method thus started had gradually become "custom", which is everything in Africa; and as the specially long run between the coast and Ujiji was required for the first time *towards their home*, a few volunteers were easily obtained. The letters so despatched reached London in seventy-eight days, and were the commencement of a splendid mail system, which (except for a few intervals in time of war) has been kept up ever since. By this means we heard at intervals of the progress of Mr. Dodgshun; but between times fearfully garbled rumours gave great cause for anxiety.

On 19th October the "English Mission-House" was formally taken possession of. On 25th November the hired boat, now fitted with sails, rigging, and accommodation in something more like English fashion, and named the *Calabash*, was launched into the lake, and her efficiency tried in a trial-trip round to Kigoma Bay, and another trip out into the lake as far as Cape Kabogo.

A better acquaintance with the language, and increasing intercourse both with the people of Ujiji and many others, were fast being obtained.

On 24th January 1879 the first detachment of Roman Catholic missionaries from Algiers arrived at Ujiji and took up temporary quarters there.

On 21st February another voyage along the east coast gave us further acquaintance with that shore and its navigation, as well as a knowledge of some of its peoples, and soon afterwards several deputations from the head chief of Ujiji enabled us to deal more personally with those natives without the intervention of the Arabs.

A few extracts from a daily journal at Ujiji serve to indicate the multifarious duties and aspects of life there during this time of living out a character for the Mission :

Monday.—Unwell, bad head since yesterday; working at boat in the morning. In the evening, put in seeds of turnip, cabbage, celery, etc.

Tuesday.—Hot and misty; both unwell; did a little work at the boat in the morning; men fetching wood, and gardening. Muinyi Heri sent us a basket of onions; very hot; shot a hyena at night just in the act of seizing one of our goats.

Wednesday.—Very ill all day with bilious fever and racking headache; compelled to put off departure of mail till Friday morning.

Sunday.—A day of quiet rest—the enjoyment of being in a house again is immense—the capabilities for quiet reading and prayer much extended. The rain came down in torrents to-day; we got into the house just in time.

Monday.—Cut out the mainsail for *Calabash,* and did a little sewing . . . went to Muinyi Heri and doctored him for fever . . . dressed out poor native patient's stump (a hand amputated after gun explosion).

Friday, 1st November.—Up early and started off with Juma and two others, and an outfit in the shape of a calabash of water, cooked fowl, and bread, a tin pannikin, and a small saucepan; kept up a good round pace all the way to Kigoma, where a little canoe served as ferry across to the little flat oval island Ruanza, on which are the houses of Muinyi Akida (an Waswahili or half-caste, or " coast " Arab) and the huts of his numerous slaves. It looks very miserable just now, all the ruins of old huts and the numerous rubbish-heaps being wet with rain. I was bade " draw near " to a very mean little house, but there was a good clean mat in the verandah. Presently the great man himself appeared, coming out of the grass-fenced enclosure hard by; found he was suffering from a very bad eye. After the usual salutations he told me that Dr. Livingstone had once given him some medicine that made his eye quite well; promised him to make medicine for it. He said I was quite welcome to bring my boat to his place, which certainly is the most snug shelter anywhere near Ujiji. I then asked him for a guide to Bangwe.

Akida told me that there was a head man at Bangwe one Mtagle (mistaken then for *mteko,* the designation for local petty chief), but that he was put there by him, Akida, for did not Bangwe and its island " all belong to him "? And now a great fat sheep was unwillingly brought before me; I gave appropriate thanks, and prepared to depart. The big sheep proved refractory, and had to be secured by rope; at last we got him into the ferry canoe, and after bidding adieu to Muinyi Akida, who came down to see me off, we launched out. But when about half over, the sheep jumped overboard, causing great excitement on both shores; but we landed him safely, and sent him home under special escort, while I proceeded to Bangwe. Crossing over Bangwe peninsula, we found Mtagle in one of the huts of his village. It began to rain sharply, and we were invited inside. The interior aspect was far from pleasing. However, the embers were blown into a little blaze, and I found quite a lot of women and children beside our host. I took the opportunity of having breakfast; so one of my men made coffee in the little saucepan, and with bread and cold fowl I thoroughly enjoyed the repast. When the rain ceased our friend gave me a guide, who, from a hill near at hand, pointed out to me and named the leading features of the country there to be observed.

Returning to the hut, Mtagle gave me a bunch of bananas, and pointed out a sheep which he said he should bring with him when he came to see me soon. We then returned by the beach to Ujiji.

This chief of Bangwe I delight to think of as my friend. A man of the fine physique and a noble countenance, of gentle yet manly aspect—he was ever ready to assist us. At the launch of the *Calabash,* and again years after at the launch of the *Morning Star,* he marched into Ujiji with the men of his village to lend a helping hand. As time after time, under his own fig tree (the village talking-place), and in the mission-house, he had drunk in gladly all the words I could give him of God and his love to us, I have rejoiced with trembling that the way is open and the people are ready, and we only are behind in faith, in ability, and perseverence.

Saturday.—The little canoe given us by Said-bin-Habib is cut out of a solid log like all the canoes here—twenty-five feet long. To-day I had it sawn into two pieces: one, fourteen feet long, is to make our dingy; of the short piece we can either make a bath, or probably Mr. Dodgshun will like to make a little boat for himself of it.

Monday.—Friendly messengers from Akida and Mtagle, whom I visited the other day, bringing presents; had a nice talk with them.

Friday.—A gang of Nassour's (our landlord) women in charge of their " mamma " clearing out the long unroofed room ready for the builders.

Monday.—Had a visit from Muinyi Heri and Abe (the leading half-caste colonist and the local native chief), and arranged with them for my visit to the head chief.

Friday.—Much better to-day; got through a lot of work, but while working at the boat felt the heat so much that I had to get a man to hold an umbrella over my head while I put the last few nails in.

Monday.—Evening, a grand row between Nassour's men and our own—nothing could be proved. Two of Nassour's men received club blows, also Maktub our postman. Farajella slightly wounded with a bullet; and Sulieman, the other postman, declared that part of his moustache was taken off by another shot at close quarters. Nassour came to me in the dark, with his friend Sali, and they stuck their spears defiantly in the ground close to me. I told them, however, the whole affair must be settled by the *Wali* (the chief authority); but having failed to scare me, and not caring for the vexation of a public inquiry, it was amicably arranged by their coming in and drinking coffee.

Monday.—Another deputation from the head chief—come " to hear our own words,"—said they were willing to give us a place to build; and although willing to send their children to be taught, they could not agree to give up their slaves to us!

The half-caste colonists, amongst other slander, had told them we should take their slaves away from them. And the natives everywhere would oppose this view of the abolition of " slavery ", though nearly everywhere they would be willing and glad to secure that peace which would prevent the " slave-trade ".

Abe's wife also called with an old lady companion, Said-bin-Habib's chief housekeeper. They were delighted to examine everything, and after looking over the medicine chest, the old lady, after some whispering with her companion, looked most pathetically at me and said: " Sir, do give me a pill!—you gave her one the other day."

Thursday.—There is a sort of by-play going on between us and the council of Arabs by means of my man Farajella: sounding him as to our intentions, and inquiring of all our doings, etc.

It is good for us in our relations both with Arabs and natives that we have these intelligent Zanzibaris as helpers. Knowing our private lives and all our doings, spies in the camp in this way have had only to report that which has helped to disarm suspicion.

I took a walk in the afternoon to the village of Gitwalo. I fund a man weaving a cotton cloth. His method and work were far superior to what I saw before, and the lath to drive home the weft was worked by two people: himself and his son. He had been working two days, and he expected to finish it in two more. I worked a few throws of the shuttle with him, at which he was pleased. As I walked through a cassava plot on my way home, six little wagtails were holding a noisy conference, fluttering and twittering. As I approached and stood still about three yards from them, they ranged themselves in a semicircle and sang to me most sweetly. When I passed away they returned to their business. The natives capture other little birds, but these wagtails are everywhere safe: I don't know why, but they are sweet little things, with their beautiful song.

Friday.—Ujiji is crowded with Wamanyuema immigrants—each party attached to some Arab. At present this plan is worse than slavery, for the injury and death of any man is not a loss to their employers, and they are fearfully ill-treated. M. Debaize (a French traveller) is now obtaining 200 of these

Wamanyuema. Notwithstanding risks and hard treatment, they are anxious to come to Ujiji for employment.

Saturday.—At 9 o'clock Mohammed-bin-Alfan's servants arrived to conduct us to his house, where he had specially invited us to breakfast and to inspect the boat he is building. We found an excellent repast awaiting us, with a table and stools specially made for the occasion. Then the model was brought in and discussed, and finally an inspection of the boat itself —a great advance on anything before done here.

This Arab Mohammed-bin-Alfan was from the first most polite and hospitable to us. He is an educated and liberal-minded man, free from many of the prejudices of the half-castes and others who have not " seen the world ". He valued highly a few hints about boat-building and other industrial work in which he showed much enterprise, as well as medical help to himself and his people. At one of the most critical times of our Ujiji experiences, related farther on, he rendered us good help; and he has since, in even more substantial manner, proved his friendship by restraining the irritation and prejudice against Europeans (during the recent troubles at the coast) of the Ujiji community.

Thursday.—About 8.30 A.M. Debaize made a start, and these 20(Wamanyuema and 150 Zanzibaris trooped out of our house in single file, a motley crowd. Some carried miserable trade guns, others spears, tomahawks, clubs, or, wanting other weapons, a sharp-pointed staff or huge porridge-stick; four or five carried small tusks of ivory; and each one some matter, as a mat, a pot, or a calabash. One man's sole outfit for the march was a huge sweet potato, which he had prudently roasted before starting, and now carried in his hand. . . .

As I sit in the window at evening writing this, the lake before me looks beautiful. At a glance I can take in the countries of Ukaranga, Ukawendi, the distant Uguha, and the tall mountain barrier of Goma; the Capes Kabogo and Kungwe, and Cape Kitanga, near the islands, their tops just lifted into view by the mirage. Close at hand, the little bay separating Kasimbo from Kawele, with large canoes drawn up on the shore, the slopes on either side of the bay covered with maize fields, scattered oil-palm trees, and bananas, with rice in the lower parts. Bright little lizards are catching flies in the verandah outside. Our pomegranate trees are alive with those tiny birds which in cages at home you may see huddled together to keep themselves warm; here *they* are at home, trim and lively. Besides these there is quite a chorus of little songsters of many and pleasing notes; and, along the path in front, the Wajiji pass actively to and fro to the market, each man with his long spear.

Tuesday.—Sambo told us his story. He says his real father was Chungu, a chief near Bangweolo. When he was very young a white man passed his village, which was on the Lopoposi River. The white man had a donkey, and wore a large hat like what Sambo sees in our house. Bangweolo was a big water near his home; he never went there, but remembers, when he was on his mother's back, her pointing it out to him in the distance. One day he went to pick up fire-wood for his mother. When he had finished he went to dig some potatoes from the garden; while at this some natives from another village carried him off and sold him to some passing Wangwana (half-castes or civilised Africans) for cloth. They took him to their camp, where there were many slaves and much ivory and copper (which he described correctly). As they went on their journey the slaves were fastened with chains, but he was fastened by himself with cord. He says they took " a year " to reach Unyanyembe, passing Tanganyika on the road, and there he became the property of Sheik Nassib, who, when Mr. Dodgshun passed by, gave the boy to him.

The old story of Joseph's brethren selling him to the Ishmaelites—the natives selling one another to passing strangers.

Sunday.—A slave of Muinyi Heri's came to us for treatment of his hand. On examination we found that an iron ring and spike had been forcibly clamped round his wrist, and that the whole hand was now mortified. Sent to Msalim (son of Muinyi Heri) to say that the man's hand must be amputated; and he said, " Do so, if the man is willing." Put the man under chloroform accordingly, and amputated about four inches from elbow—apparently a successful operation, and good stump. The man says the iron has been on for two months; that the spike was drawn out of the log into which it had been driven last Ramathan; that since then he has been loose, but tried in vain to get the iron off.

Wednesday.—Two distinct shocks of earthquake to-day: the first at 5.30 P.M., and the second and lesser shock about 6. The first shock lasted about four minutes, and quite shook the house; the roof beams creaking ominously, and everybody going outside, from whence the whole house could be seen to tremble. . . . The white ants send out new colonies (like bees) during the rains. They issue from a special back entrance in their nests or burrows, opened out for their exit, and have long loose wings to get away with. Other creatures seem to know when they are due, and gather round the entrance to devour them. Snakes, frogs, fowls snap them up, as, crowding out, they tumble over dazed in the bright light. Those that rise on

the wing are hunted by birds. Large hawks hover overhead
and snap up the dainty morsels one by one, and the fowls
stalk round on tip-toe after them in ludicrous fashion. A
short flight and they are done, and, sprawling on the ground,
become quite unmanageable. But there is a remedy: planting
his hind feet firmly on the draggling wings and pressing them
to the ground, the ant gives his body a surge forward and
is free. No more to soar aloft, he goes below as soon as
possible. The general excitement gives notice to others: men,
women, and children run with little brooms and sweep up
baskets full of the savoury morsels as they come out of the
hole. After a while the stampede is over, all is quiet, and the
earth for half a mile round is speckled with the discarded wings.

Tuesday.—Went to Kigoma in early morning as arranged; passed
on to Mbogo's village, quite a mart just now, with Mirambo's
trading-party and numerous Arabs' men come here to sell
their ivory. . . . About thirty of the elders, with Mbogo at
their head (all Wajiji chiefs), went round the corner and held
a meeting, to which, after an interval, I was requested to
come. On getting seated in the circle, I was told they had
decided to give me the land for house and garden. . . .
Adjourned to the land in question, followed by a crowd.
Mbogo's brother, as spokesman, cut a little leafy branch,
stood on a hillock waving his hand as he indicated the
boundaries and propounded the title, calling on all present
to witness the arrangement, and bade them all be friendly
to the white man who was coming to live there. Led by the
chiefs and followed by the crowd, we then perambulated the
boundaries that they might be well impressed on our memo-
ries. While thus beating the bounds we came upon a very
large snake, coiled among the branches of a low tree. I called
for my gun, but it was explained that the Wajiji wish these
creatures not to be destroyed; the elders stood and gazed at it
a short time and then we proceeded.

Wednesday.—Mtongoro, the young Mtongwe chief, came to-day,
and half a dozen of his followers; he has the logs cut that
I asked for, but cannot convey them; had interesting conference with him.

Tuesday.—A nice talk with a little party of Fipa natives come on
a trading expedition; gave me information about their country and chiefs, and carried home the news of us.

Wednesday.—Went to Mohammed's to treat a little girl, but she
could not be induced to come to me, for her nurse had before
frightened the child by threatening to give her " to the
whiteman "! Prescribed as well as I could.

Mr. Dodgshun was shortly expected, and in anticipation of his
assuming more particularly the direction of the station at Ujiji,

every information was collected and the property put in order
for that purpose. Mr. Hutley had already made furniture and other
civilised fittings and improvements to the house, and I expected
on the arrival of Mr. Dodgshun to be able to start away for a
thorough exploration of the lake.

On 27th March 1879 our brother arrived, weary and strained
with his long-continued and anxious journeyings, the last month
of which, indeed, was accomplished under most exceptionable
difficulties, but with unfailing persistence and courage. It was an
important and happy time for us all, as we recounted the long
story of stirring events since our parting at Mpwapwa, and made
plans for enlarged and extended work.

The caravan of M. Broyon had been completely wrecked. When
he started from the coast he was carrying goods for Urambo: a
large portion was doubtless the property of Mirambo, as exchange
for ivory of his taken to the coast; other portions were perhaps his
prospectively, for more ivory; all, as he expected, to be sold and
distributed in trade to him and his people. Altogether, he looked
upon it (native fashion) as *his* caravan.

Messengers of Mirambo, who had come down to us in reply to
ours, and also to see how Broyon was getting on, took vague
accounts to him of Broyon's mysterious delays, and dealings with
other clients and patrons, which awakened Mirambo's suspicions.
Now as caravans are coming up from the coast their destination is
uncertain; but by and by, at a certain fork of the road, they must
plainly announce their destination by taking this road or that. To
the neighbourhood of this fork Mirambo sent a party of his men,
to ascertain there if Broyon was false to him or not. If Broyon took
the road towards Urambo, they would welcome and escort him to
their chief; if he took the other road, they were (in African fashion,
of course) to prevent the loss of their chief's goods. That road was
taken which indicated a wrong direction (although doubtless
Broyon intended to send to Mirambo from Unyanyembe what be-
longed to him). Mirambo's men, aided by the influence and the
people of Said-bin-Salim, who was living in great measure under
Mirambo's protection, unable to divert the caravan intact, which
became broken up in the fright and confusion of these threatening
circumstances, carried off the goods to Mirambo. That is, the bulk
of the goods; for on the old principle of not muzzling the ox, Said-
bin-Salim and his men, the local chiefs, and the actual carriers of
the goods, all had their shares and fees and maintenance out of
them; or, as an eye-witness subsequently told me, " Said-bin-Salim
had the cloth and Mirambo the boxes." Mirambo, however, on
receiving what came to him, and also by report, became aware that

a great part of the property was evidently not his, and sent to Unyanyembe to invite the " whitemen " to claim their own. The fears of M. Broyon, increased by the report of certain travellers who had been to Mirambo and failed to understand him, prevented, however, any adjustment at that time; and Mr. Dodgshun, only being able to judge of Mirambo by their accounts, and being enfeebled by the long journey and its many anxieties, desired to join his brethren at Ujiji before deciding on further action.

On the subsequent arrival at Mirambo's of Messrs. Southon and Griffiths, however, Mirambo himself suggested an investigation of the matter, and gave up to them what was evidently the LMS property.

Mr. Dodgshun, after resting at Unyanyembe during the confusion arising from the breaking up of this caravan, passed on alone, through much hardship, to Ujiji, where he arrived as related above. The tedious journey, however, of over seven months, with its many anxieties and hardships, the disaster in Unyamwezi, and the subsequent hurried march without proper food or outfit, had completely worn him out. The joyful stimulation of arrival amongst his brethren, and the prospect of getting to steady work, revived him for a day or two; but fatal weakness had already laid its hand upon him, and after a few hours of sudden illness he expired on the 3rd April. In the midst of his deepest difficulties and greatest weakness his determination to devote his life to the work he felt called to had not abated, and faithful unto death, he obtained the crown of life.

The events of the next four months were both exciting and important. Rumours came of Mirambo's approach to attack Ujiji; the colonial Arab community strove to slander us as the cause. Failing that, the natives were accused of having invited him; but as they offered to vacate and leave the Arabs to themselves in proof of their denial of guilt, the Colonials fell to accusing one another of complicity with Mirambo, and each one fortified himself separately in his own *tembe*.

On 21st May the French traveller, the Abbé Debaize, arrived and was assisted and entertained by the Mission. A voyage was made to Uguha on the west side of the lake, and friendly acquaintance made with its chief Kassanga, who invited us to occupy a station in his country.

On 2nd August a small party of M. Broyon's men arrived with forty loads of general stores, the salvage of the wrecked expedition.

Soon after this several new Arabs arrived in town, and some ill-feeling was again observable. It culminated one day, when, expecting the arrival of a caravan, and according to allowed custom, I determined to hoist a flag. Having the boat's mast on shore, I thought it would make a very convenient flagstaff, so put it up, not knowing then that was just the thing to excite their anger.

The Arabs armed all their slaves, forming altogether a body of about 200 armed men, and came up to our house. According to custom, I received them in a friendly way, and asked them to sit down inside. I had then about twenty of these Arabs, nearly filling the principal room. This was a critical moment. There were Mr. Hutley and I, quite alone, and apparently helpless in the hands of this lawless crowd, who completely filled and surrounded the house. There were three large windows in this principal room, just a yard or two from where we stood, and through the bars of the windows the slaves and followers of the Arabs pointed their guns. With their fingers on the triggers, they shouted to their leaders to give the word of command, but they did not: some wonderful power seemed to restrain them, and they could only talk excitedly amongst themselves. At length one of the new-comers stood up and spoke to the rest: " The house is full of goods; let us empty it now, and destroy these men at one stroke." The excited mob were now yelling and dancing in our verandah and hall, and begging the Arabs to give the word for the onslaught to commence. The Arabs only saw two calm faces, and only heard a quiet request to state their business and talk over it quietly. But One all-powerful to save heard two earnest prayers for help; the next moment Mohammed-bin-Halfan stood up and quietly said, " Let us get out," and a moment after *those Arabs were literally pushing one another in the doorway in their anxiety to get out quickly.* It appears that Mohammed had at the same time given orders for the obnoxious flagstaff to be removed. This had drawn the mob off from the house, and so at once caused the removal of the sore point to each party; he was the first, too, to make friendly advances to us again. This event, so far from causing permanent trouble, became indeed helpful to us; the best of the Arabs were alarmed at the storm they might at any time raise, the natives were deeply impressed that we remained unharmed.

We had heard of the arrival of the African International Association's expedition at Karema, then the first news of the coming of Dr. Mullens and Messrs. Southon and Griffith for the reinforcement of the Mission, and very soon afterwards of the death, alas, of their devoted and loved leader: a loss not only to our Mission, but deeply felt throughout the whole of the Society's work and connections.

The stirring events at Ujiji were made, in the good providence of God, all to work together for our good. The suspicion and doubts of Arabs and natives alike were smoothed down towards us as they had to deal with the new arrivals. Mirambo's own admission that he should indeed have attacked Ujiji, but that " his friends the whitemen " were there, and the special despatches from Zanzibar confirming the will of the deceased Abbé Debaize in placing the management of his affairs in the hands of the English missionaries, told with great weight in our favour. The Wajiji openly declared a favourable opinion of us, after having viewed us so long " with their own eyes," and offered us a piece of land for the establishment of a station.

On 23rd September Messrs. Southon and Griffith arrived, and although the smouldering doubts and ignorance of the Arabs broke out now and again in various little difficulties, the experience gained of local affairs, and the pressing invitations of Mirambo and Kassanga, enabled us, in formal committee at Ujiji, to decide in establishing stations at Urambo by its occupation by Dr. Southon, and at Uguha by Messrs. Griffith and Hutley proceeding thither, while I should continue to occupy Ujiji, and proceed with the examination of the lake: measures which, after ten or twelve days of consultation, arrangement of business, and division of stores, were duly proceeded with, and carried to a successful issue.

On 9th October Dr. Southon started for Urambo, where, with devoted and untiring energy, he laid the foundation, under God's help and blessing, of a grand Christian work in the very capital of the savage chief who had so long been regarded with fear and trembling alike by Arab, European, and native.

On 22nd October, having sent over a hired boat two days before with various stores, we sailed in the *Calabash* to establish a settlement on the western shore of the lake. Kassanga proved true to his promise: food was brought, labourers provided, and a site being selected at Mtowa, near the southern cape of a beautiful bay of islands, temporary houses were at once erected, forming a station we named Plymouth Rock, and I returned to Ujiji.

The succeeding year was, for the two new stations, a time of settling down into the new and strange conditions, of acquiring knowledge of the language and character of the people, and of solving the problems of life for the missionaries themselves, resulting in a report, in both cases, of friendly relations with the people, and an earnest appeal for more help for the work thus rapidly opening up in their hands.

At Ujiji steady advance was made in living down the prejudices of the Arabs, and in further securing the lasting respect and friendship of the Wajiji.

Voyages were made also, during which all the countries round the lake were visited, as related in detail in the following chapter.

At home the efforts of the year resulted in the despatch of reinforcements, and on 3rd October 1880 Messrs. Wookey, Palmer, and Williams arrived at Ujiji accompanied by Dr. Southon from Urambo. Messrs. Griffith and Hutley had come over from Uguha, completing for our District Committee meeting an assembly of seven missionaries. To this meeting were brought a year's report from three stations, an account of the survey of the lake, and further openings in various countries.

The destinations of the newly-arrived brethren being decided and business details arranged, we separated again in new strength and faith: Messrs. Southon and Williams to Urambo, Messrs. Griffith and Palmer to Uguha, Messrs. Wookey and Hutley remaining at Ujiji, and I to return to England, as originally arranged by the directors, to report specially upon the lake and the proposed vessel for its navigation. Three stations were thus effectively manned, and the Mission was an established fact.

The world had already been informed on the highest authority that " the safety of a European at Ujiji would be but precarious," that a disturbance might arise at any moment " the result of which would be that the European would either have to forfeit all his goods or his life, or decamp with his people immediately to save himself." The disturbances truly had from time to time arisen, but the predicted disaster had not ensued. At Ujiji during those " two whole years " the foundations of our Mission had been laid. It was there that we so lived down those prejudices of the Arabs which on our arrival had threatened to render the establishment of the Mission impossible, that in after years some of them actually upheld and preserved its members in times of peril. At Ujiji we first made ourselves acquainted with the natives, their language, their institutions, and their modes of life and thought—lived down their suspicions and won their regard. From Ujiji our good name was so made known, by various natives who visited us there, in all the regions round about, that on subsequent visits to distant places our name had gone before and we were received as friends; and there also we gathered round us the first native helpers who aided us in voyages and the settlement of stations. And the light kindled in that dark place amidst much prayer and labour and sorrow, glimmering feebly awhile, burning up gradually under steady effort, was already, under God's guidance and blessing, spreading afar into the darkness.

V

THE LAKE

In 1890 the Royal Geographical Society named Edward Hore as the recipient of its annual Cuthbert Peek award for the advancement of European knowledge of the interior of Africa. His contribution was the completion and verification of the partial surveys of Lake Tanganyika made by Burton and Speke, Livingstone, and Stanley, and Cameron. 'Three Voyages of the *Calabash*,' Hore's record of his circumnavigation, provided the basis for his first address to the Royal Geographical Society in November 1881. This was published, along with his map of the lake, as 'Lake Tanganyika' in the January 1882 *Proceedings of the Royal Geographical Society (IV)*.

The following is a combination of the published address and of the heretofore unpublished journal. Using 'Lake Tanganyika' as the framework, the editor has added, in their proper sequence, those portions of the journal which contribute new information. Only repetitive or highly detailed geographic statistics have been omitted from Hore's original record. Segments from the journal have been indented for easy recognition.

In March 1877 I was appointed to the London Missionary Society's pioneer expedition in Central Africa; to myself was committed more especially the care of such scientific observations as could be carried out amidst our various duties, the survey of the lake, and the marine department of the Mission. To aid me in this work, I was introduced by the late Dr. Mullens to your Society, and received from the late Commander George such information as enabled me to use with effect the meteorological instruments with which we were provided, and especially a most careful instruction in the use of the hypsometrical apparatus, by aid of which I have been able to produce a section of the country in addition to my map of the route. I have presented to the Society a two years' series of meteorological observations made at Ujiji, and a three months' series made at Kirasa's, in the Mukon-dokwa valley. Mercurial barometers have also since been set up at Urambo and at Uguha.

Road to the Lake. The road we were to take, though parallel to some extent with what might be called the old road used by Cameron and Stanley, was in fact almost entirely new. The portions from Saadani to Mpwapwa, avoiding the Makata swamp, were taken on the recommendation of Mr. Roger Price, who had made a preliminary journey so far; and the portion leading through the territory of the chief Mirambo was determined on with the twofold purpose of avoiding the Arab settlement of Unyanyembe, and of opening friendly negotiations with Mirambo.

More than this, we were to introduce a new (for Central Africa, at least) system of transport-bullock waggons.

Landing at Saadani in June, we at once commenced training bullocks for this service, and at the latter end of July we really started for the interior with our bullock train. Succeeding eventually in reaching Kirasa, the bullock transport came to an end by the death of these animals by the tsetse fly. Every other difficulty had been overcome for 150 miles of the most difficult part of the road, and only in respect of the fatal tsetse can this experiment be called a failure. Returning eventually to the ordinary modes of transport by porters, the remaining part of the journey, namely from Mpwapwa to Ujiji, was accomplished in eighty-seven days, a journey which, considering the amount of goods carried and the

85

new experience to be brought, has not yet been surpassed. We arrived at Ujiji on the 23rd August, 1878.

I think there has been much misapprehension in England with regard to this old road. At one of your meetings in December last year it was stated, in comparing it with another road, that a caravan journey from Zanzibar to Ujiji occupied six months, and that the rate for transport of goods was about 400l. per ton; whereas the fact was, our first real caravan journey was accomplished in 116 days, or less than four months, the second in ninety-nine days, and I have myself walked over the same road in sixty-two consecutive or fifty marching days.[1] The 400l. per ton represented not mere transport, but most exceptional loss.

Again, in the *Times* of the 27th of March 1879 it was stated that, with the assistance of steam power on Lake Nyassa and the river Zambesi, the journey from Lake Tanganyika to Quilimane might be accomplished in forty-five days, and to London in seventy-five days, and the writer was apparently ignorant of the fact that, nearly a year before, the first party we despatched from Ujiji by the old road reached the coast in forty-five days, the letters reaching London in seventy-eight days. Of this route I have made a map and section. The latitudes of various points have been fixed by meridian observations of stars north and south. On my recent journey to the coast I measured the road distance of each day's journey by means of a perambulator which I constructed at Ujiji.

The moist and luxuriant coast region, the scrubby plains and harsh thorny jungles of eastern and western Ugogo, with the beautiful forest dividing them, the step on to the forest plateau of Uyansi and Unyamwesi, the growing luxuriance of the Tanganyika watershed, I cannot here describe; I hope to do so some day, together with the surprising advances to be observed in the arts and industries and in social order amongst the natives as we proceed further inland.

General Description of the Lake. Lake Tanganyika is 330 miles in length, with a coast-line of 900 miles, and its depth is hitherto

---

1. Hore's defence of the east-west route to the interior was prompted by pressures exerted upon the directors of the London Missionary Society by James Stewart, C.E., who had charted a road connecting Lakes Nyasa and Tanganyika, and James Stevenson, a director of the Free Church of Scotland mission at Lake Nyasa, who was prepared to finance it, to adopt that route as the exclusive approach to the Lake Tanganyika mission stations. In this section Hore is responding to James Stewart's challenge to the LMS to help open a road between the lakes. See " Lake Nyassa and the Water Route to the Lake Region of Africa ", *Proceedings of the Royal Geographical Society* (May 1881).

unfathomed. A survey spreading over such distances, although of two years' continuance, must necessarily be but a rough one.

Various theories have been suggested to account for the disposal of the vast quantities of water which drain into the Tanganyika, such as enormous evaporation, subterranean outlet, &c., &c. What I have to remark on this point embraces no theory, but is a simple account of observations made during my residence upon the lake shores. I found the lake to be 2700 feet above the sea-level, and at the time of our arrival Arabs and natives alike agreed in informing me that its waters were slowly but surely rising, and had been doing so for some length of time. But a close observation on my part failed to ascertain any rise, and desiring to obtain accurate information on the subject, I erected, in March 1879, a water guage on the shores at Ujiji. By the 27th of May I found that the waters had fallen two feet, and they continued to fall until, in August 1880, they reached a point ten feet four and a half inches below my original watermark. Most evident signs of the receding of the waters might be seen all round the shores of the lake, in belts of dead timber and bleached rock. The Arabs were agreed that, shortly before our arrival, the Lukuga obstruction was broken away, and I am inclined to believe from these reports, and from personal observation, that the lake had been rising gradually for a long term of years, until the force of water carried away that obstruction, and the Lukuga river became the veritable outlet of the lake. That the evaporation was sufficient in some years to maintain the lake at a level is very likely the case, but the loss from this cause would be overcome in heavy rainy seasons by the larger accumulation of incoming waters, and the lake would increase. The rainy seasons are extremely different in different years; hence a few successive wet years would cause an unusual rising of the lake waters, such as seemed to have occurred just before our arrival. I am convinced that the lake never, or at any rate for very many years, was at such a height as just before that time. But this is quite apart from any geological evidence of the different state of things in remote ages.

I have been understood to connect the changes of the water level of Tanganyika with earthquake movements. This I did not intend to do, but merely to admit the possibility of such a theory, and the probability that the bed of the lake is in reality a vast chasm caused by volcanic or earthquake movement, by calling attention to the fact that such movement is not uncommon even now.

Some twenty years ago, the Arabs informed me that an extra-ordinary disturbance of the lake waters occurred, a long line of broken water being seen bubbling and reeking with steam. The next morning all was tranquil, but the shore was strewed with fragments of a substance resembling bitumen, a specimen of which I have deposited with your Society. The first severe shock of earthquake I felt myself at Ujiji was at 9 p.m. on the 10th of August, 1880, which shook the house considerably. There had been two or three slight shocks at the same time the previous year, but on this occasion the succeeding vibrations lasted for two or three months longer at intervals. There seemed to be a line of vibration through N.N.W. to S.S.E., and I observed a crack in the earth right through the town of Ujiji, extending for two or three miles in broken intervals in this direction. Captain Carter, of the Belgian expedition, also noticed a shock of earthquake at about this period in Southern Unyamwesi, and Mr. Thomson, of the Royal Geographical Society's expedition, reports a shock at Kapufi's, on the Lofu river, on April 12th, about 4 p.m.

Although of such large extent, and of such variety of aspect, there is a general sameness in the Tanganyika scenery; the whole basin forms in fact a vast chasm enclosed within mountain ranges or cliffs, terminating in elevated plateaux, a few lower lands intervening, natural gaps in the ranges, banks and deltas formed by eroding torrents, and in a few localities, such as at Ujiji and elsewhere, a strip of shelving beach in a east and west direction breaks the general north and south line of the lake. North of Ujiji the surrounding mountains approach the lake shore with but a small interval of low undulating hills, and have the appearance of meeting some distance north of the lake, as described by Captain Speke.

The extreme north end, however, is low alluvial land, with banks of reed and papyrus; following the general rule on the lake, which is, that bordering a shore trending east and west, an expanse of shallow water and a low beach are usually found, as though the shore had been washed down gradually by the waves. In some places, however, this is a bringing down and depositing of matters by rivers. The peninsula of Ubwari is simply a long ridge ascending steeply from the lake on all sides.

I found the southern half of the Burton Gulf to be very shallow, obtaining, on sounding, only four or five fathoms of water right across it.

The isthmus of Ukaramba is formed of low hills, and behind Ubwari there is a considerable expanse of lower land between the lake and the mountains, which again approach the shore at Goma. The lofty and level horizon of the Goma hills is one of the sights of the lake. About half the year it is visible from Ujiji, on a clear day, though forty miles distance, and the streams, descending to the lake down those lofty hillsides, may be plainly seen like silver threads. The paths to the villages, which are placed on the ridges and peaks of these hills, are in some places mere flights of steps. Though molested by several of the lake tribes, the Wagoma are a spirited and industrious race, and have grand resources further inland in a rich ivory country, of which little is yet known.

The country of Uguha, with its bay of islands, its Lukuga, and its Plymouth Rock Mission Station, forms a decided gap in the rim of the lake basin; as such it has formed hitherto the natural gateway to the regions beyond, for those who have penetrated these regions, and as such is a position of much importance both to missionaries and travellers.

Moving south along this west coast, the mountains approach the lake again gradually till the aspect of the steep shores of Goma is repeated in the rich and populous districts of Marungu and Itawa. Another gap at the Cameron bays, and we approach the loftiest barriers of the lake at the south end.

From the Lofu river round by capes Kalambwe and Pembete to the district of Kituta, the glorious undercliff of the Isle of Wight is reproduced on a gigantic scale and with tropical vegetation. The airy but still luxuriant downs above afford some splendid and healthy localities amongst which the London Missionary Society are about to select a site for another station, at a point which will be the Tanganyika terminus of Mr. Stevenson's road between the two lakes.

The entrance to the Lofu river is itself worthy of separate description. It is in the southern corner of the bay formed by the northern coast of Ulungu and the south-east corner of Itawa. With the wind east, or anywhere from east to north, there is a very nasty chop on a bar considerably outside of what would ordinarily be considered the actual mouth of the river. The embouchure itself is not visible until one comes close upon it; then, turning sharp round to the southward, a beautiful gap in the coast-line opens to a view of broad and deep entrance. Where there are sheltered points in the river banks, there the long water-grass and papyrus accumulate in thick masses of very bright green, which are so fresh and flourishing and clear of débris as to add considerably to the beauty of the scene instead of the contrary, which is more generally the case on the lake shores. Steep verdant slopes rise up on every side, broken by gullies choked with dense vegetation, and conducting smaller streams into the general outlet.

There is no expanse of river to be seen here. Sailing into the entrance, one appears to be only running up into an inlet with

large masses of water-grass at its head and hills beyond; but as
we advance, the zigzag reaches of the river disclose in succession
vista after vista, all of similar aspect, until, turning again westward, a vast gap or basin presents itself, forming one of the
most beautiful sights I have yet beheld on Lake Tanganyika. A
long winding lake, from which ascend, with more or less intervening lowlands, immense hills, with for the most part clear
straight skylines, showing the edges of the table-lands above. On
the southern side, a long and gentle rise from the water-edge to
the steeper hillside is covered with villages and extensive gardens.
Here one may walk for miles through field after field of waving
corn and rice. Westward, the valley narrows towards the more
confined space of the incoming waters, but the outlet, where we
had now just arrived, is quite hidden at a short distance. The
whole thing is on so extensive a scale that I could not on the spot
realise the sense of confinement which the description may seem
to indicate. But we were to be much disappointed; each zigzag
hitherto had in due course permitted that progress which at first
sight it seemed to deny; now, with the view all open and promising, we were brought to a stand behind a dense mass of floating
vegetation, which proved to us quite impassable, and here we
were compelled to moor the boat. On a closer inspection of the
barrier I was convinced that I could cut a channel for the entrance
of a vessel in two or three days with a gang of ten or twelve men
with tools : a channel which would be finally thoroughly cleared
by the force of the water when it was once opened. The river now
flows clear and deep beneath. During my second visit, a good-
sized boat, belonging to a party of Wajiji, was dragged over the
floating vegetation by main force. This I tried on my first visit,
but had not men enough for any great effort.

The country of Fipa in continuation presents a lofty but less
perpendicular front to the lake, the land being broken into three-
clothed hills and ridges, gradually rising to the great inland
heights, an aspect continued as far as the plain of Musamwira.
Then the Kawendi Mountains and the lofty peaks of Cape
Kungwe frown upon the lake in sublime grandeur, broken only
by immense and beautiful chines, through which descend the
watercourses from the heights, tumbling down in refreshing cascades and waterfalls. Further north, the mountains, more or less
broken, again recede, leaving the eastern gap in the rim of the
lake basin in which Ujiji is situated.

The map of the lake, which I have pleasure in submitting to
the Society, is the result of my own survey based upon latitudes
by meridian altitudes of stars north and south, and compass bear-

ings with an error of compass allowed by my own observations of 11° west at Ujiji, increasing gradually to 14° west at the south end of the lake; most of the principal points giving the general outline being laid down from bearings by azimuth compass on shore, all the detail filled in by the boat's compass. The coast of Ulungu was surveyed with special care. The exceptions to a full survey of every bend in the coast at the south end are the portions from Pambete to the Lofu, and from Musi to Cape Kipimbwe.

The weather was frequently unfavourable for astronomical observations, but still many good latitudes were obtained. My boat's compass was a large one, fitted in a proper binnacle, and frequent comparison with a compass on shore proved it to be accurate. The names of various places were obtained by careful inquiry of natives on the spot. I had no Ujiji pilot with me to volunteer uncertain information. In the progress of my work I was unable to take extensive soundings, but I have frequently found no bottom with the 168 fathoms of line I carried with me.

Natives. In describing the natives on the shores of Lake Tanganyika, I have to deal with ten district tribes, with their separate national peculiarities and customs, all of which I cannot here enter upon. That these tribes are what we commonly term savages I cannot deny, but I say that there are manifestations of civilisation amongst these people which we should do well to recognise. We see this especially in the advance they have made in the utilisation of the produce of their country. They work their own iron and copper extensively, producing a great variety of weapons and articles both of utility and ornament. Salt is carefully prepared in the localities producing it, and distributed therefrom as an article of barter all over the lake. Palm oil is largely prepared in Ujiji and Urundi, and distributed in the same way; in localities producing china clay and other valuable materials, there are large pottery works. One of the islands of Uguha and a place in Uuira [Uvira] are famous in this respect. Rua and Manyuema produce artistic iron work, and the famous grass or palm-fibre cloth. The dairy farms of Uhha send well-known packages of butter, and the poorer districts of the lake put up the parcels of dried fish which are sent far and wide throughout the country. This fishing industry is a very extensive one. The Warundi have small catamarans, made of four or five trunks of the pith-tree strung together, from which they angle for medium-sized fish. But the more extensive work goes on at night in little hollowed-out log canoes, upwards of 200 of which I have counted at one time; each canoe with its fire to attract the tiny fish, which are caught in large hand-nets. The seine is also used in some parts of the lake, and for the larger fish immense wicker traps are sunk to the bottom. Cotton cloth is also made at several places, and the various woods and barks are utilised largely for particular purposes—one kind for canoes, another for spear shafts, a third for mortars, a fourth for pestles, &c.

The division of labour thus indicated is evidence that amongst these tribes there is a wholesome system of co-operation, which is the beginning of better things. Still, amidst all this, they have been for years isolated from the outer world; and, remembering this, I consider the small advance they have thus made to be most remarkable. A comparison of these with the poor degraded people of the coast regions shows a wide difference. Most of these interior tribes, for instance, live in well-organised villages, in which considerable social order is maintained.

The Central African natives are in the iron age, and it is believed that no stone implements have been as yet discovered by any traveller. I have brought two pieces of stone, which it remains for those more skilled than myself in which matters to prove whether they are stone implements or not. They were given to me by Mr. Hutley, who describes them as being found from time to time by the natives, particularly in shallow parts of the lake, but sometimes on shore. They seem to be quite ignorant of the way in which they have been produced, but regard them with great reverence as representatives or messengers from their deceased ancestors, storing them carefully away in little huts or baskets, carefully secured from damage. The only use I can suggest for these stones is that of weights on sticks used in cultivation, as employed by the Hotten-tots, but the natives have no knowledge of their former use.

I have brought home specimens of arms, pottery, basket-work, cotton, bark, and palm-fibre cloths, as well as samples of the lake water, the water of the hot springs of Uguha, palm oil, mpufu oil, cotton, tobacco, china clay, and the salt of Uvinsa and Ugogo, which may be seen at the London Missionary Society's museum.

Climate, Products. The lake is subject to frequent storms, especially from south, south-east, and south-west, lasting sometimes for two or three days, and leaving a heavy swell, which proves a great hindrance to navigation. At the changes of monsoon, violent squalls from the north and north-west sweep over the lake, making canoe work dangerous, and raising at times a terrible cross sea. During this unsettled weather immense masses of rain-clouds hang about the hill-tops surround the lake; waterspouts are frequent at these times, and my boat was once completely turned over on the shore by a whirlwind which swept over Ujiji from the westward.

After having been round the world two or three times, I have never witnessed such wondrous cloud scenery and majestic effects of thunder and lightning as on Tanganyika. But a small proportion of rain, however, is discharged upon the surface of the lake, the clouds being tapped by the surrounding hills, down which the resulting torrents pour into the lake.

The plants cultivated for food on the lake shore are rice, manioc (*Jatropha*), Kaffir corn (*Holcus sorghum*), two kinds of ground nuts, the oil of which is excellent, maize, uleysi (*Eleusine corocana*), pumpkin, sweet potatoes, and sugar cane, while the castor oil, tamarind, cotton, tomato, and cucumber grow wild around nearly every village.

The oil-palm is met with both at Ujiji, Urundi, and at the south end of the lake, the Raphia in several luxuriant localities, the Borassus largely on the margin of the Malagarasi river, the screw-palm in Uguha, and a single coco-nut-tree flourishes in the garden of an Arab at Ujiji.

Amongst the useful timber trees may be specially noticed the gigantic *mvule*, out of which the canoes are hewn, and the Mininga or African teak, lignum-vitae, ebony; a variety of woods useful for smaller purposes are also to be found, and are worked by the natives.

Extensive tracts of country on the lake shore are still freely roamed over by the larger African animals: two distinct kinds of crocodile were seen. Immense flocks of water-fowl abound in the river mouths and pools, amongst which are noticeable the sacred and the black ibis, three kingfishers (a large dull-coloured bird, a black and white speckled species, and a tiny but most beautiful bird with a prevailing colour of peacock blue). Stanley's water hyenas turned out to be otters, which are frequently seen in quiet creeks and bays. A collection of twenty-one species of shells from the lake have been described by Mr. Smith in the ' Proceedings ' of the Zoological Society, nine of them as entirely new. The tsetse fly abounds on the lake shores from Ujiji round the south end and so up the west coast as far as Ubwari.

Visit to Mtowa. The boat *Calabash,* in which my various voyages on the lake were made, was formerly used by an Arab to convey slaves and ivory across the lake; I myself made the sails and rigged her up somewhat in English fashion. One of my first voyages, after a trip had proved the seaworthiness of my boat, was across to Uguha, first visiting the interesting island of Kabesa and Kasenge. The former is an oval, conical hill, the top of which is 250 feet above the lake, covered with large, rough, broken pieces of granite, the interstices filled with coarse grass and bushes, and the summit crowned with a miniature forest of trees, tangled in a mass of creepers.

After getting bearings here, I sailed round to the north end of Kasenge, where I expected to find a depot or settlement, but not a vestige of such is to be found. The landward side of all these islands has grass, water-cane, &c.; while the weather side are mostly bare, being exposed to the south and south-east winds. There are two small villages upon the island, one having about ten and the other about twelve houses. Kasenge is conspicuous only because it is different from all the other islands, having a smooth, grass-covered mound at its northern extremity, while the others, are mostly rugged and tree-covered.

On the 1st of May I landed at Mtowa, on the mainland. Near the landing-place, a few miserable settlements of Wangwana and people belonging to Arab traders by no means add to the beauty of the scene. The native village, half a mile distant, shows better signs of life and activity. Here I visited the chief, Kassanga, jun., whose acquaintance I had previously made in Ujiji. He received me very good-naturedly, said he was glad to see me, and on my telling him I wanted to look at his country a little, he said it was open to me and I could go where I liked.

> He received me on the grass laid circle around the inevitable fig tree in the centre of the village, and was evidently prepared to impress me that he was an important man. He is a comfortable looking man, sleek and trim and with a sort of smirking air as if ever ready to burst into a laugh. He wore a long necklace of large blue sami-sami, a little ivory idol, and various charms; his garment was of Manyeuma grass cloth gathered full in front and there further bunched and aproned by the addition of a leopard-skin; he wore brass wire spiral bracelets and ample sambo enriched, if not adorned, his ankles. The people all gathered round whilst we had our little talk; one substantial man anxious to inform me that he was brother to mine host. Kasanga said he was glad to see me, and, on telling him I wanted to look at his country a little, he said it was open to me, I could go where I liked, and promised to give me a guide to go to Cape Kahangwa in the afternoon.

When I returned to the boat he came on board, and was much pleased with some of the white man's wonderful things, none of which, however, pleased him so much as the production of fire from a match.

In the afternoon, I climbed the lofty peak of Cape Kahangwa. Our course led us over smooth, rounded hills, covered with thick, long grass, up and through which we pushed our way with great labour. Between each hill was a deep ravine, generally containing a pleasant little running stream; each one a perfect strip of tropical scenery. After a steep climb, the peak itself was reached, and a splendid view rewarded me as I took a round of bearings from Goma and across to Cape Kungwe on the other side of the lake, and to the hills of Murungu in the south. At our feet, and between us and the river Lukuga, lay the great plain on which Ruanda, the capital of Uguha, is situated. These hills are of clay-slate, and slaty sandstone, with loose quartz rich in mica. On our return we struck a path which led us back to Mtowa, along ridges, avoiding almost entirely the deep ravines which had so wearied us. As I passed through Kassanga's village on my return, he came out accompanied by his wife, both in full evening costume, the most striking feature of which is in both cases the elaborate head-dress, so distinctive of the people of Uguha. Kassanga's wife, one of five or six, was adorned with large spiral wire bracelets, and anklets and necklaces of shells.

> As I passed through Kassanga's village he came out very kindly to ask if I was all right, etc., and his wife, also, made her appearance both in full evening dress, and they are certainly I think as fine a pair of human beings as I have seen among the Africans. Like Kassanga his wife is a sleek and smooth and just (comfortably only) filled out, not a straggle about her elaborate head-dress which is almost the same as her husband's with the addition of sundry oddly shaped projecting skewers; round her neck is a necklace of huge shells hanging down over her breast and collar-wise another of many kinds of large beads and sami-sami—her wrists are adorned with large spiral brass-wire bracelets and *sambo* on her ankles. These two are very much alike and both very pleasant. Kassanga escorted me in Arab fashion to the outskirts of his village. Later in the evening I could not sleep for thinking over the work, etc., and fearing lest the Arabs by their lies should spoil my visit and perhaps even preventing seeing the Lukuga River. Sent Farajella to Kassanga with a present of a Sahara cloth and a necklace of glass beads which apparently pleased him much.

The next day I walked over to Ruanda, to visit Kassanga, sen., who is the chief of the whole country.

> Today I planned to walk to Ruanda to see the place and to visit Kassanga Senior who is the Sultan of the whole country. The Ujiji Arab, Hamees bin Raschid, arrived from that place four days out. Hamees was going to Ruanda so we agreed to march in company.

Passing Kahangwa, we skirted by a devious path several of those wonderful rounded hills, with ravines deeper and more romantic than ever; little tropical streamlets, deep in rocky beds, with numerous little cascades over which the water pours clear as crystal. Finally descending rapidly to the plain, on the other side of which is Ruanda, we entered upon a flat expanse of black mud cracking in the sun, and overgrown with rank grass and weeds, but with very few trees; in the rains it must be in places a terrible morass. Ruanda itself is quite a wonder in these parts, and is conspicuous on this plain by a sprinkling of the Bombax or cotton-tree in and about it. It consists of at least 400 houses, which, for the most part, are built so regularly as to form long streets, giving an unusual appearance of tidiness to the place. Considerable spaces are kept clear and swept, and here and there rudely carved posts with double-faced human heads serve to remind the people of reverence due to their departed ancestors—their guardian spirits. The Uguha houses are built with a square frame and all the upright ends gathered together in a point at the top; but the thatch is put on so thickly that when finished they present a perfectly round beehive shape, with a bunch on the top where the uppermost thatching is securely fastened together.

I was pleased to observe in active operation numerous industries of a superior kind and on a larger scale than I had seen anywhere else on the lake shores : pottery, matting, and baskets of many kinds, wooden bowls and dishes, and wooden drums, were the chief articles manufactured. There were also blacksmiths and coppersmiths, but I think their neighbours, the Warua, supply them chiefly in metal wares. The people appeared cheerful, healthy, and well-behaved. I found the great Kassanga himself was absent. The people trooped together in large numbers to get a sight of the white man, but there was no impertinence or ill-feeling, only what appeared to be a pleased curiosity. I walked on to an Arab camp or settlement—an assembly of small grass houses in which the Arabs live, and smaller huts for their slaves and porters. Here they assemble and arrange their caravans before proceeding westward.

Kassanga not being home I went on with Hamees to the Arab settlement about a half mile beyond, just the other side of a small stream. This Arab settlement is a considerable assembly of small grass houses and " bandas " (little grass thatched sitting rooms with open fronts) in which the Arabs live and of grass bunks of their slaves and Wamanyuema pagazi. I was welcomed by Nassor-bin-Mussoud who invited me to sit down on a good English camp bedstand he had there. After spending some time with him, I went on and had a walk across the plain to the Rogumba river which, however, I did not reach being completely tired out. On returning to the Arab settlement I drew near to the band of two Arabs who I knew in Ujiji. Hamees and Abdulla they are both very cheerful and pleasant, and I had a long rest in their banda. Hamees then invited me to go into his house and have some food. I found he had provided for me a very nice little repast of rice and fowl etc. of which I partook heartily. He showed me his little store of trade goods, about a dozen loads. All these Arabs are shortly going in a united caravan to Manyeuma. After talking a little while longer I started back for Mtowa. I was told that Kassanga Senior was gone to punish some troublesome Wagoma near his borders but that now he was returning. When I got back to Mtowa just before sundown I found a large flag flying and was told it was the flag that Kassanga Senior flies when he goes to war and that he was now returned.

The Lukuga Outlet. I got back to Mtowa just before sundown, and had a long consultation with Kassanga, jun., about the Lukuga river. He told me I was quite welcome to go there, but it was a dangerous place, and some Arabs' boats had come to grief in the river. He seriously warned me not to attempt to reach the Lukuga by land, and refused to send two or three of his men with me. I told him I should start on the morrow. Unfavourable winds, however, in the morning prevented my doing so, a state of things to which I was easily reconciled when I was informed that Kassanga, sen., was in a village close by, and invited the white man to go and see him. I accordingly went to a small village half-an-hour's walk distant in a public place, in which I found quite an assemblage of richly dressed chiefs and warriors, most of them with huge plumes of brightly coloured feathers on their heads. They were evidently awaiting my arrival when I drew near and sat down in their midst. Kassanga's own big house was close by, and the great man being informed of my arrival, shortly afterwards made his appearance. He is an old man, but bears his age well, being sleek and clean, and of cheerful countenance. His manner was somewhat embarrassed, but very friendly; he was dressed very much plainer than most of his chiefs, with a plain calico loin cloth, a white turban, a thick bunch of scarlet feathers on the top of his head in front, whereas his inferiors all wore their feathers on the top behind. His sole ornament was a necklace of large shells, the very largest I have seen.

A friendly conversation ensued in which I endeavoured to make him understand our purpose in coming into Africa, and he replied that the country was open, I could go wherever I liked.

He soon, however (as far as I could see by the advice of his chiefs), retired personally from the conference and placed himself just inside his own door while he carried on the rest of the talk through one of the chiefs, Kadunga. As soon as Kassanga went into his hut he sent Kadunga out to me with a load (about fifty lbs.) of maize meal nicely fastened up in a leaf package for transport according to the fashion of the country, and then I continued the conversation through Kadunga. I told him what a long journey it was for the white to come to him. I asked him if he liked one to come and live in his country. He said he would not only permit it but he should be very pleased for one of those wonderful people to come and live with him. I wrote notes in my book, telling him I did so that I might tell my people all about him and his country and he said that was good. He was particularly pleased with my field glasses. After I mentioned about the white man coming to his country he said my words were very good, and sent Kadunga out with another load of maize saying while I was in his country I should have food. Here and elsewhere I hear that the Waguha have been told by the Arabs' people that the white men were bad, but as we had now been living at Ujiji so long they had heard about us from others (natives?) and did not believe those reports. Indeed, Kadunga himself had been to Ujiji and seen us, and I remember having seen him pass our house one day.

At the conclusion he retired into his hut and sent out one of the chiefs with a load of maize-meal very neatly fastened up in a leaf package all ready for transport. This was a formal hospitable welcome to his country.

Tuesday May 4th—This morning Kadunga came to the boat with more words from Kassanga who he said was very pleased to have seen me because he had heard so many different stories about the white men but now he was satisfied having seen for himself. He sent Kadunga down to the boat to see it and my things, to bid me farewell, to give me some food for the voyage (a bundle of sugar cane and a quantity of mpufo), and to tell me that if I wanted to stop in his country, stop—if I wanted to go to the Lukuga, go there, or if I want to go back home, go. Either way he was my friend and added a request: he wants me to give him a flag. I sent back to say that the words of Kassanga were good, that I had come to see him, and he had given me food, and begged me go where I liked, and now going away he had given me food for the journey, so I should send a letter to my people to tell them about Kassanga and that he was our friend. As to the flag I had not one to give him now but I would make one on purpose for him, and I will send it to him or come again myself. After showing Kadunga some of the things he departed well pleased. This afternoon some of Hamees-bin-Raschid's men came down to prepare his boat for her return voyage to Ujiji. He came here to fetch Wamanyuema pagazi. When the boat was ready they commenced shipping these poor emigrants. The Arab slaves were armed with sticks, and they used them continually in arranging and assorting out these men. Attention being called, instead of addressing a man with words or touching him, by a good wack on the head or shoulders with a stick. The hired Wajiji boatmen vied with the Arab slaves in acts of brutality, and any poor man who had wrongfully got into the boat or in any way displeased any of these brutes had either to run the gauntlet of the whole lot or to jump clean overboard and struggle ashore as he might. Many of them further out of their spite snatched away little bundles of food, properties which these poor people possessed, and threw them away into the lake. These emigrants were so anxious to ship that they returned repeatedly to the boat to see if per chance they might get a place. Doubtless, after they had come thus far from their home and being in a state of destitution they were anxious to obtain that employment that should bring them even the small pittance allowed them by their Arab employer. I found on my return to Ujiji that one of the worst of those overseers was himself one of the Manyeuma pagazi who for the sake of the brief authority and investiture for the occasion of belt and gun was willing to belabour his fellows. Having loaded the boat nearly to the gunwales they pulled round for about half an hour with drums beating and then, returning, discharged the Wamanyuema until their master should arrive; this was their trial trip. Later on the Arab Hamees arrived and the enshipment commenced. It was just a repetition, but if anything worse than the former scene. The Arab Hamees taking a prominent part in it and encouraging his slaves. He was, however, as I could plainly see much annoyed that I should be a witness to this scene. Just before the start it was quite a fright; indeed, if force had not been used the Wamanyuema would certainly have sunk the boat in their anxiety to ship. As it was, she was tacked and was very dangerously low in the water. Loud and angry were the curses that followed the boat when it went away. The Wamanyuema were packed like herrings, and so they remained all night and next day till they got to Ujiji. . . .

Some six months afterwards I had the honour of escorting two of my colleagues to this place, and Kassanga's friendship ever since has been proved genuine and lasting. Mr. Griffith, who is in charge of this station, has, up to the last mail, given us most accounts of the progress of the Mission.[2]

2. Rev William Griffith, the only reinforcement in 1879, had the services of Walter Hutley at the Plymouth Rock station. For the period when Hore was surveying the south end of the lake, the LMS station and property at Ujiji was in the charge of a Zanzibari employee.

I started the next afternoon and got well out to windward towards Cape Kungwe, in order to avoid the terrible rocks on the northern side of Cape Kahangwa, a most dangerous shore during the south-east winds which prevail here. A strong breeze coming on from the south, I ran in towards the Lukuga entrance. It was rough work with my inexperienced men, especially this running down upon an almost unknown shore in the hope that I should find a harbour. I was able to recognise the coast as I went along in the immediate neighbourhood of the Lukuga from Captain Cameron's map, which has proved in many of its local details to be most valuable and accurate. I ran right in the Lukuga about 5:30 p.m., finding from three to five fathoms at the entrance. As the entrance narrowed we found ourselves rapidly swept in. In the centre of the swift current were numerous eddies, or calm places in which the boat seemed to halt for a moment before being swept on faster than ever. My men were panic-stricken, and it was with extreme difficulty I could get the little work done that I required from them. The people of Kawe Niangwe's village ran out in alarm at seeing a large boat being swept, as they thought, to utter destruction; but we had no time to attend to their cries, and, nowithstanding the utmost exertion, we were drawn at least one mile down the river before I could bring the boat to the bank and make her fast.

I at once visited the chief Kawe Niangwe at his village. I found him to be a tall, lively, cheerful-looking man of considerable intelligence, without any of that gloomy mystery so frequently a hindrance to intercourse with these chiefs. He made and answered questions in a straightforward way and did not beg.

> Inside this Chief's large hut the floor and sides are of clean black pottery work with numerous smooth and uniform logs stuck in and on forming tables and partitions and a fortified bed place which seems peculiar to the Waguhha chiefs. These logs are finished off very neatly, some smoothed and reddened, some painted in patches and diamonds—black, red, white, the wall plaster is also painted thus, . . . I fixed a pretty picture from *The Graphic* on the wall, much to the delight of all hands.

He at once acquiesced in my request for a guide for the Lukuga, producing a sharp-looking fellow of some social rank named Mtweta My-y-ya. With this man I started on Saturday morning to explore the river, which of necessity had to be done in a small native canoe, and not in my own more cumbersome boat. Mtweta My-y-ya brought with him three little lads and a large pot of pombe, nor would he provide any other food though he knew my intention was to stop away all night; my man Farajella who accompanied us also neglected to provide food, notwithstanding my protestations; they both anticipated they would tire me and return the same evening, but they were disappointed. We descended the river to Stanley's farthest, the rapids beyond being dangerous for our canoe. Here Mtweta My-y-ya thought I should give in, but landing at once, I directed them to prepare for the march, which they all did unwillingly. However, at last, finding I was determined, they moored the canoe, and hid the paddles and the precious pombe in the grass, doubtless expecting to return in the afternoon. Going about half a mile, we passed the river Rubamba. Mtweta My-y-ya told me that Stanley did not pass here.

I had several good views of the river along the road, and soon saw that the rapids extended only for a distance of half a mile. after which the river widened as before, gently winding.

About two miles and a half on my right I crossed the river Msengela, two miles beyond that passed an empty village, and then the river Kawindi. Soon after this the three lads put their loads down and declared they would go no further. Mtweta My-y-ya doubtless thought this would stop me, but I was determined to ascend the Kiyanja ridge to see the river and to get observations for latitude, so I shouldered one of the loads, and Mtweta My-y-ya was manly enough when I put it to him in that way not to break his agreement, and so he, Farajella, and myself proceeded alone, Mtweta My-y-ya shortly afterwards taking my load in addition to his own. We were now going along a road which he said led to a fisherman's camp, but to get to the ridge we must leave this road and strike across country. This Mtweta My-y-ya hesitated to do, pleading thorns and wild beasts, and various difficulties, and hoping that I might give in. But late in the afternoon we left the road and struck straight across for the Kiyanja. We had already crossed the river Luamuwa; by this valley we crossed it again —a most refreshing little stream—and, struggling through the jungle, reached the base of the Kiyanja ridge.

The ascent was very, very steep—a climb, in fact, necessitating frequent rests; but each halt brought us to a more extensive and glorious outlook than the last. At about 800 feet I selected a camping place, and the men made me a little hut and collected firewood. I mounted afterwards about 300 feet high, from which elevation I had a bird's-eye view of the Lukuga river flowing far away to the westward. From this place I got bearings, and at night the latitude 5° 50′, which, with the latitude at Kawe Niangwe's village, 5° 52′ 45″, will serve as a basis for a sketch of this part of the river. It would have served the men right to let them hunger,

H

for it was all their own fault; I had told them to bring food. Mtweta wandered about and picked up a few seeds, which he chewed, but they looked so miserable that I gave them a small allowance from my own food. The hillside is covered with the same quartz and mica with which the sands of the little river below sparkle. The whole view from this position is very fine and extensive. Beyond lay the distant lake itself, bounded by the lofty peaks of Kungwe; and the winding reaches of the Lukuga lay at our feet as on a plain, a clearly defined and swift river, which, sweeping round the foot of this ridge, is lost to view among the distant hills of Urua. The next morning we tramped back to where we had left the canoe, and reached my boat the same evening.

Mr. Stanley's prediction has been fulfilled: recent news has come that the strength of the Lukuga current is slackened, and, provided with a solid rocky sill, it will probably become the permanent waste-pipe of the lake, maintaining its waters at a pretty constant level.

River Malagarasi.—The river Malagarasi, as one of the largest streams flowing into the lake and situated near Ujiji, naturally attracted my attention. I had to go to its entrance on several occasions to cut timber, to visit the young chief Mtongoro, in order gradually to gain the confidence of the wild and wandering tribes of Kawendi, and twice to ferry parties across the river.

In August 1879, I pulled up the river to explore. The entrance proper is through mazes of papyrus and pith-tree; after one mile, the river narrows between distinct forest-clad banks, in many places completely covered with a thick garment of creepers, then widening out again into a large expanse, with plains on the north and low hills on the south, and quantities of the Borassus palm. This place is the haunt of immense numbers of hippopotami and crocodiles, and herds of buffalo, baboons, and other animals. Narrowing again between hills the current became swifter and the river more confined as we turned into the north-easterly reaches. At a distance of five and a half miles from the lake my progress was stopped by a series of rapids formed by the stream flowing down over large pebbles and boulders.

Recent traces of the elephant and buffalo were seen, and the lion was heard at night. I estimated the dimensions of the river, just below the rapids where it is clearly defined between distinct banks, as follows: width 500 feet, average depth five feet; giving a sectional area of 2,500 feet, and flowing at the rate of four and a half knots per hour.

Two months later I again entered the river, and there was then so little water that I could only get one mile beyond the entrance. Before the rains of 1880, I again visited it; the surface of the lake was then of course much lower; I was unable even to enter the barrier of vegetation at the mouth, through which the water was slowly flowing in small quantities. The flood caused by the rains would doubtless excavate the bed deeper, but I think it will be some years before the river is able to be again entered as I had done.

On 6th Augt. I started for the Malagarasi with Father Deniaud[3] and a load of his goods. We got into the river the next day at noon, and sailed right up with a fair wind to the place where I had previously taken Debaize.[4] I then walked up stream a little and found that the boat could go no further for just beyond the bend it was all stony rapids—three kinds of crocodile here and abundant traces of elephant and other large game. While in the river we saw great numbers of hippos, baboons, buffaloes, and many other animals and birds. Being a pretty regular reach just here and obtained a good section of the river where it runs four-and-a-half knots. On the 9th after coming down the river again I visited Mtongoro's village, taking him a cloth and a felt hat which I gave to his Father, Mtongora himself being about on an elephant hunt. After ferrying over the little party I had despatched to the relief of Debaize, I set sail about midnight for Bikari in Urundi, which place I reached on the afternoon of the 11th but did not finally land at the Frenchman's camp till daylight next morning. I then stopped with them three days, made a mast, sail, and awning and fitted them to their boat, etc.

Urundi. The people are scattered all about in houses; there are no regular villages. They are eminently fisher folk, and use little catamarans of pith tree stems as well as canoes. They much resemble the Wajiji in their persons, dress, and habits but seem more alive. Their bark clothes and skins are pretty uniform and their ornaments very profuse. The Chief Mkela sent me a present of three goats and a large basket of Mhogo meal, I gave him a cloth in return and very useful the friendship proved for when I tried to shove off I found the *Calabash* had stuck hard in the mud, and he brought his people to assist in the launch.

3. The senior priest with the White Father's expedition that arrived at Ujiji in January 1879. He and Hore informally partitioned the lake into a northern Catholic sphere and a southern Protestant sphere. Throughout his tenure at the Lake Hore retained friendly relations with the Catholic mission.

4. In charge of a French sponsored expedition to the upper Congo the abbe Debaize was Hore's guest at Ujiji on his way west and was returned ill and blinded later in 1879 to die at the LMS mission house. Hore, who acted as the executor of the Debaize property, was rewarded with a gold chronometer by the French government in appreciation for his services.

The afternoon after leaving Bihari was a long remembered one. During the forenoon it was calm but just at noon a breeze came from South gradually increasing to a gale till by 4 p.m. I was scudding under bare poles for the end of the lake. As the day declined I began to wish very much for a lull but the wind continued and such a fearful sea that I dared not attempt to put the boat round. This continued for some time after dark, and I knew I must be getting so near the land at the North end of the Lake that I must put the boat round, so getting the men all ready I watched carefully for a smooth sea when all at once one big roller completely enveloped the boat carrying her ahead with a furious sweep, and I found myself in comparatively smooth water. On sounding I found six fathoms and further on about eight feet. Made fast the fine stones and anchored with them. At daylight found ourselves just about 400 yards off the shore. Went to the village of Kugera, country Mughewa, Chief Juakuma. Two head men came to see me on behalf of the chief; the second one bringing me as a present one bullock, seven goats, and about thirty or forty fowls.

I sailed along and visited the people in many villages in the countries of Uvira, Ubemba, Msansi, Ubwari, Ukaramba, and Ugoma, meeting with kindness everywhere. Chief and people friendly and no trouble. All are quiet and friendly, not excepting " the wild and fierce cannibals of Ubembe " and the " foolishly furious people " of Msansi.[5]

One night in Goma I was assailed by hundreds of the people gathering on the lofty hills overlooking the Lake and pelting me with large stones, but they took us for their enemies the Warua. We escaped however only to fall into an ambush of four canoes full of warriors. These I hailed as I approached, shouting to them that I was a white man. They said, " no you are Warua, and we are coming to fight you," but added that, if I should prove to be a white man, no harm should be done for " they knew the white man was good!" Knowing that I could easily prove that I was a white man I bade them " come on " and they were soon convinced. The row was as loud as ever but instead of shouts of defiance it was now exclamations of delight, welcome, and apology. As daylight broke I landed amongst the exclamation of hundreds; they had never seen a white man before. I asked them how they knew that the white man was good. They said the Chief of Bangwe came here and told us and once when the Wajiji were imposing upon some of our people the white man's men interfered to protect them. Thus my little friendship with the Bangwe chief and a trivial incident of which I had never before heard secured to me the friendship of this interesting

5. These are references to statements contained in Chapter XIV, " Geographical and Ethnographical Remarks ", in *How I Found Livingstone* by Henry M. Stanley.

and numerous people. The water hyaenas (Stanley) are simply otters; I saw some of them in Goma.

Uguha and Goma should be one country but there is a constant feud between them. The people are much alike.

On September 7th arrived at Mtowa in Uguha where I was welcomed by Kassanga's head man Kadunga. I had brought two flags for Kassanga, and he is very pleased that I have thus minutely fulfilled my promise to him. I said I did not want a lot of food given me but I should like a few things to show my friends as specimens of Uguha work. He accordingly had a spear made on purpose for me that very day and sent it to me together with some baskets and other little things as I requested, also a load of beans. He now sends a special message to me in these words, " You come to see Uguha but you do not stop. I want a white man to come and live here for I see they are great people and know many things." I said, " if you said your word shall stand, I will send it to my people." He repeated that he really meant that he wanted a white man to live there and show the people improvements. The last day I wanted to see Kassanga again but he did not come in time, to the great disgust of Kassanga Junior who I hear abusing the head man Kadunga something in this style: " do you not know the white man's ways by this time and when he said he will go he means to go." Kassanga Junior at Mtowa has five or six wives, all have brass wire bracelets up to the elbows and very many large beads.

Voyage to the Southern End of the Lake. In September 1879, we were reinforced at Ujiji by Messrs. Southon and Griffith, and it was determined to occupy the two stations of Urambo and Plymouth Rock.[6] In the spring of 1880 I found opportunity to at last make a voyage round the south of the lake.

I started from Ujiji on the evening of the 17th of March with a crew of six Wajiji, two Zanzibar men, and my two boys Sambo and Sievedi. Immediately before leaving I was surprised by the arrival of a party of Mr. Thomson's[7] men bringing the startling news that that gentleman had returned to Mtowa with a total loss of outfit. I hurriedly got together a small quantity of wearing apparel and cloth for his use, which I took with me. Arriving at Cape Kabogo next morning, and Kavala Island at four p.m. the

6. Urambo was the capital of the Nyamwezi chief Mirambo; Plymouth Rock, so named by Griffith because its physical resemblance to the Devonshire hills and its position on the west side of the " sea ", was near Mtowa in Uguha, and the station was a direct result of Hore's earlier visit there.

7. Joseph Thomson after the death of Alexander Keith Johnston took command of the Royal Geographical Society's expedition to Central Africa. His travels are described in *To the Central African Lakes and Back,* 1881.

next day,[8] the wind being very light, I found all well at Mtowa, and that the alarm about Mr. Thomson was much exaggerated. The next day, embarking Mr. Thomson and his men, I proceeded on the voyage, crossing to Cape Kungwe, coasting the highlands south of that cape, exploring the pretty inlet at the mouth of the Calabash river, running past the pirate's island of Kabogo with a splendid fair breeze at night, and arriving at the station of the African International Association in Musamwira on the evening of the 26th. Captain Carter, of the elephant expedition, happened to be camped near the site of the stone house which was then being built, and in true sailor-like fashion showed lights and shouted directions for the best approach. After troublesome navigation for a quarter of a mile through eighteen inches of water, with the men overboard pushing the boat, I moored close to the hill. Here we were entertained most hospitably by Captain Carter at his camp, and by Messrs. Cambier and Popelin at the village of Karema; had a ride upon Carter's elephant, and finally started again on our voyage on the evening of the 29th of March.

I was impressed very favourably with the accounts, and with what I saw, of the elephant work. The surviving animal was one which for many years in India had done no work, and Carter was about to leave Karema for the coast to receive some more elephants from India with which he was to start the work of catching and taming the African ones. Why this work has been abandoned I cannot tell. It has been proved that waggons can be got through, but we cannot use bullock waggons on account of the tsetse. I think it has been proved that elephants can be got through, but that they would not answer because of the immense labour and the number of men required to load and unload them daily, and because of the great weight concentrated on four points on shaky ground. By using elephant waggons both difficulties would be done away with, and both successes usefully combined.

The work of the African International Association at Karema appeared to be proceeding surely though slowly. A stone house of considerable size was being erected upon an elevation close to the lake shore under the care of Captain Cambier, who I must say appeared to me to be carrying out the excellent instructions laid down for the agents of this Association in a most efficient way. The chief result, up to this time, of his presence in that neighbourhood was the evidently increasing prosperity of the natives there. I had visited this place some months before and looked upon it as

8. Kavala Island. On his return to Lake Tanganyika in 1883, Hore established his marine headquarters at Kavala, which became by 1885 the most substantial LMS station at the Lake.

one of the poorest and most miserable of native settlements on the lake shore. The difference I now observed was remarkable; the people were well clothed, and I doubt if they could easily be prevailed upon voluntarily to part with the presence of the white men in their midst.

A mutual good understanding has always existed upon the lake between ourselves and the gentlemen of this Association, and I understand we are indebted to Captain Cambier's careful observations for the most reliable longitude of a position on the lake shores.

I deeply regret the untimely death of Captain Carter, in whom the work of exploration in Africa has lost one of its finest and most efficient men.[9] Wherever he has passed in the African interior I believe an honest Englishman can pass again, which is saying a great deal, and he was always ready to share his last resources with any one.

Proceeding on our voyage we coasted round the verdant neighbourhood called by Cameron Massi Kambi, rounded capes Kapendi and Mpiwbwe, visiting the few villages there, passed Cape Chakuola and entered the bay of Kirando on the evening of April 1st. Here we found several villages of considerable size, and immense farms with large rice fields. The Makomomo Islands serve to enclose an excellent harbour in this bay which at first sight would appear to afford a fine situation for a station, but in the rains I find there will be a great expanse of marsh. On the southern side, however, which would more frequently be the weather side, the rising ground affords a better site.

Here is a considerable district of villages (we are now fairly in Fipa) and very extensive and luxuriant gardens with great variety of foods. The marshy ground mentioned is covered with large rice fields; beyond these vast fields of matama and mihinde, semsem, ground nuts, pumpkins, potatoes, etc., etc. Most of the villages are, or have been, fortified but the bomas are not kept repaired; it looks as if the necessity for them was past. An Arab, one Msalim bin Hamed, has a small village here, now nearly in ruins with a few of his followers lazily hanging about. I heard also of a small Wanguana trader, one Makhib, in a village beyond Msalim bin Hamed is now in Ujiji and is shortly going to Kirando to put his village to rights and recommence trade. A few guns amongst the natives are the price of blood. A fundo of beads secured the friendship of the village head man I visited,

9. Carter and a companion, Cadenhead, were killed by a party of Mirambo's warriors in an attack on a hostile village. Although Mirambo denied wilful intent, this incident convinced Consul John Kirk at Zanzibar that co-operation with the Nyamwezi chief was no longer possible.

and messengers came to me when I was about starting with news
of a man at distant village with gun shot wound to whom I send
amadou and bandages with directions.

Village head man says : local chief is Kirangawani and he is
now away fighting. They bring slaves from Nemba and Mirangu,
and the traders buy them. Kapufi is chief of all Fipa. There are
many villages and people on the Makomomo islands.

Much more cultivation is observed as we proceed south and are
fairly centered up the coast of Fipa. This is another of the districts
of country ruled over by a chief of importance; his name is
Kapufi. At the island of Kirui I first made the friendly acquaintance of the Fipa people, a man volunteering to come on board at
night to pilot us into a harbour.

I must rapidly pass on south without notice of all the various
bays and populous villages of Fipa.

Here in Fipa more than anywhere else the people most wonderfully disguised their surprise on seeing me. One would think
white men were as common as black among some whom I knew
had never seen one before.

Getting underweigh at 3:30 next morning we pulled round the
island and along a very rocky, rugged shore a little land breeze
helping us along but a terrible Southerly swell impeding us very
much. In pulling against swell it's simply power to check the
boat's way is not the only hindrance, but the violent pitching of
the boat prevents the men exerting their paddle force efficiently.
About 8 a.m., this swell being supplemented by light Southerly
breeze, we were compelled to stop behind the islet Itsiu; this is a
small rocky islet with a little fishing village. We lay at the main
land, the swell preventing safe communication with the island.
These rocky shores require great caution in approaching them
when there is any swell. Saw the tsetse here. At noon wind
promising fair, went out and sailed along shore with fine W.N.W.
wind for two hours. When falling calm we pulled in behind
Nendeh, an island almost " let in " to a gap in the land; the
passage between is shallow, and the lake passage between will
soon disappear. One small village and the remains of another,
very dirty and neglected. A few women and children only who
said all the men were working at the gardens of the main land
where there were many villages. One old man appeared in canoe
to observe our movements. The Ujiji boat that was forty days to
Karema was here: she has a Wanywana head man, tho' the
whole concern belongs to Abe the Mteko of Ugoy. A cruise after
slaves, and they are very shy of me.

We stopped on Sunday at Msamba Island, evidently a well-to-do
place; a half-caste spy here visited us and, as events proved, carried no favourable account of us to the mainland.

While resting here a man came from the mainland in a canoe whose gun, etc., and dress and manner indicated some considerable acquaintance with Arabs or Wanguana, but he was evidently a native. He passed close to where we were sitting and very barely replied to our salutation, passing on as if on important business to one of the villages. Now this was very strange. We were told this man had come from Kapufi's (the Sultan of Fipa) but under ordinary circumstances such a man would have stopped and talked with us, however important his business might be, but he was on an island and could not be simply *passing* in a hurry (I think I got some explanation of this in Ujiji after my return when I got a letter from Mr. Thomson).

Visiting the large village of Wampembe we passed on to Polungu Island, where we were delayed a whole day by the swell that followed the south-west gale, and suddenly discovered ourselves surrounded by a force of armed men in the little creek in which we were moored; sent over, as they afterwards acknowledged, in consequence of evil reports of us made by some traders to the chief Kapufi. They were very soon assured, however, by our quiet demeanour, an examination of the boat, and the statements of my Wajiji crew, that there was no harm in the white man, and eventually left for the mainland as a deputation to carry a good report of us to their chief.

As we approached the first landing place we saw two large canoes full of people lying on their oars, or at any rate awaiting our approach in silence, and I suspect fearful expectation; as we came nearer my men perceived that they were Wajiji and hailed them; they then came towards us very pleased. They proved to be a trading party of Wajiji homeward bound from a long voyage and were delighted at meeting their countrymen; as we passed them a few friendly words were exchanged but my men requested that I would stop to permit of a fuller exchange of civilities and news. And now a most interesting scene took place, and it must be remembered that my crew were real Wajiji (not Arabs' men) most of them Gungu from whence this expedition had started. The two canoes pulled back and came close along side. Some twenty minutes was occupied in a formal exchange of civilities between each individual in the canoes and each of my Wajiji by holding out hands, etc. Then a gossip began, but this was soon silenced to permit of a business-like communication to the whole company by one of my men who was generally accepted as an orator; he stood up close to the side of the boat and, in an oration of some quarter of an hour amid deep silence communicated to the travellers all the home news, the death of the head chief, the health of Mboyo and his people, etc., etc., amongst other matter I understood. He described fully the allotment of the land to the white men (and I believe a very good character was given to myself) and the hindrances of the Arabs. A short account was then given in return of the voyage of the others, and, amid renewed salutation and expression of good wishes to my men and to ourselves, the two canoes went on their way northbound and we went on to the other landing place on Polungu Island. There were about sixty persons in all in those two canoes. A few young female slaves were concealed amidships; the chief end of the voyage, I expect. These Wajiji were a remarkably clean, respectable lot altogether, apart from their traffic. The little nook which we now entered was at the foot of a steep rocky path leading up amidst tangled underwood to the summit of the island —a big sandbeach and large broken masses of rocks.

The *one* man on the island proved to be very shy, the others were said to be away on the mainland working on the farms. But the women were not at all backward and brought us fowls and eggs for sale; otherwise, we could not make much of them. I was again disappointed for latitude by frequent passing clouds,— only getting one star. Started away early morning but such a heavy swell from S.W. that it was of no use. We were compelled to return behind the island. The heavy swell is one of the chief hindrances to the navigation of the Lake by these boats, and all day there was no chance of a start. After consultation with Mr. Thomson I now determined to start out in the evening and make across to the Lofu River on the other side. After leaving Mr. Thomson at Liendwe I could then go round the other way and explore the coast of Ulungu. The one man on the island was a poor shy, sly sort of fellow. I went up to the village to have a talk but he slipped away and left me with the women. During the morning one other man came from the mainland and shortly returned. Later on two men and one woman came from the mainland. About 3 p.m., when we were preparing food previous to a start, everybody was collected around the fires. Mr. Thomson reclining under a shade ashore; I had been doing the same aboard, I had just risen up and was about to [go] ashore to see the dinner prepared when, happening to look aloft, I saw a long string of natives (about twenty-six) coming down the steep rocky path to the boat. They were all fully armed and came down in that deliberate way—the old men wore an aspect of solemnity, and the young ones of boldness—which has become so familiarly portentous to me, of at least a shauri. These men all pushed themselves around the little nook in which we lay behind rocks and emjovences so as to command us and the boat.

Some had as many as twenty or thirty arrows and each one, two or more spears and bow and arrows. It was evident that they meant business (but surely it could not be to attack us without some good reason here in Fipa), perhaps it was something to do with the hongo. Captain Carters' men say they have paid [hongo] in Fipa. Shortly, however, a spokesman slipped

forward and gave his message; namely, he stated that he had
heard that we had come to Fipa with evil intentions and to forcibly take away their slaves from them. I laughed at them, called
for a light for my pipe and, walking down on the gunwale of the
boat, proceeded to answer their doubts. First, I said, take a good
look at us; come and look in the boat, and see if any slaves or anything suspicious is therein, and, at the same time, I ordered the
tarpaulin and hatch cover to be taken off. The man who inspected
the boat soon lost his suspicions and opened his mouth and eyes in
astonishment and wonder at the strange, but innocent things, that
he saw there. Now I said talk to the Wajiji who were with me;
ask them all about the white men. And Sainesi, a younger man,
stepped forward and told them of my living with Wajiji and of
my friendliness to all natives. Spears were stood up against the
rocks, solemn countenances relaxed, and they all gathered closely
around us smiling and chattering. An elder man stepped forwards,
and stated that a man from the island had come and alarmed
them, and they saw that there was no ground for suspicion, and
that it was true that some Watongwe had previously told them:
viz, that the white man of Ujiji who travelled on the lake in a
boat was good. I said it was good that they should thus come
and see for themselves, but I hoped they would now tell their
chief Kapufi and all the Wafipa what they had seen that there
might be no mistake in future, and endeavoured, so far as
possible, to explain my friendly purpose in visiting them, finishing by giving the elder a piece of cloth and a little salt.

I was now able to gather some better information about the
place and people and especially about the southern border of
Fipa. They all agreed that Ulungu commenced at the village of
Utundu, in which lived both Wafipa and Walungu and was
situate[d] a little south of this.

In answer to my constant inquiries the natives of Fipa agree in
telling me they have one big chief or sultan who rules over the
whole country, Kapufi (not to be confounded with the small chief
Kapufi at Liendwe), Kapufi the chief of Ufipa lives, as far as I
can understand, two or three days' journey from almost any part
of the coast. When at Liendwe, Mr. Thomson kindly undertook to
carry a present and letter for me to Kapufi, and I have since
heard from him that he delivered the same, but that an mswahili
was living with Kapufi and seemed to exercise considerable influence over him. This explains to me *fully* some of the strange
occurrences during my visit to the Ufipa coast. The present and
letter and Mr. Thomson's pains, though apparently thwarted, give
us this information which will be valuable in future visits. To be
forewarned is to be forearmed. I understand now how this coast
man's influence worked; as soon as I appeared on the coast of
Fipa, he must have alarmed Kapufi with his slander and caused
spies to intercept us at Msamba Island and at Polungu Island,
with what effect has been seen.

At Polungu Island we rested and slept, starting again at daylight next morning, and now making a closer and more careful survey of the south end. Passing three little steep capes, forming together one broad one, the shore runs well in east to a river on which is situated, I believe, the village Utunduu, described by the Wafipa as the border village then past the island and peninsula of Micongorlo, where a beautiful little land-locked harbour is surrounded by several villages and extensive farms.

My men, landing, proceeded to light a fire when some natives quietly *requested* us not to light a fire on that exact spot which was sacred. I always feel great pleasure in acceding to any such request so different to the portentous unexplained solemnity which amongst some natives precedes a shauri respecting some superstition or custom to which innocent disrespect has been offered. The people declared that the white man should be their friend, and as throughout, Ulungu were quite pleasant and sociable and, as far as we could understand one another, communicative.

I walked across the Micongorlo Peninsula and saw the Amalesa Islands adjacent. I observed several prosperous villages, and considerable cultivation. Leaving this place with a fine breeze, we passed along the Mpete Peninsula round into Liemba Harbour—a perfect lake-like, land-locked harbour. I could not make out that the natives had any name for the harbour itself, though I got names for all sides and villages round. Of Liemba they knew nothing, except that it was the Kilungu word for lake. I believe no one else has named this place; I would therefore suggest that it retain the name of Liemba Harbour which, if it means " lake-like harbour," is by no means inappropriately applied to it; the name Liemba was apparently first given to this part of Tanganyika by Dr. Livingstone. Liemba Harbour is roughly circular in form. At its head is a tiny peninsula, Ikyoni, behind which I moored the boat. It is like a little world in itself, the home of a herd of hippopotami, and very numerous water-fowl and other birds. I saw traces of numbers of buffalo in the neighbourhood, and other large game. I also observed wild grapes in a strong shrub-like form. On the mainland side the shores ascend steeply from the lake to the lofty plateau above. At night rain came on and continued without ceasing.

Swarms of mosquitoes added to the discomforts of this very unpleasant night during which none of us had a wink of sleep. About two o'clock my sailors who had been uneasy all the time began to laugh at one another, and soon all got up and began to dance. They found it was no use here sulking and pretending to sleep. The water about us was constantly sparkling with shoals of lively little fish which soon attracted the attention of the Wajiji who stripping themselves waded out in the shallow and with torches of grass constantly renewed they succeeded in catching several fish with their hands and in cloths held out like an apron; the fishes all gather to the light.

Next morning, moving across to the Kalambo side, we made friends with the natives there. I found that the chief of the district was a woman—" Sultani Mwema "—that is, " the good chief," and no other name could I get. This princess lives in the village of Katete, about 2,000 feet above the lake. As it was described to be near, I determined to pay the lady a visit. A terribly steep walk through an interminable forest of tall straight trees, the path very often almost like a flight of steps, took me up to the heights above; but, as the afternoon was drawing to a close, I put off my visit to the next day, and returned to the boat. Early next morning I was told that Sultani Mwema was coming in person to meet me. She appeared about ten o'clock, with a numerous train of ladies-in-waiting. I showed her everything I had in the boat, which she in turn pointed out and explained and criticised to her women. This princess had a self-confident manner, quite different from the ordinary look of the women. She is probably about forty years of age. Her husband was with her — " not the chief," I was told, but " the chief's husband." They appeared much pleased with what they saw, and after I had explained the reasons for our visiting her country, I really think the " good princess " really meant it when she said she should be very pleased to give a place for houses and gardens if white men would come and live as friends in her district. I gave the sultana a suitable present of cloth and beads, and a necklace to each of her women. She gave me some fowls in return, and we parted with the understanding that when I brought my brethren a place should be given them in which to live. As the princess retired, I observed that, though attired in coloured trade cloth, she still wore the national female costume, which I shall describe further on. The natives assured me that Sultani Mwema is the sister of Tafuna, who they say is the chief of all Ulungu; but the word " sister " may only mean " friend," " ally," or " equal in rank." " Mazombe," which appears on some maps, is either the name of the district just inside and south of this, or it simply means " on the heights "; there is no village of that name.

Leaving Liemba Harbour, I passed several small rock capes, and Luasi, on the river of that name, with its wall-like cliffs, then the great bluff cape Yamini, with its jagged and weather-worn perpendicular cliffs, after which the hills recede, leaving a small space of lowland about the village Mufinga, a small place of eleven huts, where we stopped for the night.

Rounding the little peninsula of Kirongo, we passed some low rocky cliffs, a tract of thick forest, and small broken hills; beyond these, towards the Malwe river, lower land at the foot of the hills permits movement along the shore, and the scenery wears a general dry, though picturesque aspect, the surface consisting of red earth, quartz rock, and hard sandstone set off with groups of Borassus palms.

The entrance to Malwe river, itself a mere torrent, is quite a gap, forming behind a sandy cape quite a snug little harbour; a delta of low land is closed in by precipitous hills, the delta itself choked up with a dense growth of palms and grasses, amongst which, in a clearing of gardens, is the stockaded village of Malwe. Although evidently stockaded for defence, there is no ditch, as in the countries north. The people, apparently poor, make up for more valuable ornaments by wearing sambo of yellow grass, which much resembles copper when seen from a distance. A strong south-west wind detained me here till late in the afternoon, when it shifted to the north-west, and with a fresh breeze I stood out and laid along to the Kowa river, which I reached in the evening. With a following sea, I could not venture to enter the river mouth, so went up into a corner on a soft bed of mud. Rain fell during the night, preventing observations. I started again at daylight, rounding Cape Nyanzowe, after which the highlands approached closer to shore again, the drainage gaps becoming deep cuttings. Kalambo river is in one of these; it forms an extensive but shallow boat-harbour, much choked with weeds. Precipitous mountains rise abruptly from a valley a quarter to three-quarters of a mile across, rising gradually and narrowing at once till it seems lost in a narrow cleft between precipices of 1,000 feet, but again opening shows two other ravines converging to this point, and each bringing down a stream which unite to form a broad and rushing torrent, that, roaring over huge boulders, washes the precipice on the south side with a noise resounding throughout the valley.

Jagged, discoloured patches of bare rock stand out among the trees with which the hillsides are elsewhere covered, except where a few clearings with waving corn testify to some perseverance on the part of the natives; for even these clearings can only be reached by a steep climb. Two small clearings occupy the level ground by the river mouth, and others are situated on natural landings at intervals on the great staircase at the head of the valley leading up into the interior. I walked up to one of these, a small village called Mukipwa, the chief of which is named Mpuliamba, who told me he had seen Mr. Thomson the day before, at Pongorlo, on the Unyanyembe route. The people seemed somewhat listless at first, but on finding we wanted to buy food they soon trooped down to the boat with various produce, and a friendly intercourse was opened. These were the last villages I found on the eastern shore. The steeper hills now retired somewhat from the shore, leaving a space of small broken hills and little stony capes.

The district of Kituta was reached on the 21st April, at the river mouth which Stanley terms the extreme south end of the lake, the extreme south however is really at Pambete. I cannot improve on Stanley's description of the dense dark grove of trees at this river mouth, which forms a very conspicuous mark from a distance. A few fishermen approached from the Lonzua river and invited me to proceed there, which, indeed was necessary if I would hold intercourse with the natives, there being no signs of habitations where I then was. I found a road, however passing round the lake and which seemed tolerably well used. We moved on therefore to the Lonzua river, approaching the steep landing-place through a wilderness of dead tree stumps and clumps of reeds. This river is a torrent, rushing down a steep and rocky declivity. On the top of the ridge are many scattered farms and small villages. A friendly native soon attached himself to me as guide and informant, and I also obtained a guide to go to Zombe's on the morrow. At daylight, putting the boat aground in a safe place on the south shore, we started. Very near our camp we found a path running east and west, and then turning north along the lake shore; this is a branch of the caravan road from Liendwe to Unyanyembe; the other, and probably the principal, one passing through Isoko and Zombe's. To go to Zombe's we crossed this path, trending east, however, for some distance, and continually mounting upwards, first through tangled wood full of rocks, and then through more regular forest. In three hours I reached what I at first supposed to be the top at 2400 feet. The country here extends far and wide in bold undulations of rich forest lands; still no villages, but in the forest I came across a party of hunters. They had an immense net about half a mile in length and six feet high and with meshes from two to three inches apart, kept in position by stakes and stays at intervals. It was placed in what I suppose was meant for a straight line, with watchers at about every 200 yards; this must be a work requiring a considerable amount of well-arranged partnership, the net being all in separate lengths of about fifty or sixty feet belonging to different men.

After leaving the hunting party I descended to the small river Muswira; half an hour further a small village of ten houses, and then a scattered series of isolated farmhouses, each surrounded with its little fortification, or *boma*. From one of these a man became our guide for a short distance, taking us to the outskirts of this farm district, and indicating to us the forest path we were again to follow. We now gradually rose again to about 2,500 feet through the same fine forest land, crossing two little rivers with very cool water. The last of these streams we followed up for some time, where it runs through steep banks crowded with ferns and mosses and other damp-loving light green vegetation, with the gigantic *moowali* palms (Raphia) arching over the verdant tunnels, completing a scene refreshing in the extreme. These Raphia are splendid trees, many of the leaves being forty feet long, and supply the beautiful and strong fibre of which the well-known Manyuema cloth is made, and serving a variety of purposes of utility and ornament. The mid-ribs of the leaves form excellent rafters for small houses, and are also used for frames of bedsteads and many other purposes. Crossing the stream we ascended to dry, bare, stony ground, and soon came again to scattered farms, which proved to be the outlying parts of Zombe's neighbourhood, whose town I reached after a march of about sixteen miles from the lake, at an elevation of 2,300 feet above its shores. Coming from the lake I continued to feel even here that I was up aloft; each horizon seemed to be the edge beyond which one would at once descend to ordinary levels. I think this was due to the change of air as well as to the actual fact of having ascended from the lake.

Zombe's is a large fortified town subdivided by other stockades into several compartments, so that in the village one is continually passing through gates. On the north side of the town is a stream descending into the Kalambo river, which I was told forms a natural barrier, and its dense margin of moowali palms and other tall trees of bright fresh verdure displays a pleasing background to the scene as approached from the west by the forest road. Extensive gardens dot the country, which on all sides is covered with a fresh bright growth, whether of forest trees or shrubs and grass. A small herd of well-favoured kine with barrel-like bodies, and the passing to and fro of the numerous people loaded with the produce of their gardens, made up a picture which I found very interesting and refreshing after my voyage, and seemed to speak of grand possibilities for the country in the future.

Mr. Thomson had told me this was a small place with a few lean cattle when he passed. Nature was not then in her luxuriance, and he had come from a more thickly populated country. For my part, I was impressed most favourably with this place, and what I saw further of it only increased that view.[10]

I was now completely tired out and crippled with large blisters on both feet and knew well that I could not possibly return to the boat on the morrow. I, therefore, determined to make the most of my visit. Having a *native* guide, with whom by reason of the companionship of the journey, etc., I had by this time established a good understanding, I thought it was all right when he bade us just follow him into the town without those formalities which had I been alone I should have considered necessary. But we had scarcely passed the first gate when our guide was stopped and rather sharply desired to state his business, etc. I was vexed that I had so depended on him, and, without waiting for him, retired outside followed closely by my Wajiji. Outside I sat down and awaited the return of the guide that I might send him with one of my own men with a message in due form. And here I may remark that these Wajiji in their own country so bold (and some would say impudent), so self-assured and knowing, are *here* almost as dependent on me as if they were following me about the streets of London. It is this childlike confidence in us that makes me love these Wajiji sailors as I have no other natives; notwithstanding that they have several times been *very naughty children,* but still *children.* But when they say so confidently, " Master, we are in your hands; we are far away from home and must just follow you," I feel as if I could do anything for them.

Having seated myself comfortably with my Wajiji round me, I sent a message to Zombe to say I had come to see him. The usual difficulties were thrown in my way, and it was not till next morning that I saw the chief, who then came to visit me.

The messengers returned to say that Zombe was absent, and the man in charge could do nothing till his return. So I sent another message, assuming an offended tone, to tell the head man that I was sure my friend Zombe would be angry if he knew that *customary hospitality* was denied his friend the white man who

10. Earlier in the *Journal* Hore had written: " Of course in my voyage here I may consider certain districts as populous which a visit further inland would prove not to be so and other parts as uninhabited which were really populous a short distance from the Lake shore, but I have always made inquiries, with a view to fuller information in these matters, but as regards this description of Ulungu, a comparison of it with Mr. Thomson's description of his journey will be most valuable, always remembering that Mr. Thomson with his impressions gathered in *very* populous districts on his Southern road is apt to call villages small and mean which I might consider fairly considerable and important."

I

had travelled a long way to see him. The result was as I expected —that the head man himself came out and requested me to state what I wanted. I said, " I am weary and hungry. I want a house and food for myself and men, firewood and water." I was at once invited to enter; an empty hut was placed at my disposal; water and firewood and pots were brought, and I was soon in a fair way to get refreshed. Before dark Zombe himself returned and wanted to see me but, hearing that I was very tired, he sent a sheep and two dishes of cooked food saying he would come and see me in the morning. The food consisted of a huge pudding of uleysi meal (Eleusine coracana) and a dish of a savoury vegetable stew, apparently of little bulbs like grass roots.

He was a rather large man, with the peculiar air of watchfulness I had noticed in Mirambo. He was clothed in a blue and grey cotton counterpane, ornaments of substantial copper sambo, and carried a neat axe—a sort of wand of office. He informed me that his river joins the Kalambo; that Pongorlo is three days' march from there; that he thought the white men were good, and would give them a place to live in either at his town or between that and the lake. He said that the Watuta used to give him some trouble, but they had gone away now; and truly he seems to keep his people under command, though I observed that men, women, and children alike approached and saluted him without fear. He remembered the party passing with Livingstone's dead body, and Mr. Stewart and Mr. Thomson had both visited him. After breakfast I walked outside, and found Zombe seated on a huge ash-heap just outside the town, a sort of quarterdeck place of observation from whence he could see his cattle and all outcomers and ingoers, and whence he kept up an almost continuous of hands in answer to the respectful salutes of his passing subjects.

Zombe's village has about 120 houses, and besides the cattle already mentioned, some fine goats and sheep. I sent him some good coloured cloths and glass beads, and he thoroughly enjoyed the exhibition and description of every article I possessed of European manufacture.

In the afternoon I returned his visit. His own house has the river close behind it. His wife was a superior sort of woman, to whom I felt bound to make a little present. Zombe continued on the same friendly terms with me during my stay, and promised to escort in the morning and he himself attended to wish me a most cordial farewell.

I told him I might come again in six months, and he hoped that if I did I would bring him a gun or something European, but he by no means begged.

I have much pleasure in drawing the attention of the directors to Zombe's as a site for a Mission station. Climate, land, friendly chief, and numerous people are its advantages. Its drawback is that the mission station would be at least twelve or sixteen miles from a suitable landing place on Lake shores which would probably be never more than a " landing place." The only harbour at the south end of Tanganyika is on the bay of Niumkorlo and in the event of launching a steamer at the south end of Niumkorlo would be the point for the camp of operation. Zombe came early next morning to see me off and gave me an escort of four men to accompany me to the boat, he bade me a most cordial farewell.

I reached the boat about one p.m. very much tired out, killed the sheep, and gave all hands a feast. Stars bright.

Returning to the shore at Kituta, I got careful observations for latitude which I made to be 8° 46' 30", surveyed closely round the peninsula of Kapata, and rounded the island of Mtondwe, where I got latitude and bearings. The south end of this island is low, and the north end bluff. Coasted with leading winds to Kasakalowa, stopping by the way at the villages of Kondo and Niumkorlo; the latter has a fine little harbour, at the north side of which is a prominent round hill on a peninsula. On Livingstone's map this, and also the peninsula of Msenga in Itawa, are marked as islands, and from the distance at which he saw them they would doubtless appear so.

Kasakalowa is a village of about forty houses. There is a space of some extent here of lower hills and bench between the Kapata ridge and the south-west corner of the lake, and in this space are the villages of Kasakalowa and Pambete at the real south end of the lake, in latitude 8° 47' 30". Just halting for rest and bearings, I then turned up the west coast. Here the mountains rise steeply from the lake shore, but still on the slopes there are numerous villages and farms; perpendicular cliffs of weather-stained rock stand out at great heights among the trees.

Leaving Mwangala in the evening, I pulled on, hoping to reach a gap I had seen in the mountains, which I supposed to be Cameron's river Kiazu; but as we made slow headway against the swell, it was dark before I made out any available landing. The night proved extremely dark, and just after sunset, a slashing breeze springing up from the southward, I determined that as I could not survey, I would at any rate make a passage, and ran into the Lofu river before the morning.

The night proved extremely dark and just after sunset, a slashing breeze springing up from the Southward. I determined that as I could not survey I would at any rate make a passage, keeping as

close as I dare to the shore. The *Calabash* flew along and
gave us some three or four hours sleep in the Lofu river before
next morning. As I ran in here in the dark with a good breeze,
for the wind followed us round West, I began to flatter myself
that I was "getting much acquainted" in these waters. As we
got up into the second reach of the river in the silence of night
we caused quite a commotion. A hippopotamus feeding on the
bank sprang headlong (in his fright) into the river making a tre-
mendous to do, and as we near the shore close to a large
tree, the whole upper portion appears to detach itself suddenly
and ascend with a loud whirring noise. The fact was that which
in the dark had appeared to be the foliage of the tree was an
immense number of guinea fowl at roost who were suddenly
disturbed by our arrival. The unusual cries of "way enough,"
"boat hook," and "make fast ahead and stern" concluded the
disturbance in this quiet nook, and all was again quiet till daylight. We then moved up to the old camp, and sent men to
Kapufi's to announce my arrival and to buy food. Kapufi visited
me at the camp and continued his friendly relations and offer of
a place to build.

Here, securing the latitude and compass variation, my survey of
Ulungu was completed. Both as regards the people and the country,
I had been agreeably disappointed. I had expected to find a
scattered and mixed people, but I found them to be a distinct tribe,
with their own peculiar customs, dress, arms and houses. The most
characteristic article of dress is the goatskin garment worn by the
women; the top part being unconfined, it hinges, as it were, at the
waist so that on sitting down it at once swings into its proper place
as a mat or carpet; the lower end is scalloped in a set pattern.

The most common grain is the *uleysi*, cultivated in circular
forest clearings, watched from huts raised on high poles. The nether
millstones used by the Walungu are neatly imbedded in a plaster
bench or table, with a receptacle for the meal.

Uganga, in its various forms of fetishes, miniature sacred huts,
and mystical performances, flourishes in every small village. The
tsetse fly was seen in all parts, even to within half a mile of
Zombe's village, the only place where cattle are kept. Cotton is
cultivated largely, and cloth made at Ujiji.

The mininga or African teak was seen in several places and many
fine tall forest trees but none of large girth. A friendly reception
was accorded by the natives throughout the survey. At Liemba
Harbour and several other places I was told on enquiry that one
Tafuna at the South and was the head chief of all Ulungu,
others told me that Zombe was equal in importance with Tafuna.
Tafuna is said to live at Isoko somewhere between Pambete and

Zombe's, but my impression is from all I have gathered that Zombe and other local chiefs are almost, if not quite, independent. Perhaps Tafuna is the most so. The same remarks about the want of easily accessible places near the shore applies to Ulungu as to Fipa. The Kapata ridge with its villages and the district containing Kondo, Niumkorlo, Kasakalowa, and Pembete is another instance of an accessible district of villages, communicable with the interior by easier roads from the Kapata ridge towards Isoko than the road by which I walked to Zombe's. The Walungu cultivate cotton more than I have seen elsewhere and make cloth like the Wajiji, but I cannot say I have seen many weaving it.

The bow of the Walungu and Wafipa is peculiar, having two elbows in it, instead of being, as usual, the segment of a circle, and a tassel of long dark hair is attached. Bees are cultivated, and large fish-traps are anchored off the shore to entice the large and oily *senga*.

After visiting the chief Muriro, at Akalunga in Itawa, and the southern portion of Marungu, a strong south-west gale decided me to run north, calling once more at the station of the African International Association and at Plymouth Rock.

On May 1 I started early in the morning, pulled down river taking bearings as I went along. One or two small canoes about at the mouth of the river pulled across towards the little bluff cape. S.E. came on and we laid just nicely on and rounded the Cape, getting bearings of the points beyond as they opened out. Got round Cape and sailed west into a little bay and moored for wind to finish. About two p.m. pulled out and along isthmus. Communicated with a few people passing along the beach and then right round the Msenga peninsula to the other side of it, Cameron's bay opening out like a large harbour. The sand hills of this isthmus are quite a novel feature. Inside amongst the houses there are luxuriant gardens with potatoes, pumpkins, nitima, ulezi, nureri, beans, etc. People with less decided characteristics than the Walungu, no distinctive dress. Arms as Walunga. I saw here a javelin of the Zulus which the people told me had been captured in a fight with those people at Katanga! They have cloth, guns and various little matters from contact, I suppose, with Wayamwezi traders. Chief Kungu, subject to Muriro. " Majolo " is the salutation here.

Coasted on to river Camba, hippopotami; rounded a little sand cap and into a shallow expanse, the river entrance. Extensive valley of drainage beyond. The people here had small hand fishing nets. Coasted on round the district of Nundo to its northern side where we stopped the night, and I got latitude. A good deal of bare sand here again. Coasted on to the bottom of the bay and so to Msika's large village in unhealthy situation. Visited Msika who is said to be Muriro's " akida," his principal subchief. He has rather an extensive village. (The sketch of King Muriro and his granary in Cameron's book has often been in my mind; it is an excellent illustration of the granaries to be seen in every village here.) Msika brought out his musicians to entertain me with a tune on an iron keyed instrument (of torture), and this followed me to the boat when I returned. Msika pleaded poverty, but still came on board the boat and brought a liberal present of food. I met a Makua man here who was very officious, but rather humbly and usefully so than otherwise. He came over the mud shallows (of which there is a great expanse here) to us as we approached shore and did a little piloting business. Told me the names of places, etc., together with his own history. He left Zanzibar the year Seyid Majid died [1870], left Unyanyembe four years ago, has been to Katanga, has been here one year elephant shooting, and has killed eight of those animals. Afterwards he shewed me his little village and what he was very proud of, a well he had made and which, he said, gave better water than any other in the neighbourhood. On going away, he gave me a fine white cock and a calabash full of his famous water. . . .

. . . A little breeze spring up we sailed on pleasantly to the Chief Muriro's at Akalunga. Akalunga is represented by Cameron as an elbow-shaped Cape but, when I arrived, the outer end of this Cape by the rising of the Lake had become an island between which and the main I passed in about two and a half feet of water. Then rounded into a very snug harbour, being an inlet into which runs the river Kirenga. Between Cape Kipimbwe and Akalunga are two or three villages and near Akalunga three large villages, Muriro's. Muriro is the head chief of the county of Itawa which extends from the river Lofu to Cape Runangwa.

A wet night, morning strong S.E. wind shifted to a moderate S.W. Went ashore to see Muriro; was asked to the verandah of his granary, and told that he wanted a small present to let me see him. I said, " very well, I am going back to the boat," but they requested me to stop, and in a minute or two invited me to come in and see the Chief. I found Muriro sitting in the verandah of a very small but neat hut with enclosure of reeds. Could not make much of him, just an exchange of salutations. However, soon afterwards, in response to my invitation, Muriro came to return my visit. Tottering and trembling he, at first, seemed to despair of getting into the boat, however with the help of a lift from two or three of his women he got aboard and squatted down at once on the fore-castle thinking it impossible to get along the thwarts. However, he was prevailed upon again, and urged by his attendants, came aft to the place I had prepared for him. Bloated and blear-eyed and trembling from head to foot he was still dressed out fully in what he thought to be finery and which he must have just donned in my honour or else to impress me with his dignity. On his head was a large mop like cap of long haired lion skin with a broad band of many coloured beads

and a frontlet of medicine sticks and lions' claws. A long garment of red and black blanket shift only just revealed his
elephantine ankles which were covered with a quantity of copper
sambo. I could not get this old gentleman to talk; he just gaped
and wondered, but could not get his attention fixed for a moment.
I am afraid he was very far gone both at that particular time and
as a permanent condition. Even when he walked on shore I
noticed that he got a shove behind from an attendant where
there was the least ascent. Muriro's people seem on the whole
pretty flourishing and were very busy bringing food and various
things for sale during my stay. I sent a couple of good cloths to
Muriro but he was too mean to return a suitable present; he
gave me a small pot of honey which was no good, and told me
that he would give one of his wives permission to sell me some
more! I have always been used to getting at least a sheep or
goat and a basket of meal from such a chief, but he was very
mean. I saw a tame ostrich and a large pig here but was told
they were solitary specimens. . . .

. . . Entered the inlet at Igangwe for the Karema station just at
sunset. Next morning I walked to Karema; as we came now
over the ridge towards the plain in which the village is situate, we
saw the elephant feeding on the plain to the great delight and
astonishment of my Wajiji. Marching into the village I met with
a very hearty welcome from Captain Carter and afterwards from
Captain Cambier. Captain Popelin had just started on a voyage.
Three of the newly arrived French Missionaries were here almost
destitute, having been brought up from Simba (where they
deserted by all of their men) by the men belonging to Capt.
Carter's expedition. Mr. Cadenhead was now expected here almost
daily. I delivered over various stores I had brought rice, honey,
etc., and took in the two sections of boat given to me by Capt.
Cambier. I was entertained most kindly during my stay here. The
very last fowl was being killed for me the day before I left. I
truly hope that these friendly relations will continue. It is wonderful how much white men can be of *mutual assistance* out
here, and how extremely pleasant it is thus to come to a place
like this and feel that one is welcome and in the midst of friends.
I am happy to say that the friendly feeling is mutual, and I have
heard that Capt. Popelin and Mr. Burdo have heard such accounts
of Ujiji that they are determined to visit it at first opportunity.
M. Cambier's house on the Lake shore is slowly progressing on a
firm footing, he is enthusiastic and constant at the work, but he is
shortly returning to England having completed his term of
service.

On May 11, I left Igangwe, exchanging signals with M. Cambier
as I passed his house. Wind squally off the land, afternoon S.W.
with bumpy sea; went into a little harbour which I knew
(Mwibo) and stopped all night. Next morning a fine steady E.S.E.
breeze took us right across to Tembe Head where we camped

for the night and then pulled in to visit my old friend, the Chief Boondo (Uguha). Tho' I never before had cause to fear the hippopotami they must now be counted amongst the dangers of the Lake, for as we near the head of the bay at this place some of them attacked us and nearly bit a piece out of the boat. The boat is a very heavy one, the bottom plank being mostly three or three and a half inches thick, but one of these heads logged up underneath and gave a sensation as if we had knocked hard against a rock; then another came at the boat open mouthed, giving us another shake and leaving its teeth marks deep in the planks. I know that it is very dangerous to provoke these animals from a boat and have always refrained from doing so, but this was a perfectly unprovoked attack and has never happened to me before. Probably, they were only playing, but it is something like a child playing with an egg for an ordinary light boat would have been quite scrunched up.

There has been warfare here since my last visit. Boondo has been driven away and his village destroyed by one Lusinga who has now built a new village. In the afternoon S.S.E. wind took us on towards Cape Kimono which we rounded by moonlight. I expected to find a good harbour here, but the swell comes right in making it but poor shelter. This is Lutuku. Waguha gathered merrily round our camp fire. First daylight moved away to more sheltered position but still not good. Went to visit Lutuku, immense and fat, something like the models of fat mandarins with great flaps of fat hanging about him. Lutuku reminded me very much of Minuyi Heri. While I was speaking to Lutuku the chief Monji from the other side of Lukuga suddenly walked up. This is quite a different man tho' perhaps bigger or taller he is not so fat as Lutuku and stood gun in hand instead of squatting. He reminded me strongly by his lively wide awake manner of the chief Kawi Ngangwe of South Lukuga. Monji was dressed in a complete suit of red blanket, a single necklace of blue singo mazi, small turban, and bunch of feathers. When I asked him what he was doing here he said, " oh, just walking around," and asked me for some gunpowder. I said I had none except what was in cartridges; he replied, " well, never mind," and forthwith brought me two fowls. I afterwards sent him one cloth, one cap and two virungu, and he sent me two more fowls with an apology that he " was only a visitor here or he would send some other food." Lutuku, to whom I sent a good cloth also, gave me nothing! but asked my Wajiji if it was not customary to give two. My men replied without prompting that it was also customary for chiefs to entertain the white man. They had noticed closely the different conduct of the two chiefs. Lutuku, however, was too fat to be angry. My old friend Boondo came down to the boat to see me. He had taken refuge in Lutuku's district after being driven from his own place by Lusinga. With a few followers he has a small village here under Lutuku's protection. He

took me ashore to see Lutuku but assumed a confidential tone
as of an old friend in the presence of that chief; his manner was
as much as to say now we have paid formal respects to the
chief let us go on to my house and have a comfortable chat. I
followed him to his little village and he gave me a long account
of his troubles. Lusinga's enmity he attributes to his being jealous
of his (Boondo's) friendship with the white men(!) and Wangwana, and now says he thinks of asking Wanguana from Ujiji
to assist him in getting back his place. I asked him if it was not
possible to arrange matters without a fight; he said if he would
stand against Lusinga he must have guns. I pointed out to him
what trouble might follow his bringing Wanguana to fight and
that the white man's method was to try and arrange matters by a
shauri. He said he would be very glad if I would so arrange
matters between them; I said I should like to do so but I had a
lot of work on hand now and must return at once to Ujiji.
Boondo held out hopes of a goat but had to know first what
he shall get in return. Soon afterwards I found out what he was
in hopes that, as I could not stop to arrange his affair, I should
give him some magic preparation to annihilate Lusinga and he
held the goat in readiness to pay me for the same. It is pleasing
to relate that my Wajiji are now so well acquainted with my
methods and principles, that they explained to Boondo this
great mistake, almost without any prompting from myself. The
poor man was much disappointed. I bartered here the whole
day, buying in goats and fowls for Plymouth Rock but after all
did not get many. The hot springs are on the Cape, water bubbling up thro' pebbles too hot for the hand to stop in it. I
brought away a sample. My men feebly suggested beads at the
spring, but a single reproachful glance collapsed them. On Saturday, May 15, with fine weather and light S.E. wind I arrived at
Plymouth Rock station about 10:30 p.m. and found all well.
Spent Sunday with the Brethren, landed nice goats and fowls,
visited Kassanga at Ruanda with Mr. Griffith and started on the
18th, two p.m. for Ujiji.

I arrived at Ujiji on May 2nd, after a voyage of sixty-two days,
costing in good, pay of men, presents to chiefs, etc., about 150
dollars.[11] The employment of the Ujiji natives in this way was a
grand success; by living with me in the boat all this time we had
got thoroughly acquainted with each other, and these men did
excellent service in speaking well of me, not only in the various
countries visited, but also among their own people on our return.
    Ujiji. It is difficult to think of Lake Tanganyika apart from
Ujiji. Ujiji is a country situated upon the eastern shores of the

11. In his journal Hore states that he arrived back in Ujiji on 20th June
after the 62 day voyage.

lake, originally ruled over by a sultan or native head chief, but actually by some two or three leading men, called Mutwali, amongst the chiefs of the thirty or forty counties or districts into which the country is divided. I roughly estimate the country to contain about 700 to 800 square miles. The population is much larger than a hasty survey would indicate, the country people on the heights living in populous villages. What is most frequently known as Ujiji, however, is the metropolis of that country, and it may be said of Tanganyika, a straggling town spreading over portions of two of those divisions, namely Ugoy and Kawele, and forming the headquarters in that neighbourhood of a colony of Arab slave and ivory traders, as well as a native mart frequented by representatives of all the tribes upon the lake shores. It is the terminus of what for years was the only safe and well-known route from the east coast to the lake, and an important station upon a line of traffic, geographically suited and by common consent adopted as convenient right across the continent, and is for all purposes of commerce and communication the centre of the rich district of the Tanganyika. This town of Ujiji is in S. lat. 4° 54' 30", and E. long. 30° (approx). I resided at this place a little over two years. From it I made my various voyages on the lake. At Ujiji we lived out a character which so recommended itself to the native mind, that after we had been there a year they volunteered to give us a site for our station, and publicly recognised us as their friends in spite of all the opposition and slander of the Arabs.

At this place, in its very stronghold, we struck a deadly blow at the slave traffic of Central Africa, so that from the day of our arrival the public exposure of slaves for sale ceased, and was only carried on as admittedly contraband. By an apparent desire to settle at this place, we were permitted unmolested to spread out to other localities in the hope that, getting there, we should abandon Ujiji to its old unmolested iniquities; for, as in African travel there are times when it needs all the stimulus of a determination to cross the continent in order to complete one day's march; so nothing short of aiming at a settlement in their very headquarters would have given us the prestige necessary to settle in any part of those regions, over which these Arab settlers undoubtedly have the power to oppose us.

No better locality could have been chosen, not only from its never-to-be-forgotten associations, but from the fact that at Ujiji natives from all the lake countries assemble; that news is to be obtained and communication kept up; and, moreover, that amongst the low-lying lands surrounding the lake (which must necessarily be the scene of pioneer work, before we can build permanent

stations on healthy elevations) there are few, if any, positions
healthier than Ujiji. It is situated on one of the few small stretches
of east and west coast, a position which opens the neighbourhood
to the healthy influences of the southerly winds. The house I
resided in at Ujiji was in the highest part of the town, and subject
to an almost continual fresh breeze.

It has been unfortunate for the good name of Ujiji in this respect,
however, that it has often been the scene of the illness and death
so frequently the result of the long and trying journey from the
coast. But a long residence there has never yet proved fatal. I think
I may say that no traveller has come out of Central African work
in better health than myself, and I resided at Ujiji longer than any
European has yet done. My colleague Mr. Hutley comes next, and
at the present moment he is the oldest of our residents in those
regions. His recent illness followed his one year's residence in
another locality than Ujiji, and from whence another of our men
is also returning disabled. Since leaving Ujiji in October last, after
a residence there of two years, I have had no fever, and the Royal
Geographical Society's traveller, Mr. Thomson, speaks most
favourably also of the place.

It is interesting to note that whilst, in 1879, 29.78 inches of rain
fell at Ujiji, there fell in London during the same year 30.13 inches,
a difference of not half an inch. In 1878 nearly an inch more than
that fell in London, and in the only two months recorded at Ujiji
in that year the rain was also in excess of the corresponding period
in 1879.

Of the rain of 1880 at Ujiji I have only records up to October,
but, adding to that the average of the preceding two years for
November and December, we have for 1880 27.34, a difference
again from the London rainfall of that year, of just half an inch.

The hottest time of the year at Ujiji has been before and after
the early rains in September and November, with a maximum in
the house of 83°; the coldest in July, with a minimum, outside, of
58°, the ordinary temperature in the house being 76° to 79°.

In both the years 1879 and 1880 the approach of the rains was
faithfully indicated by the highest range between the wet and dry
bulb thermometers, which occurred in both those years the day
before the first rain.

Your Society has proved it possible for Englishmen to traverse
these regions successfully and safely. The London Missionary
Society has proved it possible for them to reside upon the lake
shores in friendly relations with its natives, and in safe, if not
friendly, relations with the Arab colonists; but amongst these I can
point to many now whom I know would remain neutral, if not

actually friendly, who, when we first arrived, were strong to oppose us.

I wish to bear public testimony to the fact that Mohammed Bogharib most certainly saved my life on one memorable occasion, and to remind you that this good old man did a like service for Dr. Livingstone. If on my return to Africa I could convey to Bogharib some testimony of the gratitude of our friends in England, I should be very pleased to do so.

Concluding Remarks.—But to conclude. Beyond this lake lie immense unexplored regions. The London Missionary Society recognises its stations on the lake as forming only a basis for the spread of missionary operations across the continent; and I would remind your Society that while, with Zanzibar for a base, travellers have seldom penetrated much beyond the lake, if they selected some such point as Ujiji for a similar base, wide and valuable explorations still further afield could be made with almost equal facility.

A kind of depôt or headquarters might be made there, from which the explorer, relieved from the great strain and anxiety of the journey, could calmly regard and settle down to the work before him, and where a transit instrument could be set up. Even by the so-called old route a traveller, lightly laden, could march from the coast to Ujiji in seventy days, to which place supplies could be safely forwarded without his being burdened with the care and delay of a laden caravan. A party of African natives, without Europeans, are just now taking in the annual supply to our mission stations. The expense of residence would be trifling compared with that of the large party to be constantly maintained in caravan work, and the missionaries resident in the district would, I trust, ever afford a companionship and assistance, which more than one traveller has spoken of as being the reverse of depressing. For my part, I would most heartily welcome, as a means of recommending Christian civilisation to the natives, the presence of any upright English gentleman.

I cannot possibly include in this paper an account of the other voyages I made upon the lake, but each country has been visited, and wherever I have been able to come face to face with the real natives I have never failed to make some friendly negotiations, and at several points we have distinct invitations to settle. There have been cases of mistaken identity, as when the people of Goma stoned me at night from their lofty hillsides; but when daylight revealed my white skin I was heartily welcomed to their shores.

Further reinforcements to our party having arrived at Ujiji in October 1880, I was at liberty to return to England to arrange for the new vessel which we hoped to obtain for service on the lake, for the further visiting of the people and the maintenance in efficiency of stations on its shores. I left Ujiji on the 3rd of November last year, and reached the coast in sixty-two days, meeting with a friendly reception all along the road, which we ourselves may truly be said to have opened up to the passage of Europeans.

The London Missionary Society have now determined to build and send out an efficient steam vessel in sections, and also to make fair trial of the new routes by Lake Nyassa, though at the same time they see the importance of keeping open the old route, which now has four mission stations on it. The proposed new road between the lakes Nyassa and Tanganyika will form the connecting link (the steamer once being on Tanganyika), completing a chain of communication in English hands and by English means (including the coast-lines of the two lakes) of about 2,000 miles. The carrying into operation of these two last links—viz. the making of that road and the transport and launch of the steamer—will certainly be watched with interest by the friends of Africa, and, I trust, not allowed to fail.

The new results of general interest I have been able to place before geographers must be remembered to have been gathered amidst the pressure of the more immediate work of our Mission. I do not know how the cost in money of this work compares with that of other extensive African expeditions, past or present—perhaps not unfavourably—but the work has been done throughout upon the principles it has been planned to disseminate, without any bloodshed or disturbance between Europeans and natives, and with the loss of only some three or four of our porters from natural causes. I think I may say that a permanent way through the territories of some sixteen Central African tribes, representing a line of over 1,500 miles of hitherto almost unknown country, has been secured, in the course of accomplishing which I have myself walked about 2,500 miles and sailed over 1,000. Three stations have been established in important centres, at two of which at least Christian influence is at the present moment gaining ground.

Whether the *ordinary* duties and responsibilities of English residents at those stations have been fulfilled by the missionaries, it is for the British and French Governments, the Royal Geographical Society, the African International Association, and the Roman Catholic missionaries to say. Of the still greater results for which the friends of missions hopefully look, let no man hastily judge.

VI

THE PEOPLES OF THE LAKE AND THE INTERIOR

For the Anthropological Institute of Great Britain and Ireland, Hore prepared a description and comparison of the customs of the peoples encountered in the interior. He first discussed the tribes living between the coast and Lake Tanganyika, observing that many of their less admirable qualities were derived from contacts and intruders from the coast. Turning his attention to the peoples living around the lake, Hore exhibited a belief in the nobility of primitive society. While in 1882 Hore considered the slave raiders to be the destructive force in the interior, in 1888 he would point out to the foreign secretary of the LMS that " . . . Arab and Wangwana . . . small traders and settlements form the only oasis of peace and prosperity to the natives and are a cementing power to keep society together. True they want purifying of slavery but *equally* so do all the *natives* where alone they can and do commence the work of peace and civilisation far better than any European I know yet. . . . Far better these people than the South African colonial process " (to R. W. Thompson, February 11, 1888).

' On the Twelve Tribes of Tanganyika ' was published in *1883*, a year after Hore had returned to central Africa.

On the Twelve Tribes of Tanganyika*

In attempting to describe a dozen or so of the native tribes of Central Africa a large task lies before me—a task indeed which I cannot hope to complete, from a strictly scientific point of view. My work in Central Africa as a missionary involved, it is true, the study of mankind, but not always the close observation of those minute differences of colour, stature, physiognomy, or tribal marks so valuable to the Anthropologist.

There are, moreover, certain difficulties surrounding the attainment of such detailed observations, perhaps more insurmountable to resident missionaries, who must carefully avoid anything that would add mystery to their proceedings in the eyes of the ignorant, timid, and superstitious barbarian, than to a traveller whose known object is research into all scientific matters.

My account, therefore, will be a simple statement of what I have seen, in passing through or living with these tribes, from which you may cull some information valuable to the objects of your Institute, rather than an attempt to offer any theory, or to deal with the subject in a strictly scientific manner.

Many of these tribes have already been described by travellers far more competent to the task than myself. I wish simply to add to those descriptions what I have myself observed.

The *locale* of the twelve tribes referred to is the shores of Lake Tanganyika, in Central Africa, lying in from 3° to 9° S. lat. and from 29° to 31° 30′ E. long.; comprising, with its various bays and river-mouths, a coast-line of about 1,000 miles.

Distant from the east coast at Zanzibar only 540 geographical miles (as the crow flies), the caravan route from the coast to the Lake (consisting, for the most part, of a continuous zig-zag of native paths from village to village, and determined, through a long course of years, by existence of water, avoidance of natural obstacles, and other causes) is lengthened to a distance of 800 English miles—giving the Tanganyika so far an interior position as to render some short description of the tribes encountered on the route from the coast almost necessary.

* From the *Journal of the Anthropological Institute of Great Britain and Ireland* (January 1883). 2-21.

K

A hasty glance as we go westward into Central Africa reveals something like this:—a narrow margin on the sea-board of a doubtful oriental civilisation, and a broader margin of small native tribes mingled with the lowest of semi-civilised half-castes, and fast losing their distinctive nationalities. The outer band of civilisation has sucked the life-blood of these communities—quite paralysed the native germs of civilisation, and up to recent times given nothing in their place.

Then, at from 100 to 200 miles from the coast, we come upon distinct native tribes, of uneasy and apparently warlike aspect, too far from the coast to be completely overrun by the invading race, and therefore retaining, to some extent, the original native arts and customs: they seem in a chronic state of armed resistance to every one, and in most cases, as with the Wagogo, sufficiently powerful to demand a share in passing trade, in which, by their unsettled position, they are unable to take a legitimate share. They are neither far enough away from the coast quietly to produce, nor sufficiently near to it peaceably to trade. These unsettled tribes are everywhere the most difficult to deal with.

Continuing west, to come to real Central African tribes, amongst whom only we can fairly look for real samples of the native African, and amongst whom we find evidence of capabilities which only require appropriate assistance to develop into civilisation—tribes indeed, which, isolated from the benefits of communication with the outer world, have also been, in many cases, isolated from the disturbing influences of such communication, and in peace and quiet have made some considerable advance in the use of the produce of their country, and in a certain amount of social order and tranquility.

Hence in an observant journey into this region, instead of, as might be expected, going deeper into ignorance and barbarity, we regularly advance from the socially and physically degraded barbarian, settled often but a mile or two from the coast, to the real healthy active savage of the far interior, living in large orderly settlements, and pursuing the industries he has patiently acquired. It is not without substantial reason that extensive missionary organisations have sought a field of labour in the far interior.

Off-shoots of the doubtful civilisation, referred to have penetrated even to the far interior, and settled, leech-like, upon some of these tribes, but except in certain isolated localities, and in the case of some small weak tribes, they have not taken possession. The slave trade, however, the original end and purpose of those distant representatives of civilisation, has left no part wholly untouched.

I will not attempt to describe fully the coast natives, forming the outer margin of disturbed and degraded tribes. From the coast to Mpwapwa (200 miles) we pass through Useguha and Usagara, in which districts are settled the representatives of many other tribes. Eight or ten miles from the coast, we may see the real barbarian living in a tiny beehive hut—a kilt of grass his only garment, and bow and quiver his constant companion. Since the commencement of the active suppression of the slave trade the countries covering this first 200 miles between the coast and Mpwapwa are, however, evidently recovering from their miserable condition, and though original tribal distinctions are most difficult to trace, their obliteration is perhaps partly conducive to the gathering of industrious communities, which are even now showing promise of what more peaceful times will do for these regions.

Two smaller belts of country remain to be described on either side of the apparently warlike tribes referred to, and serving still further to isolate them from the tribes to the east and west. These smaller belts form a sort of unsettled or debatable ground, for the most part badly watered and serving as a refuge for wanderers and outcasts from all directions, and especially for those bands of robbers or bandits, the terror alike of passing travellers, and of the settled tribes whom they frequently molest. These desert tracts, however, are nominally portioned out as belonging to certain adjacent tribes. They are represented on the line of our route by the Marenga Mkali in the east, which is nominally included in the country of Ugogo, and the Magunda Mkali in the west, nominally the possession, in parts, of the Wagogo, the Wanyamwezi, the Wakimbu, and the people of Uyansi.

At Mpwapwa (200 miles from the coast) we come to the borders of Ugogo, and may suppose we see something of the Wagogo. We see, at any rate, the tribal house, and something of the tribal dress and ornaments, but they are here much mixed with the Wasagara. We must cross the Marenga Mkali in order to see these people with their true character developed in their native home. Ugogo may be roughly described as a vast plain, draining, where it does so at all, south into the Rufigi river, and divided into eastern and western Ugogo at a verdant strip of lofty forest, and extending from the Chunyo Pass at Mpwapwa to the steep step on to the forest uplands of Uyansi, a distance of seventy to eighty geographical miles. I estimate the country of Ugogo to contain from 3,000 to 4,000 square miles. The line of unsettled and apparently predatory tribes here represented by the Wagogo is continued north in the Wamasi and Wahumba, and in the south by the Warori and Wakimbu.

Our line of route from Ugogo, probably by far the most populous part, passes through ten distinct districts of villages, each containing from fifteen to fifty houses or villages, varying from seventy to eighty people. At Mvomi, the first of these districts, I counted, from a slight elevation, forty of these houses.

In these houses, or tembes, we find the first district tribal characteristic. They are of a rectanguar shape : two stockades, one from six to eight feet within the other, form the framework of the house, closed in above by a flat roof of rafters covered with earth; the walls are then filled in and plastered over with clay. One central door or gateway affords the only means of ingress and egress, and the cattle, sheep, etc., the general property of the villagers, are placed in the centre. The surrounding house is portioned off into small compartments for families. The one door being closed at night shuts in effectually the whole community.

The Wagogo have often been described as a bold, impudent, warlike tribe. They are necessarily so, to some extent, from their situation in the country as before described. Their system of *hongo*, or customs dues, is almost the only means they have of sharing in the commerce of the country, and perhaps they are entitled to this in return for a free and peaceable passage through their territory. They certainly afford the protection and supply to caravans which would be expected under similar circumstances in any place. In the Wagogo, the traveller comes, almost for the first time, upon real distinct tribal customs, dress, ornament, arms, and manufactures.

The Wagogo are generally rather short, thick-set people, with thick lips and woolly hair, although the latter is seen to grow to considerable length in many instances, encouraged by the tribal custom of lengthening it out in little plaits weighted with beads or pieces of metal. The clothing is very scant, consisting, in the males, of a short mantle of well softened goatskin, often fringed or embroidered with white beads, and covered with bands and spots of bark dye. The tribal ornaments, however, are very profuse; iron bracelets and anklets, as well as those of hide, necklaces of beads, and chains and earrings of every imaginable description and material, serve to give the people an appearance of being elaborately clothed. The young children very seldom have any clothing at all, and the women more frequently use imported cloth, according to their means. The Wagogo are generally well armed; their spears, of immense length and size, are noted amongst all the tribes. They also carry a short two-edged sword, evidently imported from the coast, as well as clubs and bows.

Circumcision is practised by the Wagogo, amongst whom it is evidently an important rite. The youths are secluded apart in a hut, on an open plain, away from the immediate neighbourhood of villages. This hut is decorated profusely with charms, etc., consisting of bones, feathers, pots, skulls of animals, etc. The particular hut I observed was without roof. A close inspection was angrily denied; in fact, I found I had incurred displeasure by approaching it. Exercise is allowed to the patients while still in retirement, being marched about under the care of a responsible person. During all this time the youths wear a conspicuous apron, hanging behind and before from the neck, and consisting of little pieces of hollow reed strung on cords so as to rattle with every movement. They are further made conspicuous by means of daubs of a white substance upon the face and body.

The districts are ruled in orderly manner by their several chiefs, each appearing to be well nigh independent in his own small territory. Although subject to frequent attacks from the cattle-stealing Wahumba in the north, those people may still be seen in frequent friendly relations with the villagers, especially in western Ugogo. On the south side of western Ugogo the Wakimbu also mix in friendly intercourse with the people, their villages being frequently side by side. In the debatable border beyond western Ugogo may be seen, near together, villages of Wagogo, Wakimbu, Uyansi, and Wahumba, although they all seem to retain markedly their own tribal characteristics. The Wahumba, especially, seem to be a distinct race, with tapering limbs and much finer features. They are very fine representatives of what I shall call the Abyssinian type, which seems to come in from the north upon all the districts I am describing, to be traced especially in these people and in the Wahha, Wajiji, and Warundi.

Passing rapidly over this district we come to Unyamwesi. We have now to deal with the more prosperous, intelligent tribes inhabiting those inner regions, which may be described as forming the equatorial Lake Regions, for the most part well watered countries. Unyamwesi proper is a large country, comprising, probably, about 12,000 square miles, divided roughly into two portions, respectively under the control of the Arab colony of Uyanyembi, and the famous native chief Mirambo. Mirambo himself describes his country as extending from the shores of the Victoria Nyanza to the south end of Tanganyika. No doubt his influence does extend to those limits, but his own proper possessions may be included within much smaller bounds. To give an adequate description of Unyamwesi would fill a volume. I hope shortly that Dr. Southon, our missionary at Urambo, will give us the benefit of his careful research into the history, manners, and customs of these people. A mere glance must suffice here. In my rapid visits to the Wanyamwesi I saw amongst them two types: one a short, thick-set people, somewhat similar to the Wagogo, the other tall and slight, but both are equally active, and have the beautiful sharp merry eye almost everywhere characteristic of these people. Almost every tolerably well-to-do individual is clothed in European cloth. They are settled in large well protected towns. Except upon the western borders of the country, the square *tembe* is seldom seen. From 100 to 200 large round conical-roofed houses are protected by a tall stockade with fortified gates, the houses themselves, indeed, being well fitted to withstand an attack, as they are surrounded with an outer gallery of strong logs. In Mirambo's town, especially, the houses are very fine and large, being built with a floor above in the roof, and the town itself is surrounded by a double wall, forming, in fact, a huge *tembe* enclosing several hundred large round houses. Mirambo's own establishment being in the centre. Numerous blacksmiths' shops, factories of bark boxes, pottery works, and other industries, indicate that we have arrived among the industrious tribes I have referred to. The Wanyamwesi are doubtless an energetic race. Under their chief, Mirambo, they have successfully protested against the tyranny of the Arab colonists, and bid fair, under his effectual leadership, to become a prosperous and peaceful, if not a civilised nation. A mission station has been successfully conducted in the immediate neighbourhood of Mirambo's town for the last two years. Wonderful influence for good has been gained over this chief, who is determined, he says, that his country and people shall learn to take their place among civilised races.

In the natural order of things we should now come to the Lake shores, but another tribe, the Wavinza, intervenes between the Wanyamwesi and the Wajiji, which will probably ere long be included in the former tribe, having many of the same characteristics, only perhaps in a less advanced degree. This tribe holds the ferry of the Malagarasi river, which has, in fact, long been a natural barrier to prevent their assimilation with the Wanyamwesi.

We now advance to the territory of the Wajiji, the first of the twelve tribes of Tanganyika, and the first, not only for convenience of description, but because in this country all travellers from the east have found it a convenient point of approach to the great Lake. The town of Ujiji itself, in fact, is the metropolis of the Lake, and has become the centre of trade and communication for the whole district. Ujiji is a country ruled over by a sultan, or native head chief, but actually by some two or three men called Mutwale among the chiefs, or Wamteko, of the thirty or forty counties or districts into which the country is divided. I roughly estimate the country to contain from 700 to 800 square miles, with a coast-line on the

Lake of some 40 to 50 geographical miles. The population is large —larger than a hasty survey would indicate, the country people on the heights living in large populous villages. Ujiji is bounded on the north by the river Mohala, and on the east by Ruiche river. What is most frequently known as Ujiji, however, is the metropolis of that country, and, as I have said of Tanganyika. It is a straggling town, spreading over portions of two counties or districts, viz., Ugoy and Kawele, and forming the headquarters in that neighbour-hood of a colony of Arab slave and ivory traders, as well as a native market frequented by representatives of all the tribes upon the Lake shores. It is the terminus of what for years was the only safe and well known route from the east coast to the Lake, and an important station upon a line of traffic adopted by common consent as a convenient course right across the continent.

The most noticeable feature in Ujiji is its market, which, however, has often been described. It is rather an exchange for produce from many of the lake countries than representative of a large producing country; the only export of great extent from Ujiji itself being the famous packages of salt, current all over the Lake shores as a medium of barter. This salt is manufactured once a year on the banks of the Ruguvu river, east of Ujiji, where from 2,000 to 3,000 persons sometimes assemble at the proper season, just before the commencement of the rain, forming quite a town for the sole purpose of manufacturing the salt. It is packed up in cylindrical leaf packages weighing from twenty to thirty lbs. each, and valued at Ujiji at about two yards of good calico. The market of Ujiji town consists generally, of an assembl-age of from 200 to 300 small booths or stalls, exposing for sale almost everything that the Lake countries produce, as well as meat, vegetables, fruit, and grain. Here for the first time we find a regular currency or money in use by the natives; it consists of strings of blue and white cylindrical beads, each string containing twenty beads. Bunches of ten strings are called *fundo*. From nine to eleven fundo are given in exchange for four yards of thin Man-chester calico, and from twelve to fifteen for four yards of good heavy American calico; the value varying daily, according to the quantity of cloth in the market. The four yard piece, or *doti*, and the two-yard piece, or *Shukka*, are the lengths generally used in trade. One-yard pieces are also used, but are then of less pro-portionate value. *Kanika* (Indian blue-dyed cloth) is about the same value as the Manchester calico. Coloured cloths, with nails and coils of copper and brass wire, are used for more extensive purchases.

Besides the market in Ujiji town proper, which is frequented by the Arab and Swahili community as well as natives, there are the country markets, some of them frequented almost entirely by natives, and in their hands, especially one at Gungu, about six miles from Ujiji, where large quantities of palm oil are brought from Urundi. The natives frequent these markets daily for their supply of food. Mtama corn is largely imported into Ujiji as they produce maize themselves. A small quantity of palm oil is produced also in Ujiji, but Uvira salt is the principal export. The famous pottery and iron ware is disposed of in considerable quantities at Ujiji, although they are already vieing with Uvira in pottery work.

The houses in Ujiji town are first the large square flat-roofed Arab houses built in the same style probably as that of centuries ago, and smaller square houses imitating this style to some extent. But a walk of three or four miles is sufficient in order to see the real native type of house, dress, etc. The Ujiji house is of a large beehive pattern, very frequently without any internal support, the whole thing depending upon the beautifully made framework or skeleton of bamboo and branches, which is thatched over with grass. A little porch is frequently made before the door. Slightly raised bed-places covered with mats, and the regular African three-legged stool, represent most of the furniture. The villages are numerous but small, each one ruled over by a village headman, or elder, who himself is subject to the district chief, or Mteko.

Although the tsetse fly may be found within a few miles of Ujiji the country is so far cleared as to enable the people to keep considerable numbers of domestic cattle. There is a large and long-horned breed of cattle highly valued by the Arab settlers at Ujiji; they are also found in Uvira and Urundi, and have many of the characteristics of the Galla ox. There is also a smaller breed kept in large numbers by the natives on the inland heights. Goats, fowls, and pigeons of many kinds are plentiful, the latter being rather kept as pets in the villages than as food. Pombe is manufactured from malted Mtama, and a weak spirit or wine is made from the banana. Dishes and drinking-vessels are wooden bowls or baskets. The principal foods are Mtama, maize, and Mhogo, or cassava. The latter is used in many forms, either simply cooked and as a vegetable, or dried in slices and pounded up into a coarse meal, which is made into a sort of loaf or pudding.

The Wajiji may be said to be a tall race. I think I have nowhere seen finer looking people, straight and well made for the most part. They aid their own natural good appearance by an upright carriage, and some attention to neatness and smartness of dress and ornament, without any superfluity. The common garment is of bark or cotton cloth, tied over one shoulder, and open at the side. The distinctive national ornament is a crescent-shaped piece of hippopotamus ivory. European cloth, however, is being largely introduced. The women anywhere near the Arab colony like to imitate those settlers in the manner of attire and dressing the hair, which is neatly divided into narrow ridges from back to front. The men usually shave the head, leaving a round or crescent-shaped patch on the top or side. They are not profusely ornamented. Copper or iron sambo bracelets, bound with wire, are common, and serve also for purposes of barter and exchange. Chiefs and well-to-do men often wear solid brass or copperware bracelets, and carry in their hands a small tomahawk. It is noticeable that I have never seen an Ujiji in possession of a gun. The Arabs have been able to prevent the introduction of firearms where it suited their purposes. The weapons of the Wajiji are spear, bow, knife and club. The bowstring is made of the fibre of the rafia palm-leaf, of which they also make fine cord for various purposes. The spear is rather roughly made to be inserted into the wooden shaft, but the famous Uvira spears, which fit to the shaft in the reverse way, are largely taking the place of the former. Cotton and bark cloth are also manufactured.

The long two-edged knife, with central ridge, is also an importation from Uvira.

I have failed to find that fierce untameable character which has been described to the Wajiji. In a normal state there is found in the villages a peaceful, social, and family life. Perhaps no people on the Lake shores have had more difficulties to contend with in order to a peaceful condition : polygamy, although perhaps not the rule, is quite lawful and only limited by the means of the individual. I suppose there are very few families without one or more domestic slaves, but they are really domestic slaves, mostly bearing the relation of members of the household.

As in most of the Lake tribes the work of the field appertains to the women. The young girls invariably accompanying their mothers, assisting in this work, and early learning to carry loads on their heads. The smallest article, to be carried any distance, is placed upon the head and carried with wonderful precision and skill. Much has been said about the unfair division of labour in such circumstances, but when it is considered that a wild man finds scarcely anything to his hand, but must himself cut the wood and the grass to build his house, manufacture his spear and cooking vessels, take his part in tribal duties, and is frequently compelled to seek food in long and laborious hunting expeditions, it will be seen that he often gets his fair share of work.

The Wajiji are famous for their extensive fishing journeys. In fleets of from six to twenty canoes, they remain away often for a month or two, accumulating large quantities of the small *dagga* which, dried in the sun and packed up into large bundles, are sent far and wide throughout the country.

The Warundi (proceeding northwards round the Lake shore) are in many respects similar to the Wajiji. Physically they are almost the same; for the most part of good height and shapely build. Were Ujiji stripped of its market and metropolitan character, it would be a much poorer country than Urundi. Urundi, including in it the district of Uzige, has about 120 miles of coastline abutting on the Lake, and from such information as has been collected, extends to some considerable distance north-west of the Lake. As in Ujiji, they admit allegiance to the big sultan " who lives up in the hills," but many of the Mtekos, or district chiefs, are probably supreme in their own locality. Urundi has also several markets. The principal export is the palm oil, which is put up and sold in large and fine egg-shaped jars, containing about two or three gallons. They are also famous for medium-sized lake canoes, which they build to a set pattern, but which are not so fine or so strong as those built in Goma.

The Warundi are famous fishermen. This industry is carried on, as well in log canoes as in small rafts, or catamarans, made of the trunks of the pith tree pegged together. Five or six of these small trunks form a raft sufficient and safe for one or two men, with their fishing-tackle, and are easily drawn up on to the beach, or into the villages when not in use. Into the canoes which go out fishing at night, they place long torches or bundles of reeds tightly lashed together, and often longer than the canoe itself. One end is lighted, and is pushed over the bow of the canoe as it becomes expended, but they last nearly all night.

The Warundi are apparently more fierce and unapproachable just in proportion as they are less acquainted with strange travellers from a distance than the Wajiji, but where I have landed in their country I have succeeded in making friends with the people.

They have a splendid and rich country. Immense groves of bananas, large corn-fields and gardens cover the verdant slopes from the Lake shores to the hills, and aid in giving this people a generally prosperous appearance. The beads used as currency at Ujiji are here largely used as ornaments, as well as the crescent-shaped hippopotamus-tooth referred to in Ujiji.

It is doubtful whether Céige should be considered separately from Urundi. The chief certainly is powerful and probably nearly independent, but still the natives say " it is all Urundi ".

Explorers seeking to traverse the country between Tanganyika and Victoria Nyanza, will have to make negotiations with the people of either Uzige or Urundi. I have myself no doubt concerning the success of such negotiations if made in a cautious and friendly spirit, but the Warundi are a courageous and spirited people, and will doubtless, and with good reason, demand a full explanation of purpose from all visitors.

The extreme north end of the Lake, with its long low approach of reeds, and the openings to the Rusizi river afford a home for the hippopotamus.

The people of Uzige and Uvira hunt this animal in specially fitted canoes, with spears having long ropes attached. A lump of the pith-tree wood is put on the end of the spear shaft to serve as a float.

Coming round now to the west side of the lake we find at Uvira another extensive mart, but this time not so much so from its central position among other tribes as from the value and quantity of its own produce. Uvira proper presents a coast-line of only about twenty miles to the Lake, but it is the port, doubtless, to a rich and large-interior region whence ivory is collected in large quantities. Uvira is famous for its iron and pottery works, both of especially fine quality, and is a favourite locality for Arab traders to reside for a few months, or sometimes for a year or two, collecting ivory and trading in various local products. The Waviri have found considerable assistance in this way to their local industries, which are encouraged by the Arab traders. It is also recognised as one of the healthiest positions upon the Lake shores. The people are a smaller and darker race than the Warundi, with very thick woolly hair and dark eyes, although by no means the coarsest of negro features. Some of them are very small.

The next fifty miles of coast-line is that of Msansi and Bemba. The latter name, however, I think only applies to a small locality immediately around Cape Bemba, famous for its kaolin, or china clay, and regarded by the natives as a very sacred locality.

The Wamsansi have, I think unfairly, received a name for morose inhospitality. I had no difficulty in landing at various places, and received ordinary hospitality. Some trade in ivory is carried on here, but they are far poorer and more unsettled than the people of Uvira or Urundi. They have, however, many canoes, and carry on considerable intercourse with the Warundi.

The peninsula of Ubwari is one of the curiosities of the Lake; a little country complete in itself. This peninsula, nearly thirty geographical miles in length, and from six to twelve in width, appears to be formed of one single mountainous ridge, and would probably be a very healthy locality. The Ubwari in general appearance, feature, and manner, are quite distinct from other tribes. Rather below the ordinary stature, they are of a lighter colour than their neighbours, and their limbs are very tapering, with especially small hands and feet. They are much more poorly off in the matter of clothing and ornament than their neighbours on the east side, having but little cloth and but little native produce in its place. Their poor and unsettled condition it attributable very largely to their being the objects of periodical raids by the warlike Warna, but doubtless they must industriously collect such riches as to make them worth these attacks. Parties of these Ubwari may be seen at intervals at Ujiji bringing small quantities of ivory for sale, and probably slaves. They are expert fishermen and grow large quantities of Mtama.

We must class with these people the inhabitants of Ukaramba on the south end of the peninsula. They, however, are darker in colour than the Ubwari, and form a sort of connecting link between them and the people of Goma. All these people have a peculiar way of dressing the hair: cut all round, it appears like a black skull-cap with a central tuft, the whole being arranged in horizontal ridges.

The country of Goma has a coast-line of about 70 miles for the most part approaching the Lake very steeply. The villages, being situate on the ridges and tops of these hills, are often reached by extremely steep paths or steps. These people are also subject to the attacks of the Warna and give one the idea of being continually on the defensive. My first approach to the shores of Goma was in the middle of the night. The people assembled in large numbers and threw large showers of stones down upon us, but daylight revealed, what I had expected, that they were not aware their visitor was a European, and that being known, they received me cordially on the strength of good reports they had had from Ujiji. They are a lively and active people, almost as light coloured as the Ubwari. Their chief characteristic is an appearance of cheerfulness and happiness. Their houses, unlike those of the Wajiji, have distinct walls and separate roofs. They do not wear a large amount of clothing or ornament, and have but few arms. The country is governed, as far as I could observe, only by local chiefs. Traders settle at one or two points in Goma, trading with salt, cloth, and beads, for ivory. But the famous produce of Goma is its canoes, which are made of solid logs up to sizes of forty feet by seven or eight, and are triumphs of native African art.

Where Goma ends and Uguha commences it is difficult to say; for purposes of description I place the boundary about the north side of the islands, which give Uguha a coast-line of about 90 miles. The grand feature of maritime Uguha is its bay of islands and Lukuga river. Uguha, further investigation will doubtless reveal, is but a principality of the large country of Rua, but for all purposes of government and trade, Uguha is a separate country, ruled over by several rich and powerful chiefs, amongst whom it is difficult to say which is senior: the honour probably fluctuates. This country presents a very rich field for the investigation of native habits and customs, and of possibilities of a considerable state of advance in industry and social order amongst still savage tribes. In the people themselves the most noticeable feature is the head-dress; they might well be described as the " head-dress people ". Men and women alike are got up in the most elaborate style. The hair is encouraged to grow long by every possible aid of combing and stretching over rolls and puffs, which are built up into shapes resembling crowns or turbans, and ornamented with iron and copper ornaments, bands of cowries and beads and terminal points and cones, forming a structure requiring great care to preserve from damage. This is achieved by the use of little wooden head-rests, or pillows, which are used in sleeping to keep the head from contact with the ground or bed; the women, especially, are extensively tattooed. The usual dress, whether of skin, European cloth, or native grass-cloth, is gathered about the waist, with a great bunch in front. In the case of chiefs, however, it is ornamented frequently with a sort of leopard-skin apron. Ornaments are extremely plentiful; a conical shell, brought from the coast, is ground down with flat surfaces, and strung together to form huge necklaces for the chiefs. The large blue and white beads, of the size of pigeons' eggs, are most popular for neck or waist ornaments. Large spiral bracelets of copper wire adorn the arms and legs of the well-to-do women, whose dress is distinct in shape and form from that of the men.

In the villages of the Waguha, even in the smallest of them, there is an attempt to arrange the houses in regular rows or streets. This is finely illustrated in the town of Ruanda, about ten miles from the London Missionary Society's station. This town contains from 400 to 600 houses, arranged in straight rows. A long central street runs the whole length of the village, and its beauty is enhanced by the presence of several fine bombax trees, placed at regular intervals at cross roads. The houses, though at first sight of an ugly shape, are really very beautiful structures, built on a square plan, tapering from the top of the walls to the point of the roof. So much thatch of coarse grass is placed over and around them as entirely to hide the shapely form of the house, but inside the intricate and beautiful work is fully seen. Fine clay, such as is used in pottery, is smoothly plastered over the floor and around the walls, generally of a rich chocolate colour. Into this are built smooth upright logs, forming stands or legs for bed-places, racks for firewood, or enclosed fortified places of retreat from an enemy. They are of equal size, smooth, clean, and even coloured red or brown. Beautiful mats are spread upon the bed-places, richly carved stools, and stands for arms; and almost invariably an image representing the guardian spirit or ancester of the family is placed in a safe and prominent position; the cooking-pots hung up in the roof in a netting, firewood neatly piled up in its own place, and the floor cleanly swept give to some of these interiors a most clean and comfortable appearance.

In some of the larger houses, and those of the chiefs, elevated tables are made, on which are placed packages of corn, meal, salt, etc. The images or figures of spirits and ancestors, to which I have referred, are a noticeable feature in this country. They are placed at the entrance and principal parts of the villages. They are certainly not idols, as we accept the term, but are regarded as sacred objects, although it is not difficult to purchase specimens.

Some of the well-to-do chiefs referred to have very many wives. Casanga, the chief at Ruanda, for example, is said to have 200 or 300. But they deal largely in domestic slaves, and many of these, doubtless, must be regarded rather as slaves than as wives. The general appearance of the people is bold and self-possessed, and though not perhaps of so gainly an appearance as the Wajiji and Warundi, they are stronger and more hardy. In south Uguha the same amount of prosperity does not exist, although tribal characteristics continue. They have not the same benefit of traffic and intercourse with others as have the people of north Uguha, and for many years there have been poverty-bringing troubles between neighbouring chiefs.

One of the chief products of Uguha, or perhaps more properly Rua, is the famous grass-cloth and iron ware. The Waguha themselves also produce very beautiful mats, basket work, pottery, wooden bowls and platters, and various small carved work. On one of the islands, Mtowa, there is a famous pottery, and here, and in Uguha generally, they produce some of the largest vessels to be obtained anywhere on the Lake shore. There are some special peculiarities about the arms of the Waguha. The bow, for instance, is quite unlike that of any other tribe. The bowstring is made of hide or tendon, and is carried through a hole at the end of the bow, which is not carried to a point, but is bound through with iron. The spears of Rua and Uguha are very finely made, and sometimes beautifully ornamented and carved. They, however, are inserted into the wooden shaft, unlike those of Uvira, and the shaft itself is armed at the butt end, not with a spike as in other tribes, but with a small axe or chisel-shaped piece of iron. The tribes, with the pointed spear-end, explain its use to be that of sticking into the ground. The Wajiji explain the use of their chisel-shaped end to be that of digging a hole or cutting roots.

South of Uguha, the country of Marungu extends with a coast-line of 140 miles, having an extremely varied aspect, but towards the south presenting a very bold front to the Lake. It is, perhaps, at the present time one of the principal slave-producing or trading countries around the Lake. Voyages are frequently made from Ujiji to Warungu, but I know of no produce coming from there in any quantity. The salt and palm oil of Ujiji here attain an almost fabulous value.

Possessed of many populous villages and an extensive country, hospitable too, as far as I have seen them, the Marungu have not yet received the visits of many travellers, and a large field still lies open in their country for investigation. They are famous makers of bark cloth. They are a rougher-looking and darker race than the Waguha.

Itawa, next to the south, has a coast-line of about eighty miles. King Muriro of Akkalunga is supposed to be the head chief, and the Msika in Msumbu the second in authority. As we might expect to find, from its position, the people of Itawa show indications of communication with the west. They are probably near a line of traffic from the Katanga copper-fields to Unyanyembi. Very many of them are in possession of guns, and here and there Swahili traders and elephant hunters are settlers, but for the most part these are poor and isolated individuals. They are a large-limbed, dark, and coarse-looking race generally, though some of the women have a very fine appearance. Local chiefs have considerable power in their own districts, and it is well it should be so, for the chief, Muriro, is in a continual state of drunkenness and imbecility. When he came to visit me in my boat he had to be pushed along by three or four of his wives, and exhibited but little interest or care for anything beyond himself. The women are famous smokers of tobacco, which they also manufacture into cakes here and at the south end of the Lake. Sugar-cane is produced in some places, and large luxuriant corn-fields fill the damp hollows.

The river Lofu is supposed to form the boundary between Itawa and Ulungu, which latter has a coast-line of at least 100 miles, forming the south end of the Lake.

I had expected to find a scattered and mixed people, but I found them to be a distinct tribe, with their own peculiar customs, dress, arms, and houses. The most characteristic article of dress is the goatskin garment worn by the women; the top part being unconfined, it hinges, as it were, at the waist, so that on sitting down it at once swings into its proper place as a mat or carpet; the lower part is scalloped in a set pattern.

The most common grain is the *uleysi*, cultivated in circular forest clearings, watched from huts raised on high poles. The nether millstones used by the Walungu are really embedded in a plaster bench or table, with a receptacle for the meal.

Uganga, in its various forms of fetishes, miniature sacred huts, and mystical performances, flourishes in every small village. The tsetse fly was seen in all parts, even to within half-a-mile of Zombe's village, the only place where cattle are kept. Cotton is cultivated largely, and cloth made as at Ujiji. The bow of the Walungu and Wafipa is peculiar, having two elbows in it, instead of being, as usual, the segment of a circle, and a tassel of long dark hair is attached. Bees are cultivated, and large fish-traps are anchored off the shore to entice the large and oily *senga*.

The people of Fipa, occupying a coast-line of 120 miles, are somewhat allied to the Walunga in appearance and manner, being decidedly a dark race. They own allegiance to Chief Kapufi, who lives in a central position a short way inland. They have many rich and populous villages, and have doubtless been great slave traders, but have no produce to export, to any great extent, beyond the interchange of food and a small quantity of ivory. The borders of Fipa and Ukawendi are a short distance south of the Belgian station at Karema.

Ukawendi, or Utongwe, is perhaps the least known country upon the Lake, at least as regards its inhabitants. With a coastline of about 140 miles, extending from Karema to the Malagarasi river, it includes some of the most beautiful scenery upon the Lake shores. Many of the heights are well nigh inaccessible from the Lake, into which numerous rivers flow from a great elevation.

The people of Ukawendi are much scattered, and have the name everywhere of being robbers. They have little or no trade anywhere upon their seaport, hence it is known to them only as a way of access for probable enemies. Visits have been received by them in former times which have probably been from slave hunters, and it is difficult for them to understand any friendly visitors. At one or two points, such as Kabogo island and Cape Kungme, bands of wandering robbers have learned to seek opportunities of plunder in boats seeking shelter at those places. Altogether the people have a bad name upon the Lake, and are especially feared by the Wajiji boatmen. There are capabilities, however, amongst these people, doubtless as good as of any tribe on the Lake. I have succeeded in visiting and forming friendship with the young chief Mtongoro, at the extreme north end of this coast-line, and through him I hope to make the people understand that our intentions are friendly. At this village I found indications of prosperity and order which promise much. The small but respectable houses, made principally of reeds, were surrounded by a stockade of bamboo neatly ornamented. The young chief Mtongoro is a great hunter and himself collects ivory.

As far as I have seen, they are a poor, because an unsettled people. Cultivation is irregular and limited, and little clothing beyond skin is worn except by chiefs. Many renegade Wanyamwesi have also cast in their lot with these wandering people. I also saw something of the Ukawendi at Karema, which place I visited before the arrival of the Belgian party. Every village is fortified, and in a doubtful state of friendship with its neighbours. The chief employment seemed to be buffalo and elephant hunting, and a certain amount of prosperity was due to the extreme luxuriance of the neighbouring moist plain. They also produce and manufacture tobacco, and place great value upon the palm oil and salt of the northern countries. They are a dark unpleasant-looking people, with very little of distinct tribal ornament or dress.

There seems to be a general vague idea amongst the tribes of the existence of one all-powerful being, superior to the other spiritual beings or influences they believe in; but of worship, save the offerings placed in miniature huts in the fields and village, I have seen none.

It is a great mistake to suppose that uncivilised and so-called savage tribes are necessarily wicked and murderous.

After living nearly four years amongst the tribes I have described, I have to report that I find among them every natural affection and friendliness, general protest against abuse, and often an earnest desire for light and improvement.

Much has been said of the dangers to Europeans in visiting these tribes; but if any, it is incurred by a hasty disregard of the very natural shyness and timidity of such people on first beholding powerful parties of strange people entering their country for unknown causes.

We have heard even of travellers murdered by the natives. I know nothing of Europeans being murdered by Central African

L

natives, except in cases (parallel with cases in Europe) where hordes of banditti both rob and murder their victims; but only one even of such cases has come under my notice in Central Africa—viz. : the case of Mr. Penrose, of the Church Missionary Society—and that, just as it might have occurred in Europe, did not necessarily involve the guilt of the inhabitants so-called. There are cases in which upon evidence—strange evidence, perhaps, but certainly upon, to them, stronger evidence than would be necessary in the case of one of their own countrymen—Central African tribes have passed sentence of death upon a visitor for what they deem to be gross offence against their moral code and peace of society. In one case I have myself been condemned to death under such circumstances.

There are cases also in Africa (as in Europe) where neutral persons have fallen by accidentally coming between belligerents blinded with the flurry of battle and mutual animosity, as in the case of my lamented friend, F. F. Carter, and his companion.

There have also been cases of mistaken identity, as when the supposed murderous and cannibal people of Goma on Tanganyika stoned me at night from their lofty hill-sides, but who, when daylight revealed my white skin, received me with acclamation to their shores, saying they knew the white man was good. And there have been cases where want of tact has failed to convince the alarmed and instinctively armed savage that he was not himself about to be attacked or enslaved; but of actual *murder* I know nothing, and I think it unfair to pass such a sentence upon distant, and doubtless ignorant and savage, tribes, among whom I have lived in friendship and safety, and whom I assert not to be degraded (except inasmuch as all men are so), but who have made some small advance, isolated as they have been from the benefit of intercourse with their fellow-men, in the use of the produce of their country, and a certain amount of social order, and several of whose chiefs have deputed me to send " good, true men " to live among and teach them.

After visiting every one of these tribes, I am able to say that whenever I have encountered the real native African face to face, free from the intervention of the Arab slave trader, or the disturbing influence of a doubtful civilisation, I have succeeded in making friends with them, and there is among them a universally expressed desire for intercourse with their visitors, and a vague longing after something better, socially and morally, as well as with a view to the immediate gain which such intercourse seems to promise them.

There is yet opportunity in these comparatively undisturbed tribes of the far interior fairly to test the effects upon the African race of Christian civilisation—before the disturbing influences of fortune-hunters overwhelm such germs of civilisation as they possess.

Such effort is being made by the London Missionary Society, in connection with whose work I have been enabled to gather what I have laid before you this evening.

VII

A WOMAN'S VIEW

Not only was the life of a missionary in central Africa isolated and lonely, but, without a wife, there were unpleasant, time-consuming, household chores to perform. Furthermore, as Africans believed that a man was something less than a man without a woman, there were inevitable embarrassing questions and suggestions. By mail Hore proposed to Anne Boyle Gibbon, a member of the Wesleyan Missionary Society in Bedford and, soon after arriving in England on furlough, married her in March 1881. She and their infant son were part of the massive LMS caravan under Hore's command which left Zanzibar for the interior in June–July 1882, but, when the expedition was forced to await delayed supplies, Hore, fearing the effect of fever, dispatched them to England.

At Lake Tanganyika, Hore established his marine station on a small island off the west coast, built a house for his family, and, travelling to the coast, escorted them back, arriving at the beginning of 1885. The journey had been unique for several reasons. It had been made during the unhealthy, uncomfortable rainy period across land hard hit by famine. Secondly, although the caravan was small, it included the first European woman and child to venture so far inland as Lake Tanganyika. With her husband's encouragement, Anne Hore decided to publish her adventures, and *To Lake Tanganyika in a Bath Chair* is the account of the expedition plus the following chapter describing the daily life of a missionary wife on Kavala Island, Lake Tanganyika, in 1886.

Our Island Home*

Kavala is an island about five miles long, by half to one mile in width, and formed of an almost continuous high ridge, more or less parallel with the mountain ridges of Uguha, to which it lies adjacent. It forms one of a group of islands to the north of the promontory of Kahangwa, the northern head of the bay from which the river Lukuga, (the outlet of the lake,) flows out.

In its normal condition the island is a great heap of granite, interspersed with slate and quartz, and covered from water's edge to water's edge, with a dense jungle of trees, bushes, and creepers, free indeed from beasts of prey, but swarming with many kinds of venomous and beautiful snakes and insects.

The natives of Uguha have often used these islands as places of refuge from the attack of foes on the mainland, and Kavala, the largest of them, has for some time been permanently settled upon by one of their chiefs. On the principal clearing, where a suitable formation gives a level for the plantations and a landing for their canoes, the natives have built a large village; and three or four smaller ones, always increasing, exist on other parts of the island.

Kavala lies right in the course of the boats, which convey caravans across the lake, between Uguha and Ujiji, and as it is surrounded by deep water, and possesses two excellent natural boat harbours, it derives some benefit from passing trade, especially as the natives, having some splendid clay on the island, excel in the manufacture of cooking-pots, which are eagerly purchased by all visitors.

By the accompanying map of Tanganyika, it will be seen that this group of islands projects somewhat into the lake, hence most of the currents of air to which it is subject are lake winds, free from malaria.

Edward had, long since, considered this to be a healthy and convenient site for the station of the Marine Department. The harbour on the side next the land, was just the place suitable both for the shelter of the boats, and for their convenient starting in any direction; while a good elevation above the water could be got for the residences, without going away from the boats and workshop. Here accordingly he had placed such stores as were not in immedi-

* From *To Lake Tanganyika in a Bath Chair* (London, 1886).

ate use, under the care of three trustworthy men, who were to build some additional huts to accommodate us, when we should arrive.

Edward had already been made welcome to the place of his choice, both by the local chief, Kavala, and by Kassanga, the head chief of Uguha, and the people had long been expecting our arrival.

Such descriptions and considerations, however, had little room in my thoughts, when once I had embarked on board the *Alfajiri*, which with her first erratic movements, seemed to promise anything but the brightening prospects her name implied.

Edward was soon compelled, for safety and convenience of sailing, to take down the little tent-like awning which covered the after-part of the boat, and the prospect of a small open boat in a rough sea, out of sight of land, was opened to me in all its strangeness and awe, for the dark gathering clouds and approaching night, hid the receding Ujiji land from all but the accustomed eye. I had never been to sea before in such a small boat, and it seemed to me the extreme of risk and peril; each wave appeared as though it must come over into the boat, but as the boat rose lightly over each as they came along, and Edward assured me of our safety, I was fain to devote my attention to a series of experiments upon stowage, in the shape of certain struggles and shiftings about of myself and Jack, in a sort of pit or box without a lid, which I was told was the " stern-sheets ", a place of honour. Here I at last found the angle of least inconvenience, and sought to go to sleep, while Edward with a blanket and waterproof sheet fitted up a screen to shelter us from the drizzling rain, and the spray from the paddles of the crew. Sleep, however, was out of the question, the lifting and heaving of the boat was incessant, and I was compelled frequently to respond.

We had a good run of some hours twice through the night, and my chief idea was of rushing, bubbling water. At other times the men worked the paddles, and then all thought was lost in a clashing and groaning of every plank, only equalled by the loud songs indulged in by the rowers. To me the night was perfectly black in its darkness, but Edward told me he could see the land nearly all night.

For a long time I lay and watched his dark figure, apparently swaying to and fro on the seat above, and now and then he would strike a match under a corner of the blanket, to consult the compass. Altogether it was a night to be remembered, and one calculated, if anything could, to cool one's enthusiasm. That

I was on the path of duty, I had and have decided, both before and since.

Morning brought finer weather, and some relief, but the boat made slow progress, being propelled only by paddles. About nine o'clock Kavala was sighted in the distance, and soon after a fine, fair breeze enabled us to hoist the sail, and spin along at a splendid rate. It proved a fine day, and just as we approached the strait between the island and the mainland, and could distinguish the trees and rocks, I was able to sit up and enjoy the prospect. Jack also somewhat revived, and was delighted with the boat and the awning, and especially with the songs of the crew, amongst whom he recognised some of the carriers of our chair.

At about two p.m. we entered our little harbour, with the chief's village on the one hand, and straight before and above us, the few small huts which formed the nucleus of the settlement we were to establish.

A very steep climb up a narrow path, between dense bush, took us to the huts on the top, into one of which we speedily brought our present outfit, and proceeded to arrange the boxes and furniture, for immediate temporary accommodation.

Our house was a mud hut, consisting of two rooms, respectively nine and sixteen feet by fifteen feet. The door was a frame of reeds, which hung on two loops of cord for hinges, and another cord formed the fastening. The house contained one good piece of furniture, an ample table, which had formerly served our missionaries at Ujiji; for the rest we furnished with what we had brought in the boat. But worst of all, the walls were full of holes, having only received the first plastering, which drying and crackling, left gaps all round which gave the house rather the character of a cage.

The floor also was quite damp, the men, in their anxiety to show some work on our arrival, having just finished stamping it with new earth. Edward was very angry with them, and set them at once caulking up the walls with more mud.

When he had arranged our camp gear in this hut, and began to look round, although I was deeply thankful that I had come to my journey's end, I did feel rather downhearted. However, I knew that our boxes contained a valuable outfit both of furniture and provisions; I knew also that Edward had determined at once to build here, on Kavala, so that after all we should be much sooner settled, than if I had gone to the south end of the lake.

The natives now began to collect around to see the new and wonderful arrivals, but it was some days before we had much intercourse with them. Both Jack and I were still unwell, and all the time we could do anything like work was taken up, for a day or two, solving the immediately pressing questions of first settlement and household arranagements.

The first rain proved that the roof of the house was well nigh as bad as the walls, and it had to be covered with tarpaulins; supplemented over the bed, and other important spots, by waterproof sheets.

But outside, the daily busy hum of voices indicated the quick gathering of poles and grass for a new house, and Edward, busy amongst this work, found time also to introduce me to the secrets of the African cuisine; and from time to time produced luxuries from our stores for the furnishing out of our new home.

On the 6th of February, our good old canoe, the *Calabash*, arrived from the south end of the lake, bringing our colleague, who had proceeded by the Nyassa route, and news of the welfare of our friends, and the advance of the work of building the *Good News* [the steamer].

Edward proceeded at once to Ujiji in the *Calabash*, to receive the two rear parties of our caravan, one of which had already arrived, and the other with our friend who had been left at Urambo, got to Ujiji soon after Edward arrived.

The *Calabash* was then immediately despatched to the south end with a load of provisions for our friends there, and instructions to Mr. Swann[1] to launch the vessel in readiness to bring to Kavala.

Edward, having completed the business at Ujiji, then came back with our recently arrived friend; and Mr. Jones[2] having come over from the mainland, the annual committee meeting was held, the new arrivals appointed to their stations, and general business transacted. This was scarcely settled, when Mr. Swann arrived in our beautiful steel boat, the *Morning Star*, and by his cheering accounts of the successful launch of the *Good News*, completed a good month's work of prompt business.

Shortly afterwards, Mr. Swann again sailed for the south end in the *Morning Star*, carrying thither the new missionary and his stores, and to pack up the stores of the Marine Department, and prepare them and the vessel for the voyage to Kavala.

Thus, within six weeks, the general annual business of the Mission, and its extended organisation, were set in order and arranged.

Edward was to proceed to the south end, to bring the *Good*

1. Alfred J. Swann, hired by Hore in 1882 as first mate for the missionary flotilla. See his *Fighting the Slave Hunters in Central Africa* (London, 1910).
2. Rev. David Picton Jones.

News on her first adventurous voyage, as soon as he had somewhat advanced the work of settlement and preparation on the island.

I was realising, if not in my own person, at least in what was going on all around me, that missionary life in Central Africa was by no means one of dull monotony, but capable of affording scope for every energy and accomplishment, in all the various auxiliary works of housebuilding, social economy, conveyance, preservation and maintenance of people, goods, and mails, *and the problem of existence apart from the aids of civilisation;* to say nothing of the many-sided questions and difficulties, arising from our contact and connection with various native tribes, and the Arab colonists and adventurers, a peculiar position requiring all the tact of a political agent, without his freedom of action or authority. All these affairs have to be dealt with, and successfully accomplished, before a missionary in Central Africa can hope to commence the direct and actual work of his mission, upon a basis giving hope of life, success, and permanency; and, moreover, to be accomplished with the very wise and necessary restrictions, as to getting involved in native politics, or assuming any position of authority, placed upon our actions by instructions from head-quarters.

The ultimate object of the missionary is to preach and to teach, but his first necessity is the accomplishment of those matters I have referred to, and unless they are already effected by local government, by Consul, Commissioner, or by some special department in his own mission, the individual missionary must be qualified himself to deal effectually with them before he can effect the object of his mission. It is in this part of the work where so many have failed and died, before getting at the work which they were specially fitted for carrying on.

In various ways I have realised, that the missionary life is by no means what I was led to suppose. I received considerable advice and admonition at home, both from those who were themselves experienced, and from those who, without actual contact, were, from more enlarged and general views, capable of wise consideration of the subject, which has been valuable and correct. Other views I find inapplicable to my life.

I was told it would be necessary and advisable, to " stand at my own wash-tub ", both to get the work done, and to set the example of household industry and thrift. I find, on the contrary, that the work can be done well for fair pay; that I should lose influence and respect entirely by doing such things myself, and that the drudgery and overwork of the women here is already such, that a better example would be set to the natives if I could persuade my husband to do it, than if I did it myself.

With regard to food, I was assured that the African women prepared certain dishes which were superior to our own preparations of the same things; but my experience is, that although some of the simplest native foods are wholesome and palatable enough as nature produces them, in the hands of the natives, they almost invariably become dirty and unpalatable. If the old adage is true, my efforts to effect reform in this direction, would be only secondary to the main object of our mission.

As to our own food, although there is a good assortment of native products procurable, we are thankful to avail ourselves, very largely, of the regulation transport weight in importing European provisions.

It would perhaps be possible to exist on native food, with the addition of a few imported condiments, etc.; but both muscle and brain power would suffer in time, and the effect felt, both upon our own persons and in the work of the Mission.

Meantime, we are ourselves introducing certain fruits and vegetables which promise to flourish well here, and this, together with the greater regularity of the supply of wheat from the Arabs, will soon enable us to exercise economy in regard to expensive imports. That which applies to the " groceries ", applies in almost similar manner to the " upholsteries ". The eye and the mind require rest and nourishment as well as the bodily powers; and it is not without effort and the assistance of some little civilised surroundings, that that civilisation is retained to ourselves, which we would fain communicate in some measure to our new friends. It is not impossible for isolated representatives of civilisation to be swamped in savagedom.

Let not my readers judge, however, that we live luxuriously here, but what I wish to convey is this, that although (and because) we live in a mud hut, and necessarily lead a somewhat hard and rough life, I deem it essential to our own health and happiness, and the welfare of the work we are engaged in, to strive to retain every sign and comfort of civilisation we can.

The building of the new house and stores went on apace, the whole being joined to the part we were living in, forming altogether a large L of one room in breadth. The one side contained verandah, sittingroom, and bed-room, a semi-open room for boxes, &c., and a store; and the other side the official store, the office, tool-room, mill-room, and chambers for the engineer, who was working at the *Good News*.

A separate house, a hundred yards' distance, was erected for Mr. Swann, with its own offices and kitchen; and the settlement really began to assume some form.

The walls of these houses are formed of poles stuck in the ground, afterwards wattled on each side with long thin sticks, lashed with strips of bark; the mud is then thrown into the interstices in a soft state, and left to dry, when it receives another deposit on the outer parts, and is smoothed down by the hands. A whitewash is made by pounding a soft stone procurable here, (which we suppose to be kaolin or decomposed granite), mixed with the gummy sap of a plant found on the spot. The roofs are simply thatched with grass, laid on rafters, wattled like the walls.

Our own sitting-room has four little windows, like old-fashioned ships' ports, made by inserting a single square of glass in a wooden frame, which hinges upwards; the wood-work and also that of the frames, etc., being stained with the dye which is easily extracted from some of the cheap Indian trade cloth.

The floors are simply beaten earth, but become very comfortable when covered with mats, made by the natives here.

By the middle of April the new houses were completed, and Edward prepared the new boat for the voyage to the south end of the lake. I, however, decided not to shift my quarters until my husband's return, that the house might be quite dry.

On the 18th of April, having made new sails for the boat, and set out a plan of work for our faithful headman, Ulaya, during his absence, Edward sailed in the *Alfajiri* for the south end of the lake, to bring the *Good News* to the island.

I felt rather uneasy for the first few days I was alone, but the steady and respectful conduct of our Zanzibar men soon gave me confidence; and as I gradually recovered health, set myself to work to get acquainted with the natives.

I had no lack of visitors. At first there could be little communication between us, but we soon got familiar as they learnt my harmlessness, and I got accustomed to their ways. The distribution of a few bright buttons amongst the children, and the exhibition of pictures and various common objects astonishing to them, soon placed me on friendly terms with the children, who at first were afraid to come to me.

The Waguha, the natives of the island, and the adjoining main, live together in villages of considerable size, the characteristic of which is the arrangement of the houses in straight rows, forming streets. The houses, although low, bee-hive like erections, are often fitted very comfortably inside as to sleeping-places, mats, and utensils, but the all-prevailing smoke keeps us out of them.

The tribal dress and ornament of the people is very distinctive and peculiar. The dress is made of the fibre of the raphia palm, imported from Rua and other countries, and consists of a short skirt gathered round the loins, variously ornamented and fringed for the women, and plain for the men; the latter, however, further dress themselves in monkey or leopard skins, displayed apronwise in front, when they can get them. Both men and women have most elaborate *coiffures*, padded and pomatumed to an extraordinary extent, and ornamented with coronets of cowries, with iron bands, forming a sort of skeleton crown, and with numerous long ornamented iron and wooden bodkins stuck artistically about, in the huge cushion formed by the hair. These, as well as being ornaments, are useful to introduce into the structure without disturbing it, for the purpose of soothing local irritation on the surface of the head, which it may be supposed affords a well-sheltered home for certain enemies of mankind.

The waist, neck, and limbs are used to display beads and rings of brass and iron wire as much as can be procured, and, as regards the women, the decoration is completed by an elaborate tattooed pattern of dots and ridges all over the front of the body, which in a complete toilet is oiled up to show the pattern to advantage.

There are many splendid specimens of humanity of both sexes to be seen among them, and the unmixed Waguha are by no means repulsive of countenance, whereon is often indicated character both gentle and energetic. The children for the most part, when clothed at all, are clothed with any bit of rag or skin suspended to a piece of string round the waist; a fair-sized cotton handkerchief completely sets them up.

The life of the natives, when undisturbed by war, is a round of seed-time and harvest, and the time of waiting for seed-time again. But the women are always at work; the household duties, which as elsewhere is their department, though certainly less elaborate, go deeper into the matter than with us. The food stuff they dish up to their households they must first sow, reap, pound, and grind, and the water they must carry on their heads from its source. Their lives are a continual round of drudgery, but many of the well-to-do women have slaves who do most of this.

The men seem to lead a lazy life, but still, on closer consideration, there is a considerable fishing industry, and a large production of mats, as well as the manufacture of tools and arms, all of which is done by them. The women, however, do the pottery work, for which the island is famous.

My first visit to the chief's village was a great occasion. Intending to take a quiet walk, to get the air and promote my acquaintances with the people, I found my proceedings were regarded by others with astonishment and curiosity. All our own men with their best clothes on followed me to " take care of me ", and the small village close at hand emptied itself completely into my train, till it became quite a formidable procession.

The chief received me on a bare space opposite his house, providing stools and mats, and a crowd soon collected. I was somewhat alarmed, as though I had called an audience and had nothing to say; but I soon saw they were perfectly satisfied to gaze in silence, that is *my* silence, for they were as clamorous and eager for a good view, as any Zoological-Gardens crowd. After an exchange of the few civilities then at my command, I asked the chief about his wife; the use of the singular number, however, was unintelligible, but on explaining that I was interested in the *one* who had paid me a visit, she was produced, and I offered a present of cloth. The lady happened to have a toothache, which enabled me to take my departure with credit, for the purpose of giving her medicine, for which she followed me home.

The return procession, now including the people of the other village, must, I think, have nearly reached from one end of the journey to the other.

As I entered my house, I soon found that the women and children of the party were by no means retarded in their progress by my doorway, and I should have been completely mobbed inside, but for the active and forcible aid of Ulaya, who, seeing the state of things, came and turned them out.

For weeks and weeks the slow process of making acquaintances and gaining confidence was continued, until gradually the women would come and sit and gaze, and, as far as we were able, converse; while the peeping children ceased to scamper off when I rose up or advanced towards them.

Although I was still far from well, I began now to be able to move about more, and to attend to household matters, but poor Jack was a mere shadow of his former self.

One evening, as just at sunset I was walking outside the house, three guns were fired in the offing, a signal agreed upon by Edward to announce his approach. Ulaya came running in great excitement, saying, " Mistress, the big ship is coming;" and in a few more minutes, the white hull of the *Good News* appeared rounding the southern point of our harbour, and, compared to anything else on the lake, she certainly did look like a big ship.

The whole place was at once in a state of excitement, as every one rushed out to see the new wonder, which had been long talked of here, and which I saw now for the first time.

I was also greatly relieved by my husband's safe arrival, for I viewed the voyage as a rather dangerous adventure, the vessel being only jury rigged, and having no other auxiliary power than some very awkward paddles which were of little use.

It turned out, however, that notwithstanding this she had made the quickest passage yet known on the lake, having been only two days and a half from the south end.

The *Morning Star*, not to be behind, arrived the same night.

The engineer who had been working at the *Good News* came also in her with my husband; but he was very ill, and, as it proved, too far gone already to benefit by the change to Kavala, which it had been hoped would have brought him round. He died only ten days after his arrival here, regretted by all.[3]

In the *Good News*, the whole of the stores and property of the Marine Department was brought away from the south end, which station was now left to the superintendence of our colleague, who had come to the lake by the Nyassa route. The various materials and parts, however, to continue the construction of the vessel, had not yet arrived, and a series of voyages with the *Morning Star* had to be made, to bring the same to Kavala as they accumulated at the place of delivery, nor was the last consignment brought here until early in November (1885).

Meantime, while the vessel was waiting for material, the work of preparation went on; a large workshop and shed were constructed close to the beach, and timber cut down and sawn into planks; doors and windows prepared, and roads and clearings effected about the station.

On his return from the first of these voyages, Mr. Swann brought us the sad news of the death of our colleague at the south end,[4] and as soon as all the *Good News* materials had been delivered, everything was brought to Kavala, and the south end station now remains unoccupied, till reinforcements arrive from England.

Soon afterwards, our two friends on the mainland opposite started for home, and that station had to be given up, and all the stores and property brought to the island.

What with the delay in the delivery of the materials, and all this accumulating work, it is not to be wondered at that the construction of the vessel, which we here cannot but regard as the principal present work of the mission, was delayed.

Early in November the *Morning Star*, having arrived with what purported to be the last load of material, the ship-building work was proceeded with. A closer inspection now showed that the

3. James Roxburgh.
4. John Harris.

damage and loss to this material was much greater than had been supposed. Edward characterised the material as "a mass of wreckage," and a great number of important pieces were found to be missing altogether.

Since that time, the shipbuilding has been the daily work of the station. At six o'clock every morning, Edward and Mr. Swann go down to the vessel, and work there all the morning, having their breakfasts sent down to the shed. What with engine-fitting, blacksmithing, and carpentry, it is a busy scene of industry. The afternoon is also generally taken up in various other work, such as building, storekeeping, etc., and both my husband and Mr. Swann keep their health best under these busy circumstances.

Returning health, both to myself and my little boy, as well as the natural call to share in the work of the Mission, encouraged me to join still more actively in the proceeding business, and to attempt the long-cherished scheme of imparting some instruction to the native girls.

The chief had already challenged Edward to fulfil his promise of instruction to the children, but as two of our missionaries were then located close at hand on the mainland, and he had already work more than enough to take up all his time, he did not feel justified in commencing school work. It was quite appropriate, however, that I should commence a girls' class, and one day, the chief being in our verandah, I announced that I should commence a class for the girls, and he promised to send me his children. The very next day I commenced work with those girls, showing them pictures and various things, and keeping them amused. Soon a few more came, and having overcome the first shyness and fear, a regular course of instruction in reading, writing, and sewing was soon established. Each girl was permitted to carry off, and wear the garments she had suceeded in completing in the sewing-class, and soon, thus decently clad, began to present an appearance of some respectability.

The numbers of my scholars rapidly increased, until our verandah became both too small and inconvenient for the work. A school-house was therefore built containing a room twenty-six feet long, furnished with table, and forms, and shelves for the books and slates. This has proved a great convenience and improvement, and with few exceptions, has been the daily scene of useful work.

Having no nurse, I am obliged to have Jack always with me in the school, and this has given rise to many amusing incidents, although on the whole it has scarcely been a hindrance to the work.

Many ludicrous scenes occur frequently in school, but as a rule

M

they are now wonderfully amenable to discipline. Soon after confidence had been somewhat secured, I was beset by grown-up women requiring instruction, or perhaps, the, to them, more solid benefits of the school, in the shape of garments. I tried to include them, but found it impossible, and was obliged to restrict the class to girls.

I now get from ten to fifteen scholars to the daily school; the variation is chiefly caused by the various household and field duties they have to fulfil, and at sowing and harvest times nearly all are kept away.

Some five or six girls, forming a first class, are now able to sew nicely, and can read from a book words of two and three syllables, as well as being able to repeat by heart various texts of Scripture and the Lord's Prayer. A little advance has also been made in singing, enough to sustain a hymn in our Sunday service.

The different feeling awakened towards these girls, under the advantage of decent clothing, and the little indication of intelligence acquired by the instruction they have received, is wonderful indeed; they seem quite different creatures to the rude young savages I commenced with. A continuance of the work will, I believe, bring about some permanent change for the better, not only in the girls themselves, but in their families.

Meantime, the chief still asked why the boys should be left out, and my husband, after long consideration, determined to devote half an hour each day to them. The boys' school was commenced, and has ever since been running parallel with that of the girls, and about similar advance made.

The bugbear of such efforts in Africa, the desire of scholars and parents to be paid for their " work ", has also been overcome by quiet and determined resistance.

The question of the adults was still urged upon us by the natives, and our colleagues, the missionaries on the mainland, having now departed, a regular meeting for public worship was established on Sundays, open to all, and has been regularly continued, with an average attendance of twenty persons.

A Sunday afternoon class is held for instruction in, and explanation of, the worship, and in the daily schools instruction is also given, designed to enable the children to join intelligently in the religious service.

Thus it is sought, at least, to keep together the threads of the work, until those specially fitted for its conduct shall arrive to our help.

After a year upon the island, we have fairly well proved the healthiness of the situation, having all gradually improved in health, so that I have now fully taken that charge of household duties, which releases my husband to his much-beloved ship-building, while Jack has almost fully recovered the liveliness and activity of his age. Here we are free from malaria and stagnant air, being literally at sea, although by no means isolated.

But we are very short-handed. With the advent of a missionary to conduct the special objects of our work, and a medical officer to minister in his department to the needs of the natives and ourselves, Edward and Mr. Swann would still have their hands full of their own special work, with the addition, (until its completion), of the ship-building, and this island barely provided for.

All round the lake other health sites are to be found, where it is hoped to establish stations, for the maintenance of which a perfect organisation will shortly be completed.

It is to be hoped that amongst the thousands in England, who long and wish for the emancipation of the African people, from the chains of depravity, ignorance, and slavery, there are large numbers who see in Christian missions, a means to that end which goes to the root of the matter, by aiming at the purification of the blood, while other organisations are endeavouring to staunch the outward wound.

From those of such views is drawn great support for the Tanganyika and other missions, *but now and here is specially needed the personal presence and aid* of the friends of Africa; men of power to influence and organise, of education both for impartment and for self-support, and of religious fervour for preaching the truths of the Christian religion; which personal testimony and historic evidence, combine to proclaim the source of individual happiness, and national advancement and prosperity, before which the bonds of moral and physical slavery are done away.

The bath-chair is put away in the store, and my story must end. If, by its relation, aught has been done to increase the evidence of the accessibility of Central Africa to humanising efforts, its end will have been served, for in Christian England such must surely lead to increased effort to save Africa.

VIII

A SUMMING UP

In failing health and with flagging spirit Hore left Lake Tanganyika for the last time in June 1888. Although he had remained constant to the idea of a chain of mission stations circling the lake's shores, his society was in the process of shifting its emphasis to the Nyasa-Tanganyika Plateau, leaving the lake to the Catholic White Fathers. Although he had sought co-operation with the Muslim traders and settlers, the dominant European mood was to eradicate their economic and political power. Although he hoped to protect African societies from the corrupting effect of European exploitation, the partition, which would divide Lake Tanganyika among three empires, was almost complete; as Swann was to joke two years later, the lake had so changed that he half expected to see Mr. Cook escorting a party of tourists round its shores.[1]

Africa had changed and so had the public response in England towards returning missionaries. In 1881 Hore had been the featured and praised speaker at his society's annual public meeting in London; in 1889 he spoke to an annual meeting of young men. Again the Royal Geographical Society, of which Hore was a fellow, invited him to present a paper, this time to the Geographical Section of the British Association at Newcastle, which if no less prestigious than the 1881 London meeting, was considerably less exciting or newsworthy. Published in the October 1889 *Proceedings,* this address, even more than his later book, marked Hore's last significant contribution to the knowledge of Africa. While he continued to speak on his adventures as an African pioneer to 1910, his objectivity faded with the years as his bitterness with being forgotten increased.

1. Swann to the LMS foreign secretary, December 23, 1890.

Lake Tanganyika*

THE general form of the continent of Africa has been very aptly compared to that of an inverted saucer—the idea of central plateau-like elevations sloping on every side down towards the sea. The comparison is understood, of course, to be general rather than exact, but it is a very intelligent aid, and especially in connection with our subject.

A distant vertical bird's-eye view of this central plateau-like elevation would present an aspect, if denuded of its beautifying elements of wood and water, very much like some of the crater scenery of the moon. In these crater-like cavities, at varying elevations, lie the great lakes of Inner Africa, and through the gaps in their irregular surrounding ridges flow the great draining streams of the continent, rushing through narrow channels, bounding in beautiful cascades over steep steps, and again, flowing slowly over elevated flats, well nigh lost in grass and papyrus. But a more horizontal view would reveal the fact that one of these crater-like cavities, notwithstanding the superior height of a few elevated peaks and ridges, and notwithstanding the superior elevation of at least one other of the lakes, shows the ridge of its surrounding barriers so far above the others, and is so central amongst the watersheds, that, for purpose of general description, we may compare it to the cavity in the centre of the inverted saucer and its surrounding annular ridge.

In this central depression the rainfall is retained, while without it descends in accumulating streams down to the sea on every side, for on the outer sides of this mountain barrier and its buttresses are born the Nile, the Congo, the Zambesi, and the Rufigi.

The form as well as the outline of this mountain ring is irregular. There are passes and elevations, there are places where its sharp edge cuts the raindrops and abruptly decides their destiny, whether for the ocean or for the central cavity. Such is the ridge in Usui dividing the Nile waters from those of the Malagarasi, and that in Uguha, which separates the waters of the Lualaba from those of Tanganyika; there are places where the top of the wall is flattened down, and the water hangs in swamps and sponges with its destination uncertain, as in the neighbourhood of Rikwa in the

* From *Proceedings of the Royal Geographical Society* (October 1889).

east, and probably the head waters of the Kitangule in the north, but still the boundary is known and defined.

Outside this annular enclosure, although step-like expanses and lake cavities exist, the general form down the sloping sides of the saucer is that of vast radiating ridges descending towards the coast on every side, as conjectured long ago by Sir Roderick Murchison, but, from every side, this interior hilly boundary must be mounted to reach the central depression I am describing.

The area contained within this mountainous ring-fence is, in horizontal form, an irregular oval, whose greatest length is nearly 600 miles from the parting of the waters in the north, of the Kitangule and the Lusizi, to the parting in the south, between the Lofu and the Chambezi, and a width of about 300 miles, from the eastern water-drain of the Gombe in Unyamwezi to the eastern sources of the Lualaba in Uguha, and narrowing towards the north and south extremes of the oval. In vertical aspect it is a deep depression, and in the bottom of the hollow and occupying about three-quarters of its longer diameter, lies Lake Tanganyika, from 2000 to 3000 feet below the higher parts of the mountain ring, and lying more or less close along the western side of the depression.

A section of this great central depression, taken across its minor diameter (a line indeed which is part of an ancient commercial route), almost exactly resembles the details of a fortification. Approaching from the east the " rampart " is ascended in steps— the " crest " of the parapet is crossed as the country of Unyamwezi is entered—a long gently sloping " parapet " and an equally long and steeper " escarp ", together about 200 miles, bring us to the " ditch," occupied by the lake, from the opposite side of which a steep " counterscarp " of 2000 feet ascends to the " glacis " form- ing the western boundary of the depression, from which, at no great distance, the waters descend towards the Atlantic.

This great central depression, shut off on all sides by its con- taining ramparts, has ever been the source of what of mystery and fable has been connected with African geography. Its form in large measure agrees with the old conjecture of the Mombasa missionaries, gathered from native reports, of " a general sinking of the land commencing about three degrees from the Indian Ocean till the general depression sinks into the bed of a huge lake," and the Kinyamwezi source of the information would naturally give the depression the largest extent, for that route enters and crosses it at its widest part, while it is also small enough to justify the criticism on that conjecture, that " the fall, if such exist, must be of circumscribed limits."

From three sides, at least, the boundary wall of this depression has been viewed or reported by ancient travellers as the " Mountains of the Moon " and the source of the great rivers, while, if we could imagine the gradients of its ramparts to be carried upwards to a culminating height, the reported snow-clad character of those mountains would be realised, and the four fountains of Herodotus also, which Livingstone hoped to see. It is not impossible. If we leave out, what I have included as part of the area of the central depression, the hilly table-land of Unyamwezi, for I have strictly followed the actual watershed, if we regard that country as the parapet only of the rampart, the shape of the depression is strictly long, narrow, and trough-like, a chasm in fact, with Tanganyika in its bottom, with all the appearance of a violently produced opening in the earth's crust, its sides more closely resembling the walls of a cañon than the undulation of mountain and valley. The Lake itself is not a basin, but the bottom of the chasm, 400 statute miles in length, an average width of about 20 miles, and a depth, along its centre, of 500 to 1000 feet. Not only the appearance of the depression and the Lake lead one to think of volcanic action and earthquake movement: still more practical and impressive evidence has been forced upon me, during ten years of residence there, in the frequent recurrence of shocks of earthquake, sometimes so severe as to open cracks in the ground, as well as the presence of several hot springs, and jets of steam and petroleum, while still more frequent, gloomy rumblings beneath the surface (the complaints and warnings of the storm-demon " Kabogo ") indicate that the fires below are still active.

For several years the direction of movement of these earthquakes was recognised as being about N.N.W. or N. by W. In August 1880, a shock of unusual violence opened a narrow crack in the earth for a distance of several miles with corresponding cracks in the walls of houses at Ujiji and, in October 1887, a series of shocks, lasting over twenty days, felt at Kavala Island in the Lake, and reported also at Ujiji, appeared distinctly to be right under foot without horizontal wave-movement. To Sir Richard Burton, the first European traveller to visit Tanganyika, its containing cavity " suggested the idea of a volcano of depression " and Mr. Cooley rightly described it as lying parallel to " the line of volcanic action drawn through the Isle of Bourbon, the north of Madagascar, and the Comoro Islands." Still more interesting would be a scientific study of a line of volcanic action of far greater extent, for I think it will be found that the containing chasm of Tanganyika lies lengthwise along a great circle drawn through the magnetic poles, on either side of which cluster the chief volcanoes, and sites of volcanic and earthquake phenomena, of the eastern hemisphere: and, in the western, the Sandwich Islands and New Zealand. In connection also with the suggestion of volcanic origin for the Tanganyika chasm, is the remarkable evidence of the peculiar distribution of the natives of that region, noticed further on.

The native name " Tanganyika ", meaning " the mixture ", or the " coming together " of the waters, is of the most apt significance, for the water of the Lake is drawn from all sides of the depression, taking toll of the waters which would, otherwise, flow to the Atlantic, the Mediterranean, or the Pacific. But the natives now living on the Lake shores certainly have no knowledge of that, and the name therefore seems to point for derivation to some such natural convulsion, as is hinted at in several native legends, bringing about the mixing of the waters in the cavity then formed.

In this unique position it is no wonder that Tanganyika has been the subject of much enquiry—no wonder that, as the highest watershed was reached from either side, the explorer should regard the Lake and its system as feeding one of the other great drains to the coast, but further examination has proved its isolation, and that, for generations, the Lake has been the reservoir, without other outlet than evaporation, for the whole of the drainage of the central depression. For long years, no doubt, there was pulsation between the rainfall and the evaporating power, and also that throughout a long term there was a gain inch by inch, of the water upon the evaporation, eventually making the Lake brim-full, for at two points great breaks occur in the mountain ramparts of the depression, viz. near Karema on the east, and in Uguha on the west, and, at the time of the visit of Commander Cameron, the Lake had become brim-full, that is, it had reached the level of these two lowest places in the surrounding barrier. But that the Lake had ever reached that level before, I cannot believe in the face of the existence, all round it, of large forest trees, then partly submerged, which had required ages of growth on the dry land, as well as the submerged sites of villages and cultivation.

The eastern gap presented no facility, in the shape of rapid descent, for the flow of the rising lake water, beyond, perhaps, the filling of an independent depression at Rikwa, which, known successively as " river ", " lagoon ", and " lake ", I believe attained the dimensions entitling it to the latter term at that time. But the western gap was close to a steeper edge of the barrier, and its material being soft, and with no buttress behind, the irresistible force of rising water, after gently flowing over the top for a time, burst the dam, and is still cutting out this soft channel between two hill-sides forming the Lukuga river. When all the soft material is gone, and a rocky sill remains, it will exactly resemble, and act like, a waste-pipe to a tank.

When the lake was brim-full, and before it had washed the soft material out of the gap, the condition of the Lukuga inlet was probably, for a short time, alternately an indraught, an outdraught, or at rest, and this would reconcile the somewhat varying reports we have had of it.

When I got to Tanganyika in 1878, the Lukuga channel had already been, to a great extent, excavated, and become not a mere overflow, but a rushing torrent. The lake at that time, as near as I can estimate, was at least four feet lower than when visited by Cameron. During the succeeding ten years, it has gone down eighteen feet, and is still flowing, but much more slowly, out through the Lukuga. All round the lake there is now a perpendicular height of about ten feet between the water's edge and those forest trees which must have taken many years to grow on the dry land; and about half that space between the water and the stumps of similar growths, which have been destroyed by the lake as it rose and remained about them, leaving a space of about four or five feet quite bare, except for grass and creepers, the growth of a season or two. The evidence of old residents places the level of the lake nearly up to these old stumps, at about the time of the visit of Sir Richard Burton. Everything goes to show that there has been but one great rising of the lake. A partial submergence of five or six years has sufficed to destroy large forest trees, the remains of which show every indication that all trace of them would be lost by a submergence of ten or twelve years. During the last four or five years, the annual ebb and flow has been from twelve to eighteen inches, but the flow always failing by a few inches, the extent probably of the Lukuga discharge beyond the balance between rain and evaporation.

With the breaking of the Lukuga, and the overflow of the Lake waters, the central depression lost its unique character, and is now, in vertical importance, a twin reservoir with that of the Victoria Nyanza.

To some of us but a little blue patch upon the map of Africa, Lake Tanganyika, to the natives of those regions, is " the great water ", and the source of many industries, both directly from what it produces, and indirectly, through the facility for transport and communication it affords to the ten different tribes whose territories are fringed by its 1,000 miles of shore.

Owing to the immense evaporation, the opposite shores, even where only fifteen miles distant, are visible only in the rainy season —then, sailing down the centre of the lake, one realises its trough-like character, but coasting inshore there is a great variety of scenery; here for 30 miles at a stretch you sail in deep water close alongside the mountains, which rise steeply to over 1000 feet, showing broad patches of rock amongst miles of beautiful trees; again, in a few places, shallow flats only permit access to the shore by poling in canoes. Steep rocky islands with dry soil, set out in the lake so as to be always ventilated, supply sites for residence, and many fine natural harbours give facility for navigation.

We find around the shores all the beauties and the grandeur of the lake scenery of our own country, on a much larger scale, and in places diversified, while not hidden, by tropical luxuriance.

Pebbly creeks with clear water and pretty shells fringe the drier and more scrubby forest regions of lower elevation, and invite the visits of the buffalo, the zebra, the elephant, and all the larger animals. Muddy river mouths, choked with reeds and papyrus, and swarming with hippopotami and crocodiles, afford a home for ducks, geese, the ibis, kingfishers, the beautiful crested crane, and many other aquatic birds. Again, there are deep quiet inlets with lofty and almost perpendicular sides, ending often in a deep chine with a cascade; the turtle floats in the water below, and the otter glides in and out after its prey with scarcely a splash; the weird cry of the fish-eagle, echoing from side to side, only serves to impress on the visitor the solemn silence of the place, while far above all, on the lofty heights, far overhead, the virgin forest of gigantic trees revels in perpetual moisture, sheltering tree-ferns, and festooned with lianas and rattan, affording a home for brilliant butterflies below, and rare monkeys above.

On those parts of the shore which have become the haunt of man there are two distinct kinds of scene. In the more unsettled regions, where from long and sad experience all strangers are viewed with suspicion, native villages, with houses in close array within stockades, are seen perched upon peninsulas and other easily defended positions, their stores of corn and dried fish stacked upon rocky islets, and their canoes drawn up amongst the rocks close at hand. In happier countries mile after mile of scattered houses, peeping out from amongst groves of bananas, indicate peace and plenty, and wide-stretching fields of corn and cassava are spread over the country. Here and there an open space is preserved for the market, to which the natives of both sexes and all ages may be seen hurrying by land and lake, to barter their various produce—oil, mats, fish, salt, goats, honey, and all kinds of wares; along the beach are lightly drawn up canoes of all sizes, cut out of the solid log, and the little catamaran of the fishermen—the whole array of African scenery, alike in its more arid and its most luxuriant form, its saddest and its most peaceful aspect.

Turning to the lake itself, with its long open stretches of deep blue sea, all sense of confinement is lost upon the watery horizon, rarely broken by the triangular sail of the Arab merchant's dhow, or the long low log canoe of the native adventurer, both of which coast along shore as much as possible, only crossing the lake after careful observation of the weather. The former, when caught in rough weather, are sometimes left entirely to the mercy of the winds and waves, and being excellent sea-boats, are not often lost. The natives, with their generally deep-laden canoes, have a unique method of riding out a storm; the more robust, and if necessary all hands, go overboard, and holding by the canoes with one hand, at once lightly sustain themselves and serve as a break to their craft, out of which, in case of still greater necessity, they will throw their property in the order of its least value. As a lake, Tanganyika has many aspects. In fine weather there is no more delightful sailing ground, there being but very few reefs and shallows; most beautiful of all, perhaps, is its aspect on a clear night, when, relieved of the sun's glare, the voyager is able to enjoy the scene. The busy and perpetual hum of insects on the shore gauges the distance from the beach as the boat recedes or approaches, and seems, with the flickering will-o'-wisp, marking out the water's edge, to welcome the home-coming voyager, arrived, may be, after long rain and storm, at the desired haven.

Another aspect is given by the south-easter of the dry season, sometimes lasting as a gale for four or five days, only lulling slightly at night, and causing a bad sea, running the whole length of the lake, and against which it is almost impossible for a small craft to beat. At daybreak huge masses of clouds, piled up on one of the great mountain capes of the eastern shore, begin literally to drop down over the lake, till, overshadowing all that side, as the wind begins to rise with a low moan and the water is lashed into little waves, showing their crests white under the overshadowing cloud; then in separating masses, and in long perspective procession, the clouds seem to rush off across the lake to the table-like heights of Goma on the opposite side, where, one after the other, these separate masses, retaining a separate and pillow-like form, pile themselves in regular order, like gigantic hammocks on a ship's rail. Meantime the wind has increased till it is blowing a gale, with a fierce driving sea the whole length of the lake. The sky clears, and a great dryness ensues; the long row of cloud-masses on the western shore remain discharging their moisture amongst the luxuriant forests on those heights, while the lake basin is hot and dry. This is the windy weather. There is also a watery aspect, of which I will relate one experience.

Leaving Kavala Island one afternoon, bound to Kigoma in Ujiji, I made an unusually long passage. In the early morning I got a light fair wind, but it had ceased by daylight, and set in again from the north. The heavy clouds on the mountains of the west side commencing to move north, discharged rain very heavily; clouds then collected along the eastern shore, also moving north and gathering ominously. Meantime we, in mid-lake, were still getting north wind coming down between the two cloud-currents, which were moving in the opposite direction. About eight o'clock the western clouds were in great confusion, and several waterspouts were formed and moved along with the squall. The mass of clouds on the east side at the same time broke up over Ujiji, discharging heavy rain and much thunder and lightning.

To the north, where the lake shores approach each other, the cloud masses on either side drew gradually together, until, colliding with much electric discharge, they seemed to return together down the middle upon us in mid-lake. The thunder-claps fairly shook the boat, the lightning crossed and recrossed overhead from horizon to horizon, and the rain came down in torrents and cold as ice. The last glimpse of brighter day went out overhead as the cloud-masses joined together, like the closing of a skylight in a vaulted roof. The group of waterspouts off Goma now seemed to rush out to sea in our direction, and one huge pillar came so dangerously near to us that I was able to closely observe its shape and movements. The base consisted of a pegtop-shaped cloud of spray with its big end just touching the surface of the lake; out of its centre arose a vast glass-like cylinder, forming the body of the waterspout, smooth and solid; all around, outside this central solid column, loose masses of broken water or close spray appeared falling down from the cloud in which the upper end was hidden, and the whole was gently swayed by the wind, but without losing its form or varying in diameter. Glad, indeed, we were when a mass of cloud, lower than the rest, swept down upon our dangerous neighbour and broke it up.

All this time I had half of my crew keeping the boat head to sea in the constantly varying squalls from north-west to north-east, while the other half, with myself, were constantly employed in baling-out the rain which threatened to fill the boat. Four or five other waterspouts were seen at the same time in every stage, from the dipping waving cloud-point, gradually approaching the rising vertex of the whirlpool below, to the long waving attenuated column about to disappear. With the density of the rain and clouds it was as dark as twilight, and so cold that we were all literally shivering and shaking. This continued for some three hours, nor did the sun again show himself till five o'clock. A couple of hours of calm succeeded the subsidence of the rain, and then a fresh breeze from the west took us at full speed into Kigoma Bay, where we anchored late in the afternoon.

But perhaps the most dangerous, and certainly the most disagreeable, is the bad weather at the changing of the seasons, in which both wind and water unite in most alarming aspects.

Fierce squalls, suddenly shifting in direction and causing a dangerous cross sea, are accompanied by driving rain and hail, and at night a terrible darkness makes navigation still more difficult. At these times I have seen the natural electric lights, " St. Elmo's fire ", for hours together, at each masthead and spar-end.

It will be seen that the seasons are the wet and the dry, following the general arrangement in Tropical Africa, with the greatest meteorological disturbance at the changes. The various observations I have taken were at Ujiji, in S. lat. 4° 54' 30″, from 1878 to 1880, and at Kavala Island, in S. lat. 5° 40′, from November 1885 to June 1888.

Whilst in 1879, 29·78 inches of rain fell at Ujiji, there fell in London, during the same year, 30·13 inches, a difference of not half an inch. In 1878 nearly an inch more fell in London, and in the only two months recorded at Ujiji, in that year, the rain was also in excess of the corresponding period in 1879. Of the rain of 1880 at Ujiji I have only records up to October, but, adding to that the average of the preceding two years for November and December, we have, for 1880, 27·31 inches, a difference again from the London rainfall of just half an inch. But at Kavala Island, in 1886, 52·07 inches was measured; in 1887, 52·25 inches, and for the earlier part of 1888 an amount which promised for the whole year about 58 inches.

The hottest time of year is in November and February, and the coldest in July. At Ujiji a maximum of 83°, a minimum outside of 58°, the ordinary temperature being 76° to 79°; all but the minimum, inside a house with thick walls and roof. At Kavala, in a much slighter built house, a maximum of 86° and a minimum of 60°.

The position and formation, however, of the Lake, and the depression in which it lies, much lessen the value of a few isolated observations, which can scarcely be taken as representative of the region; perhaps, however, those I have given are as valuable as could be got from any *two* positions, being taken on opposite shores of the lake.

The climate on the whole is by no means unhealthy, far healthier indeed than the coast regions in the same latitude, and the unhappy experiences hitherto of travellers and missionaries have been due rather to the difficult conditions of life and work than to insalubrity of climate. Many of those who have visited the region have been already debilitated by long journeys under conditions of hardship and anxiety. I have no doubt that, as a few civilised surroundings are secured, and the country and conditions of life become better understood, there will be no complaint of the climate.

Although large patches of the country appear to be dry and scrubby, water would be found nearly everywhere by sinking good wells, and only water is needed to fit the land for enormous production of everything that would flourish in a tropical country.

Careful observations of the boiling-point thermometer confirm those of other travellers in placing the height of the lake above the level of the sea at about 2700 feet. The water of the lake is fresh, and during several years' residence I used it for all purposes. The taste resembles that of distilled water rather than that of springs, and some I brought home has been submitted to Dr. Frankland for analysis.

In the nature and condition of its inhabitants the Tanganyika region may be said to be equally central as in its geographical relation, as truly the scene of a mixing as its original position amongst the watersheds.

Around the shores of the lake are ten distinct tribes, truly native so far as century old traditions and customs, locally stamped characteristics of personal marks, and territorial claims, and yet representing distinctly all the different families of Africa, the negro, the negroid, the Zulu, the Semitico-African, the African branch of the dwarfs, and that inner group of warlike people west of the Nyanzas not yet distinctly classified. All these have converged on, or sent offshoots to, Tanganyika, not as might be supposed, to mix in perpetual conflict, but to range themselves peacefully around the shores of the great lake, where, becoming essentially children of the soil, they yet retain sufficient of their physical characteristics and art to be identified.

The geographical radiation is evident; the ethnological convergence may also be traced. The warlike tribes from the northwest are represented in Usige, where, although to some extent settled as Lakists, they still present the greatest difficulties to the penetration of strangers into their country; but it is the point perhaps at which their opposition is most vulnerable, and, by reason of this, and also of the secure base afforded by the Lake,

Usige is the best available starting-point for operations in that direction for connecting with the territories of Emin Pasha.

The Semitico-Africans from the north-east, in a distinct line or belt right away from Abyssinia and the Galla country, developing on the way into nomads, pastorals, or shepherd class amongst other tribes, according to circumstances and surroundings, have on Tanganyika, as the Warundi and northern Wajiji, become naturalised and nationalised. Retaining their cattle, they have also become essentially agricultural, and, notwithstanding such prejudice against "the water" as to consider it unlucky for their principal chief to see it, have acquired maritime habits, being in fact the most expert canoeists and fishermen, and the only users of the catamaran. They retain the splendid physique and superior features of their forefathers, their cattle, the portico to their huts, and, under the favouring circumstances of settlement, have redeveloped the talent for working in iron and copper, weaving, and very extensively the institution of village markets.

A line has been touched by travellers at various points, commencing at the West Coast, of dwarfs and cannibals. This line, or lines, reaches Tanganyika at Ubemba; it is but slightly represented, and, for want perhaps of friendly welcome into the Lake circle, has scarcely been assimilated; but they are undoubtedly small people, with a strong suspicion of cannibalism amongst them, and all are agreed that "there is more of it," i.e. cannibalism and dwarfishness, inland from that point.

The negro type, in irregular but traceable lines, reaches Tanganyika from the west, where it is represented in Marungu, and perhaps Uguha and Goma.

The negroid family extends, in two or more lines or patches, from the East Coast.

The Zulus, as the "Mazitu," have been pressing on towards Tanganyika from the south as far back as we have records, and the Watuta and other offshoots, wearing the distinctive Zulu head-ring, after years of wandering and occasional short settlement on the south-west edge of Tanganyika, have found a home with the Wanyamwezi.

All these families (except the Zulus) have developed talent for navigation, in exact ratio to certain conditions of the presence of suitable trees for canoe-carving, suitability of coast and harbour, and necessities of exchange. The Warundi and Wajiji alone have become the best sailors under the least favourable circumstances.

But although the lake shore is thus surrounded and occupied by representatives of nearly all the African families, who would

N

seem to have come to the lake from a distance, the greater part of the central depression in which the lake lies, in fact almost the whole of that depression and its rampart not immediately adjacent to the lake, is occupied by the Wanyamwezi, "the people of the Moon country," of ancient origin, and not recognisable as one of the racial rays converging on the region from a distance. Records and local traditions of this people as the original inhabitants are as old as those referring to the Mountains of the Moon, and both from the East and the West coasts, and indicate that the present tribe and its many divisions were once more united and powerful. Yet these Wanyamwezi have never assimilated amongst the Lakists; indeed, the Watongwe, one of their offshoots, occupying over sixty miles of the lake shores, do not navigate, and scarcely utilise the Lake at all. The many colonising parties to distant countries, such as Katanga (now called Garenganza, an ancient name for part of Unyamwezi), have, either in their dread of the lake ferry, or before its existence, gone round about its southern end. None dread the water or are so incapable of canoe management as the Wanyamwezi. The same thing is noticed on the East Coast, where so many of their adventurers, after braving the arduous journey from up country, cannot be prevailed on to cross the strait to Zanzibar.

These conditions and characteristics of this ancient and enterprising people, and the comparatively recent arrival at the lake shore, of the representatives of families from remote points of the continent, would all agree with the suggestion already made as to the origin of the central depression and the lake.

Here then may be studied representatives of nearly all the families of Africa, in a position far removed from that disturbing influence of contact with foreigners to which the natives on the coast are subjected.

The "mixture" has served to promote and encourage native art and industry, and extend the exchange of produce. Improvements in this direction too, introduced by the Arabs in a way not too overwhelming for native acceptance, has served, in some measure, to aid a condition which, whatever the origin of these people, would certainly be one of progression but for the depressing and demoralising curse of the present form of slavery and the slave trade, only still further encouraged by these Oriental visitors, who in other respects may have benefited the Lake community. Nor can this curse be considered native; the original condition of slavery in Africa was doubtless the natural one which obtained in early ages, in all countries; the present unnatural form (concentrated too upon Africa as the only and last source of supply for other countries) has come from where a more artificial condition of society has developed the worst and the lowest, as well as the highest and best, of the human character.

Certain conditions of society, under which men remain stationary when surrounded with every advantage, may safely be termed retrogressive. I think these natives of Inner Africa, who at least have not lost a condition of moral and social orderliness in which the family tie and the rights of property are regarded, in which physical development also may be considered as well-nigh perfect, and the rudiments, and even the considerable development of all the useful arts and industries have been maintained against overwhelming disadvantages, must, with equal justice, be considered as progressive.

The metals are worked into useful implements and weapons, pottery clay into every form of vessels. All kinds of vegetable fibre are spun, woven into cloth, or plaited into mats and baskets; salt and oil are manufactured, fish is caught, preserved, and distributed; and wherever peace permits, markets for exchange are established. Nothing but security of peace and government, with a gentle introduction of art improvements, is required for rapid progress on every hand.

Of the produce of the lake region, there is to be seen already exploited, cultivated, or wrought by the natives, besides rice and various cereals, the oil-palm, the ground-nut and sesamum, with their oils, tobacco, cotton, and many useful vegetable fibres, india-rubber, dye and fancy woods, besides admirable large timber for local needs. Of minerals, iron and copper, of which beautifully fine wire is drawn, slate, lime, and alum, and splendid clay for pottery of all kinds. An extensive fishing industry already exists, and vast quantities of the animal products, oil, hides, horn, and ivory, are available, both from the lake and its shores. The probability of the existence of still more precious minerals, and of workable petroleum, give promise of yet undeveloped resources of great value.

In view of large commercial undertakings, involving wholesale export of produce, and import of manufactures, there is scarcely a temptation for enterprise. For development of the country for the benefit of its inhabitants, there is ample resource; and the funds otherwise expended in some vast system of transport to effect exchanges, which, in great measure, are unnecessary, would be far better expended in developing, on the spot, the native industries with native material and workers.

Although in a different form (but in a far more wholesome manner), profit would, in due time, accrue to the promoters and supporters of the improvement.

The lines of communication in Africa, to a great extent following the rivers, and always being towards the centre, necessarily converge towards Tanganyika, to which therefore, there are several means of access: but the elongated form of Africa would give two foci to these radiations, leaving a central space, in great measure crossed by east and west lines, and this is indeed the fact. In Eastern Tropical Africa the lines of communication, both by reason of the geographical features, and of connection and intercourse amongst the tribes, lie for the most part east and west: as though, in a descent from the north, the tribes of compatible characteristics had become shaken together in sediments or strata, hence it is always easier to travel from east to west than from north to south, and the difficulties of various African travellers correspond exactly to their progress in the latter direction. But when by settlement and intercourse the difficulties of language and the non-existence of native routes become of less importance, there are natural features in the great lake system that point to the possibilities for an easy great north and south line of communication from the Nile to the Zambesi. Till that is achieved, the most natural, and indeed, the easiest mode of access to Tanganyika is along one of the natural east and west lines to which I have referred, and which is actually a great natural route right across the continent from Zanzibar, by Tanganyika and the Congo, to the West Coast, a route crossed in the Tanganyika region by such irregular and zigzag north and south communication as has, from time to time, existed by means of European travellers and others. During the early part of the effort to reach Emin Pasha, letters passed through my hands, on Tanganyika, from South Africa for Emin Pasha and from the Congo for Zanzibar. The way of access to Tanganyika at the present, and for the last ten years, is and has been, the overland route from Zanzibar. The difficulties of this route have been much exaggerated, both more than doubling the time necessary for traversing it, and unfairly abusing the Zanzibar porters, who afford the ready and efficient means of conveyance. The most laggard of the Arabs, who stay a month or six weeks at Unyanyembe, do it in five or six months with laden caravans. The usual time taken by the London Missionary Society's annual caravans, laden with goods, is three months. I have walked over the route myself, under those conditions, in ninety days, another time with several Europeans, heavy loads, and a boat on six carts, in 104 days. Without loads, I have walked it in 62 days, and with my wife and child, I accomplished the journey, last year, with the greatest comfort, in seventy-two days. As compared with the Nyassa route, it is native means and methods perfected and ener- gised by Europeans, as against unperfected European arrangements clogged and hindered by all the difficulties of a new country, a case of utilising and improving what already exists, rather than introducing wholesale an entirely new system. With the details perfected, and further expenditure in providing means, the European system ought in time to excel, but up to the present the old road has been the only dependable one, and for the due comfort and well-being of passengers, the two routes are not to be compared. On the old road one gets a through carriage in the shape of an organised party accustomed to discipline, and who, together with the tent and other travelling appliances, are the same to the journey's end. On the Nyassa road, the constant changes from a water route to overland, and *vice versâ*, and the deadly marsh region, which has to be passed through, are utterly wearying, whilst at the end of the route there is still 200 miles of overland journey through an almost untraversed country, to be commenced from a point which is not a caravan depot. As to expense, the *nominal* cost of transport is in favour of the Nyassa route, but a comparison of actual achievements and delays and losses, leaves a decided balance in favour of the old road. When the central lake route comes into existence, the old road, still further perfected, will form a valuable route by which to tap the Lake region from the east, as well as to afford access to the rich countries it passes through.

Tanganyika was the first of the great Central African lakes visited by Europeans and thus laid open to accurate description. Sir Richard Burton thus opened out the mysteries of Central Africa, and his records and descriptions are yet unsurpassed. Investigation of the other lakes rapidly followed, and from time to time they have been visited by travellers, and, for some years past, become the scene of Christian missionary effort. Tanganyika especially, as lying upon the great trunk route across the continent, has been visited by many African travellers since the time when Livingstone and Stanley met at Ujiji. Not only has it been visited, but, since 1878, there have been Englishmen living on its shores. In that year the first expedition of the London Missionary Society arrived at Ujiji, and, through considerable hardship and isolation, has persistently prosecuted its work. A friendly acquaintance has been made with all the tribes around the Lake shore, and at two stations Christian teaching is now being carried on. As boatmen and builders, general workmen, and servants, many natives have been trained, and a good feeling exists in favour of the English. Even the Arab merchants and settlers have to a great extent lost their first prejudice, and by hospitality and friendly action, and even protection, have aided the objects of the mission.

As well as native-made boats, the London Missionary Society now possess a steel lifeboat and a powerful sailing vessel, fifty-four feet in length, with auxiliary steam power. The lake shore has been surveyed, the resources of the country and the character of the natives are known, and, together with the Victoria Nyanza, where similar work has been proceeding, is, equally with Nyassa, entitled to such attention and such claims to English protection and influence as English enterprise and work can give.

The position of the lake with regard to the several European spheres of occupation or influence is peculiar: according to some maps, it is entirely surrounded and shut in, but I am not aware that the Lake itself is claimed by any. Its importance in any future arrangement for opening up Africa and putting an end to the slave trade and the present unnatural condition of slavery can scarcely be overestimated, whether as a rich country of itself (for Tanganyika should include the whole of the depression which drains into it), a centre of commerce and administration, or, simply taking the Lake as the best 400 miles in the great central watery highway of Africa, it is all-important.

For scientific enquiry, for investigation of the native character and languages, the Lake offers peculiar facilities in its central position and relations, besides affording healthy residence for Europeans. Especially is it suitable for an effort to develop the people with the country, by assisting native art and industry in the way I have already suggested. It is to be regretted that the sudden flooding of some regions of Africa with cheap European goods has simply obliterated many valuable native industries, which, under careful encouragement, might have been more profitably preserved. Sad will it be if our operations are to be confined to commercial enterprise simply to enrich ourselves and the Africans shorn of their native enterprise, and yet not lifted out of native ignorance, drop into subordinate drudgery scarce better than their present condition. The Africans have a splendid country which only requires development. They have ample arts and industries, and only require encouragement and assistance to utilise the resources of their country and become themselves elevated; but the one or the other can only be possible—any enterprise of ours can only be justified—be it political, or commercial, or scientific, if, in its first action and its most stable principle, it aims at the effectual eradication of Africa's curse—the slave trade.

SELECT BIBLIOGRAPHY

of published works relating to Captain Hore and the Lake Tanganyika
Mission

By Edward Coode Hore (in addition to works previously cited).

' An Arab Friend in Central Africa ', *The Chronicle of the London
Missionary Society* (August, 1891), 235–238.

' The Heart of Africa ', *National Geographical Magazine*, III (April,
1891), 238–247.

' How I Went to Lake Tanganyika ', *Transactions of the Royal
Geographical Society of Australasia, Victoria Branch*, Melbourne,
VIII, 2 (1891), 27–33.

' The Lake Tanganyika Mission ', *The Evangelical Magazine*, new series,
XX (May, 1890), 210–213.

' On the Way to Tanganyika ', *Juvenile Missionary Magazine* of the
London Missionary Society (August-December, 1878).

Public address, annual meeting of the London Missionary Society, May,
1881. *The Christian World* (London), May 17, 1881.

Public address, annual meeting for young men of the London
Missionary Society, May, 1889. *The Christian World* (London)
May 9, 1889.

By his contemporaries.

Becker, Jerome. *La Vie en Afrique ou Trois Ans Dans l'Afrique
Centrale.* (Bruxelles, 1887).

Brode, Heinrich (trans. H. Havelock). *Tippoo Tib: The Story of his
Career in Central Africa narrated from his own Accounts.* (London,
1907).

Broyon-Mirambo, Phillippe. ' Description of Unyamwezi, the Territory
of King Mirambo, and the Best Route Thither from the East
Coast ', *Proceedings of the Royal Geographical Society*, XXII
(1878-79), 721-726.

Dodgshun, Arthur W. *From Zanzibar to Ujiji: The Journal of Arthur
W. Dodgshun 1877-1879.* Edited by Norman R. Bennett. Boston:
Boston University Press, 1969.

Fotheringham, L. Montieth. *Adventures in Nyassaland: A Two Years'
Struggle with Arab Slave Dealers in Central Africa.* (London, 1891).

Giraud, Victor. *Les Lacs de l'Afrique Equatoriale: Voyage d'Exploration Execute de 1883 à 1885.* (Paris, 1890).

Moir, Frederick L. *After Livingstone: An African Trade Romance.*
London, 1923).

———————————, ' Englishmen and Arabs in East Africa ', *Murray's
Magazine* (November, 1883), 623–636.

Moir, Jane. *A Lady's Letters from Central Africa.* (Glasgow, 1891).

Moller, P., G. Pagels, and E. Gleerup. *Tre Or I Kongo.* (Stockholm,
1888).

187

Mullens, Joseph. 'A New Route and New Mode of Travelling into Central Africa', *Proceedings of the Royal Geographical Society*, XXI (1877) 233–244.

Rabaud, Alfred. 'L'Abbè Debaize et Sa Mission Geographique et Scientific dans l'Afrique Centrale', an extract from the *Bulletin de la Societé de Geographique de Marseille*, (April, May, June, 1886), Marseille, n.d.

Stevenson, James. *The Water Highways of the Interior of Africa with Notes on Slave Hunting and Means of Its Suppression*. (Glasgow 1883).

Stewart, James. 'Lake Nyassa and the Water Route to the Lake Region of Africa', *Proceedings of the Royal Geographical Society*, new series II (May, 1881), 247–274.

Swann, Alfred J. *Fighting the Slave Hunters in Central Africa*, (1910), second edition, with a new introduction by Professor Norman R. Bennett, Frank Cass, London, 1969.

Thomson, Joseph. *To the Central African Lakes and Back* (1881); second edition, with a new introduction by Robert I. Rotberg, Frank Cass, London, 1967, 2 vols.

Wissmann, Herman von. *Unter deutscher Flagge von west nach ost, von 1880 bis 1883*. (Berlin, 1889).

By others:

Bennett, Norman R. 'Mirambo of the Nyamwezi', in *Studies in East African History*. (Boston, 1963).

————————————, 'Mwenyi Kheri', in Norman R. Bennett, (ed.) *Leadership in East Africa, Six Political Biographies*, (Boston, 1968), 139–164.

Cairns, H. Alan C. *Prelude to Imperialism: British Reactions to Central African Society, 1840-1890*. (London, 1965).

Chergwin, Arthur Mitchell. *Arthington's Million: The Romance of the Arthington Trust*. (London: 1931).

Coupland, Reginald. *The Exploitation of East Africa, 1856-1890: The Slave Trade and the Scramble*. (London, 1939).

Hanna, A. J. 'The Role of the London Missionary Society in the Opening Up of East Central Africa', *Transactions of the Royal Historical Society*, fifth series V (1955), 41–59.

Lechaptiois, Mgr. *Aux Rives du Tanganyika*, Appendix: 'Les Debuts, 1878-1891' by "A.W." (Algiers, 1932).

Lovett, Richard. *The History of the London Missionary Society* I and II. (London, 1899).

Oliver, Roland. *The Missionary Factor in East Africa*. (London, 1952).

————————————'Some Factors in the British Occupation of East Africa", *Uganda Journal*, XV (1951), 49–64.

Rotberg, Robert I. *Christian Missionaries and the Creation of Northern Rhodesia, 1880–1924*. (Princeton, 1965).

Smith, Edwin W. *Great Lion of Bechuanaland: The Life and Times of Roger Price, Missionary*. (London, 1952).

INDEX